Praise for *Schooling the Prophet*

"Painstakingly researched and carefully written, Gerald Smith's *Schooling the Prophet* shows how deep—as the subtitle of the book states—was the influence of the Book of Mormon on Joseph Smith and the early restoration. Gerald Smith's study demonstrates how profoundly—and paradoxically, since Joseph Smith only occasionally cited it—the Book of Mormon shaped early Latter-day Saint theology and practice, including baptism, the sacrament, the temple, and the concept of Zion. Warmly to be recommended."

—Stephen D. Ricks
Professor of Hebrew and Cognate Learning,
Brigham Young University

"With great attention to historical detail, this book brings to light the critical and often overlooked influence the Book of Mormon had on the restoration of the priesthood, church administration, temple, and other ordinances revealed to Joseph Smith. Gerald Smith's portrayal of the Prophet's schooling illuminates a pattern God still uses to teach his children."

—Barbara Morgan
Director of Boston LDS Institute and
Assistant Professor of Religion,
Brigham Young University

"Gerald Smith has written an extraordinary book—original, insightful, and rich in detail. This book represents a major achievement in our understanding of the fundamental role played by the Book of Mormon in the development of church doctrine and practice. It will be of great interest to everyone—LDS or not—to whom these issues are vital."

—John M. Lundquist
Adjunct Professor of Religious Studies,
Pace University

Schooling the Prophet

How the Book of Mormon Influenced Joseph Smith and the Early Restoration

Gerald E. Smith

NEAL A. MAXWELL INSTITUTE *for* RELIGIOUS SCHOLARSHIP

Brigham Young University
Provo, Utah

Library of Congress Cataloging-in-Publication Data

Smith, Gerald E., 1953– author.
Schooling the prophet : how the Book of Mormon influenced Joseph Smith and the early restoration / Gerald E. Smith.
pages cm
Includes index.
ISBN 978-0-8425-2936-5 (trade paper : alk. paper) — ISBN 978-0-8425-2937-2 (e pub) — ISBN 978-0-8425-2938-9 (kindle)
1. Book of Mormon — Influence. 2. Smith, Joseph, Jr., 1805–1844. 3. Mormon Church — Doctrines—History — 19th century. I. Title.
BX8627.S58 2015
289.3'22 — dc23 2015007869

Cover design: Caranine B. Smith

♾ The paper used in this publication meets the minimum requirements of the American National Standard for Information Sciences—Permanence of Paper for Printed Library Materials. ANSI Z39.48–1992.

Printed in the United States of America

maxwellinstitute.byu.edu

Contents

Illustrations

Foreword

It has long been recognized that early Latter-day Saints were much more attuned to biblical doctrine and culture than to Book of Mormon influences. First-generation Mormons were raised in a world saturated in a biblical grammar. No surprise, then, that Brigham Young was considered an American Moses, not the American Lehi; it is the Jordan River, not the Sidon, that waters the Salt Lake Valley; it was the camp of Israel, not the clans of Lehi, that trekked across the plains. Old Testament names and places occur some fifteen to twenty times on Utah maps. Utah place-names originating from the Book of Mormon are confined to three prophets, one city, and a honeybee. The Book of Mormon has been strikingly absent from the church curriculum until recent decades, and Mormons are hard-pressed to trace their distinctive doctrines to that scripture. Premortality, theosis, degrees of glory, distinct divine personages—these and many other teachings are utterly absent or seem vaguely alluded to at best.

In early proselytizing, as in the modern missionary program of the Church of Jesus Christ of Latter-day Saints, the Book of Mormon was seen as keystone less for what it contains than for what it points readers to: one Joseph Smith, vested with the authority to translate, and who thereby has God's authority to restore the keys and ordinances pertaining to salvation. This principal function of the Book of Mormon, together with its relative neglect by the LDS faithful, has obscured an entirely different role the Book of Mormon played in the restoration—that of powerful influence on Joseph Smith.

It may seem odd to speak of the Book of Mormon's influence on the Mormon prophet. And yet, whether you believe he produced that record "by the gift and power of God" or in a brazen act of pious deception, the ideas, doctrines, and practices detailed in that volume undoubtedly pervade the restoration project of Joseph Smith. Gerald Smith has done important work in exploring just how extensive that interpenetration was. While it may be true that the Book of Mormon functioned primarily as a sign, or an evidence, of Joseph's prophetic authority, the fruits of research like Gerald Smith's tell us we have inadequately appreciated how extensively Joseph drew upon the record in conceiving and executing his vision of priesthood, theology, church organization, ordinances, temple building, and other areas.

As Grant Hardy once noted wryly, if the Book of Mormon was only intended as an evidence that Joseph Smith could translate—a pamphlet would have sufficed. The almost 600 pages of the original edition, in actual fact, were a vast resource that Smith drew upon—consciously and unconsciously—as he unfolded the organization and teachings of the LDS Church. Gerald Smith has done the best job to date of uncovering an impressive array of Book of Mormon connections, parallels, and influences that shaped the Prophet and his work. In so doing, he has shed new light on the prophetic process, enhanced our appreciation for the value of the Book of Mormon in the restoration, and given us all motivation to continue our efforts to plumb the riches of this New World scripture.

—Terryl L. Givens

Preface

THE BIBLICAL CITATIONS IN THIS BOOK generally use the King James Version (KJV) rather than other newer versions. Joseph Smith himself used the King James Bible throughout his life and ministry. Because this volume studies the influences that shaped Joseph Smith and the early restoration, we explore the topic through the biblical lens that was most influential on his work—the King James Bible. Unless otherwise indicated, the King James Version is cited in the text, but other translations, such as the New Revised Standard Version, are provided as reference in the notes throughout.

Quotations from Joseph Smith Papers (JSP) original documents, accessed from the Church History Department of the Church of Jesus Christ of Latter-day Saints, have been quoted verbatim, including crossouts, spelling errors, and apparent edits contained in the original document to provide a truer sense of the original writings from the early restoration. However, quotations disregard minor JSP editorial markers, such as a vertical bar, which indicates a sentence has reached an end of line and then continues with the next line. To illustrate, see the following sentence from Joseph Smith's narrative, *History, circa Summer 1832*, from the JSP: "we were deprived of the bennifit of an | education suffice it to say I was mearly instruct | tid in reading and writing and the ground <rules> of | Arithmatic which const[it]uted my whole lite | rary acquirements."[1] Here the end-of-line markers "|" have been omitted. Also, text insertions in the original document, marked by <xxx>, have been retained (as in <rules> in the passage). JSP editorial insertions in the modern document, marked by [xxx], also have been retained (as in "const[it]uted" in the passage). Thus, the above passage is quoted in this book as: "We were deprived of the bennifit of an education suffice it to say I was mearly instructtid in reading and writing and the ground <rules> of Arithmatic which const[it]uted my whole literary acquirements."

Acknowledgments

I HAVE BENEFITED FROM THE KNOWLEDGE, goodwill, and encouragement of a number of colleagues and friends, leading to new friendships in the process. The Neal A. Maxwell Institute for Religious Scholarship has been very supportive and helpful in taking this project from early draft to final conclusion, for which I am grateful. Shirley Ricks has gone beyond the call of duty in making suggestions, editing, and helping me obtain photographs and permissions. Don Brugger and Leah Davis were helpful in creating the indexes. Blair Hodges provided especially useful editorial guidance and advice in refining the manuscript. I have benefited from Joe Bonyata's expert guidance and input throughout the publishing process. Also helpful were Morgan Davis, Brian Hauglid, and Jerry Bradford.

I am indebted to Terryl Givens of the University of Richmond, gifted scholar and faithful friend, for providing the impetus for this work and making suggestions, revisions, and improvements along the way that led to deeper research and clearer writing. Reverend Charles Healey, S.J., of Blessed John XXIII National Seminary in Weston, Massachusetts, Jesuit author and dear friend, provided many helpful insights into contrasting religious observances. Caranine Bigelow Smith of George Washington University—talented researcher, writer, art historian, and my daughter—gave especially perceptive thought and counsel with every chapter, for which I am so grateful. Noel B. Reynolds—professor emeritus of political science at Brigham Young University and leading educator, philosopher, and scholar of ancient texts and Mormon studies—provided particularly thoughtful and beneficial suggestions on ancient texts and the manuscript. Matt Bowman of Bowling Green State University, eloquent

American religious scholar and friend, provided valuable insight and suggestions relating to nineteenth-century frontier worship. And I thank friends Nathaniel Givens, Fiona Givens, and Ron Nickle for their careful reading, comments, suggestions, encouragement, and helpful conversations about the learnings that came from this study. Finally, I thank my wife, Betsy, for her faith and constant encouragement that made this exploration possible.

Introduction

One of the elusive paradoxes of nineteenth-century Mormonism is the relationship between founding prophet Joseph Smith and the church's founding scripture, the Book of Mormon. Scholars and historians have documented Smith's apparent avoidance of citing the Book of Mormon during sermons, discourses, and writings. "During the seven years of the church's Nauvoo period, when Joseph was preaching in public on a regular basis," wrote scholar Terryl Givens, "the hundreds of recorded pages of his sermons contain only a handful of brief allusions to the Book of Mormon—and none of them involve sustained discussion of doctrine or any other content."[1] Mormon scholar David Whittaker concluded in 1987: "In spite of critics' statements to the contrary, Mormonism is a biblical religion. Its founding prophet and his followers grew up with, respected, and regularly used the biblical text in their quest for self-understanding as well as in rationalizing and defending the restored Church. Joseph Smith never taught that the Book of Mormon was a replacement for the Bible. . . . He loved and believed in the Bible, and no serious study of his life and thought can ignore this fact."[2]

Yet, there is evidence too that during the early days of the restoration—what Latter-day Saints, or Mormons, embrace as *the* restoration of the primitive New Testament church of Christ—the Book of Mormon provided what the Prophet perceived as a reliable and trusted source document of ancient religious observances, including among others sacrament, baptism, and priesthood. Early Mormon rites and ordinances borrowed extensively, sometimes word for word, from rituals found in the Book of Mormon as Smith and his early followers began constructing and organizing their new religion. Historians Scott Faulring and Robert

Woodford initially pointed to this important connection in one of the church's earliest founding policy documents, the 1829 "Articles of the Church of Christ," penned by cofounder Oliver Cowdery.

The very question of the Book of Mormon's influence on the Prophet calls for an explanation since one might fittingly dismiss that influence simply because it was derived from Smith himself. Yet such an assumption is a heuristic one and prematurely precludes further exploration of the Book of Mormon as an original source document. On the title page Smith increasingly distanced himself from the notion that he was the book's author, as opposed to mere translator: in the first 1830 Palmyra edition he described his production role as author and proprietor,[3] but in the second 1837 Kirtland edition simply as translator ("Translated by Joseph Smith, Jr.").[4] The distinction was subtle but significant. In the preface to the 1830 edition he elaborated awkwardly, telling of his earliest translated section of the Book of Mormon text: "I would inform you that I *translated* by the gift & power of God *& caused to be written,* one hundred and sixteen pages,"[5] a description the Prophet used frequently throughout his life.

Yet the Book of Mormon asserted its own historical validity as a sacred document of an ancient people. Its title page began with a statement of historical origin: "It is an abridgment of the Record of the People of Nephi; and also of the Lamanites . . . which are a remnant of the House of Israel. . . . Also, . . . a Record of the People of Jared, which were scattered at the time the Lord confounded the language of the people when they were building a tower to get to Heaven" (see title page).[6] At the conclusion of the translation project in 1829, the Book of Mormon appeared to Smith and his associates not only to be a legitimate historical source document, but an especially accessible one as well as they contemplated their forthcoming mission with the restoration.

For Joseph Smith the Book of Mormon translation project was a prodigious effort lasting nearly seven years, from 1823 to 1830—including what I term *schooling visions* he reported experiencing annually from 1823 through 1827 under the tutelage of an ancient prophet identified as Moroni, then the translation and printing processes from

1828 through early 1830, and finally publishing the book itself in March 1830. Lasting as long as a university doctoral education, this project alone occupied one-third of Joseph's lifetime by 1830, and over two-thirds of his young adult life after his first vision in 1820. It seems inconceivable that such an endeavor would not have had a profound impact on his life, his religious views, and even his prophetic vision of how to shape the pending restoration. Could it be that the Book of Mormon was not merely *derivative* from the Prophet, but actually may have been *formative* on his life and work as a prophet? This question needs exploration, for, as we see in this book, it goes to the very core of Mormon belief and identity: of Mormon temples, Mormon Christology, Mormon priesthood, Mormon ritual and ordinances, Mormon doctrine, Mormon culture—even the meaning of the Book of Mormon itself.

It is my thesis that the Book of Mormon had a profound formative influence on Joseph Smith's doctrinal and institutional development during the nascent days of the nineteenth-century Mormon restoration. For Smith there was a confidence in, a comfort with, and consequently a willingness to draw on the body of this ancient text because he knew it well and was certain of its origin. Of course, determining influence is difficult to do. Smith's critics have tried to trace parallels in Mormonism to his contemporary environs and upbringing; apologists have sought to uncover parallels to ancient scripture; historians have explored connections more broadly to ancient and contemporary American history. Many believers attribute the developments of the restoration directly to revelation from God to the Prophet—some recognize the possibility that environment, ancient scripture, history, and revelation all played a role and that these influences can hardly be separated. In this book I do not explore these alternative parallels in detail but leave it to the reader to consider those views elsewhere. Here I am interested in what kinds of ways the Book of Mormon might have contributed to the schooling of the man who translated it, as he claimed, "by the gift and power of God,"[7] and I proceed on the assumption that the Book of Mormon translation project itself involved exposure to all four domains of potential influence.

What was it in the Book of Mormon itself that he found so resonant, so relevant, and so compelling to his unfolding mission to lead the restoration? The familiar themes found in the core identity of the book itself invited confidence: it appeared to be an ancient Judeo-Christian record with sacred writings that cross-referenced and correlated with themes from ancient biblical texts. The purpose articulated on the book's title page was resonant to many antebellum Christians who were steeped in biblical theology: "to shew unto the remnant of the House of Israel how great things the Lord hath done for their fathers; and that they may know the covenants of the Lord, that they are not cast off forever; and also to the convincing of Jew and Gentile that Jesus is the Christ, the Eternal God" (see title page).[8]

The book's very presence as a volume of ancient sacred scripture invites a cascading line of inquiries: Which Book of Mormon teachings, practices, or institutions were relevant to the Prophet while he fleshed out the budding restoration? How did the presentation of these ideas in the Book of Mormon contrast with Smith's own understanding of similar ideas found in traditional biblical-based religion of the early nineteenth century? What were the similarities and differences between these two parallel religious paradigms—Book of Mormon scripture and biblical scripture—and how did they inform his own understanding of the meaning and direction of the pending restoration?

Consider, for example, the appearance of Mormon temple worship during the early nineteenth century, a development that many Mormons and non-Mormon observers believe happened spontaneously by revelation to the Prophet in 1842. However, we can see significant imprints of Book of Mormon temple influence on various dimensions, the most visible of which is the Mormon temple vision. For example, within just nine months of the formal organization of a new church, Joseph Smith received revelation in December 1830 that a temple should soon be built: "I am Jesus Christ the Son of God Wherefore gird up your loins & I will suddenly come to my temple even so amen."[9] Seven months later the location of this *first* temple was revealed to be "in this land which is the *land of Missorie* [*sic*] . . . [in] the place which is now called

Independence [and] is the centre place, & the spot for the Temple."[10] A year and half later, in December 1832, another revelation called for the building of a *second* temple, in Kirtland, Ohio, where the majority of the Latter-day Saints were living. The Kirtland Temple was dedicated in 1836. Two years later, on April 26, 1838, the church was directed by revelation to begin construction of a *third* temple, the Far West temple: "Let the City Far West [Missouri], be a holy and consecrated land unto me . . . to build an house unto me."[11]

Only four months later, following the election riot against the Mormons on August 6, 1838, in Gallatin, Missouri, Brigham Young and his fellow apostles dedicated land at Spring Hill, Missouri (35 miles from Far West), for the building of a temple at Adam-ondi-Ahman,[12] the *fourth* temple of the latter-day church.[13] Then in 1839, as the Latter-day Saints settled a new community in Nauvoo, Illinois, "the best and most suitable site within the limits of the city as planned was selected, purchased, and duly set apart as the temple ground. The cornerstones were laid April 6, 1841."[14] This was the *fifth* announced temple of the church, the Nauvoo Temple. After Smith's death in 1844 Brigham Young and his successors replicated yet again this unique temple vision in the American West, with the commencement of the Salt Lake Temple in 1853 (dedicated in 1893), then the St. George Temple dedicated in 1877, followed by the Logan Temple in 1884 and the Manti Temple in 1888. Since then LDS temple building has grown dramatically—10 temples by 1956, 20 by 1981, 102 by 2000, 144 by 2014, and at this writing another 29 under construction or announced—a total of 173 temples expected by the middle of the decade.[15]

Yet, for a new American religion proclaiming the restoration of the simple gospel of Christ—*the restoration*—Mormonism's temple-centered rendition of Christianity was an anomaly among traditional Christian religions. What was the genesis of Joseph Smith's ambitious latter-day temple vision? He had virtually no viable temple templates to work with. At the dawning of the Second Great Awakening in nineteenth-century North America, searching Christians had no expectation that temples might someday dot the earth. Protestant Christians believed that Old

Testament prophecies of the temple had been fulfilled with Christ in the meridian of time, such as the coming of the Messiah to the temple prophesied by Malachi 3:1, or the veil of the temple being rent at Christ's crucifixion (Matthew 27:50–51), or Daniel's prophesied destruction of the temple (Daniel 9:24–26), seemingly fulfilled by the Romans in AD 70. Protestants broadly believed that the great spiritual body of believers had replaced any physical notions of modern temple architecture. Alexander Campbell, nineteenth-century Protestant leader and vociferous critic of Joseph Smith, asserted:

> The Most High God dwells not in temples made with human hands; yet He condescended in the age of types to have a temple erected for himself which He called His house, and glorified it with the symbols of His presence. In allusion to this the Christian community, organized under the government of His Son, is called His house and temple. "You are God's building," says Paul to a Christian community. This building is said to be "built upon the Apostles and Prophets—Jesus Christ Himself being the chief corner stone. Know you not that you are the temple of God? The temple of God is holy, which temple you are." 1 Cor., iii. 16,17.[16]

Jews were keepers of the temple heritage of the Hebrew Bible, which might have seemed akin to Joseph Smith's temple ideal, except that his expansive vision of community temple worship was precisely the opposite of the resolute orthodox Jewish temple ideal of only *one* central temple, a view promoted early in Jewish history by Deuteronomist scribes and historians. The First Temple of Solomon built in Jerusalem in 957 BC was destroyed by the Babylonians in 586 BC and rebuilt as the Second Temple of Zerubbabel in 515 BC. Following renovations by Judas Maccabeus in 164 BC and Herod the Great in 20 BC, the Romans destroyed the Second Temple in AD 70. Since then Orthodox Jews have offered a formal prayer three times a day for the building of the third temple of Jerusalem long prophesied by the Nevi'im (major and minor prophets) of the Hebrew Bible (the Old Testament).[17] During the interim, Jews have worshipped not in temples but in local synagogues throughout the world.

If Joseph Smith, however, somehow sensed a broader yearning for Judeo-Christian temple worship, his instincts were at the very least prescient. Jewish temple aspirations erupted in 1817 when a faction of German Jews called for community temple worship in one's own neighborhood, similar to Smith's vision. Renouncing Israel's prophetic return to Palestine to rebuild the prophesied third Jerusalem temple, these Reform Jews instead called for more elaborate worship services that would reframe synagogue worship as local temple worship—in the community and not in Jerusalem. They added the title "temple" to the local synagogue name, a practice evident in many Reform Jewish congregations today—for example, Temple Ohabei Shalom in Boston, Temple Israel of New York City, or Temple Sinai in Atlanta.[18] Of course, Joseph Smith never knew of these Jewish temple reforms since Reform Judaism migrated to America only in 1850, thirty years after Mormonism's beginnings. These parallel innovations in temple theology—in Mormonism and in Judaism—are remarkable nonetheless, pointing to a deep longing for the presence of higher forms of temple worship in the daily lives of both Jewish and Christian believers.

Students of the Book of Mormon often miss the rich temple culture that seems evident among its ancient American peoples because there is only one explicit reference to the actual construction of a temple in the entire Book of Mormon text. Other temple references are implicit, embedded in the narrative as if temple and altar worship were ubiquitous, ever present in the lives of these ancient people. Paradoxically, the Book of Mormon people originated from the highly conspicuous national temple culture of ancient Jerusalem, documented in depth in the Old Testament, that stressed the sole legitimacy of centralized temple worship—seen in the *one* tabernacle of Moses and then the *one* Temple of Solomon in Jerusalem. Ancient Roman-Jewish historian Josephus summarized this idea: "There ought also to be but one temple for one God."[19]

However, the Book of Mormon described a temple culture in the New World of the ancient Americas marked by a temple that was similar to the Jerusalem temple but then went much further. It depicted a vibrant, diffused temple culture centered not in Jerusalem, but in the disparate lands and locales of the Book of Mormon narrative—in the ancient Americas. Rather than one central temple, the Book of Mormon spoke of various major temples surrounded by numerous smaller temple altar sanctuaries dotting the land. Their temple worship was patterned after the altar worship of the ancient Israelite temple, their temple teachings quite openly centered in the creation and Eden narratives that Smith would have recognized in part from the Genesis accounts of the Old Testament.

In the Book of Mormon narrative the first temple of Nephi appeared in the ancient Americas in the mid-sixth century BC. Later it was abandoned to enemies by fleeing exiles under Mosiah who, without notice or fanfare, built a second temple in the second century BC in a nearby land, the temple of Zarahemla. Then a century later a third temple appeared alongside this temple in the same land, the temple of Bountiful. Interwoven among these noted temple centers were temple sanctuaries; ancient prophet Alma recorded that he preached "in their *temples,* and in their *sanctuaries,* and also in their synagogues"[20] dispersed throughout the land (see Alma 16:13). These sanctuaries were altar sanctuaries (Alma 15:17), suggesting parallels to similar altar sanctuaries only briefly mentioned in the Old Testament (see Amos 7:9).

This brief sketch raises a host of fundamental questions about the temple in the New World among this devout Judeo-Christian people, revealing surprisingly diffused temple worship patterns that the Prophet would never have encountered so visibly in biblical scripture. Yet the very idea of a pervasive Book of Mormon localized temple culture suggests that the question be asked in reverse: in the Israelite worship documented in the Old Testament, how pervasive was localized altar sanctuary worship—similar to that described in the Book of Mormon—that was practiced alongside the central temple orthodoxy of the Jerusalem temple? Though unknown to Smith in the early nineteenth century, biblical scholarship of the late twentieth and twenty-first centuries suggests that in ancient Israel such suburban and exurban altar worship patterns were indeed ubiquitous, with sanctuaries "numerous and scattered throughout the country."[21]

Could it be that this archetype of diffused temple worship became prophetic prologue to Joseph Smith—a type or model that influenced his earliest expectations of a religion whose worship would be first and fundamentally centered in the temple? Among the Book of Mormon peoples, temple worship was vital and prominent, yet woven into the very fabric of community worship and local life. Constructed, utilized, and even abandoned if necessary to build again, Book of Mormon temples were a symbolic place in which heaven and earth came together. In the Book of Mormon, Christ was the center of temple worship, and the central theme underlying the temple's teachings focused on the meaning of life as contained in the stories and narratives of the creation of the world and the choices made in Eden. It seems unlikely that Smith would not have noticed that during the holiest event of the Book of Mormon narrative—the visitation of the resurrected Christ to the ancient Americas—Christ came to the people assembled at the temple in Bountiful. Most important of all, *he came to a temple.*

We see striking parallels between this vibrant Book of Mormon temple culture and Smith's expansive Mormon temple vision that began in the early nineteenth century and continued growing into the twenty-first century. His vision commenced with plans revealed in December 1830 for a large central temple in Independence, Missouri—with the expectation that Christ would come to this temple. Saints later laid cornerstones for a temple in nearby Far West (July 1838) and dedicated a temple site in Adam-ondi-Ahman (October 1838), also in Missouri. The Kirtland Temple was constructed in Ohio by early 1836 but was abandoned a year later because of persecution. And after the completion of the Nauvoo Temple in the 1840s, it too was left behind to enemies just months after its dedication.

Perhaps most striking was the significance of the new latter-day temple: the Prophet's temple worship was Christ-centered temple worship—evoking precisely the meaning of the Book of Mormon temple—now restored and reinvented nearly two millennia after the long-destroyed Second Temple of Judaism had vanished into history. Of the scriptural precedent available, only the Bountiful temple account in the Book of

Mormon documented Christ-centered temple worship in the world following the cessation of the law of Moses. Then, in the last several years of his life, in 1842, Smith instituted a more complete temple narrative in Nauvoo that infused temple worship with familiar themes of the creation and the meaning of life found in the Garden of Eden narratives.

These ideas were almost certainly known to the Prophet much earlier than 1842, even if they were not codified as temple theology until later. Beginning with his immersion in the Book of Mormon translation project in the 1820s, the Prophet became familiar with the rich creation and Eden images that were interwoven in the book's temple texts. These became an impetus for later temple-themed revelations, such as the revealed Moses and Enoch texts of 1830 that included, as Givens pointed out, "Enoch's rather surprising assertion that he makes to God, 'thou hast made me, and given me a right to thy throne' (Moses 7:59)"[22] or Smith's Vision revelation of 1832 in which God revealed that those who inhabit the celestial kingdom "are Priests of the most high; . . . they are Gods even the Sons of God (see D&C 76:57–58)."[23]

Despite all this, researchers broadly agree that the Book of Mormon received surprisingly little recognition during the early restoration. Historian Grant Underwood's content analysis of early Mormon theology found that "compared to the Bible, the Book of Mormon was hardly cited at all. . . . [I]n the early literature the Bible was cited nearly twenty times more frequently than the Book of Mormon."[24] What do we make of this paradox—this benign neglect of the Book of Mormon? Could nineteenth-century Mormonism have survived without biblically driven missionary proselytization? Probably not. Yet despite this clear biblical proclivity among early Latter-day Saints, this vital unanswered question remains: Was lack of public citation of or reference to the Book of Mormon evidence that the book therefore had no influence on Joseph Smith and the early restoration? Or perhaps did it exert more subtle, unobtrusive, inconspicuous influences—things that might not have been evident on the surface of official Mormon dialogue but nonetheless were discernible in Mormon practice, culture, and spiritual observance—in the tacit development of the church?

Could it be that the Book of Mormon had a formative influence on Joseph Smith and the founders of the Mormon restoration? Woven throughout its narratives were models, archetypes, and exemplars that Smith drew on to help formulate, define, create, and specify elements of religious structure and practice for the budding restoration—for example, how ordinances were performed (such as the sacrament), how institutions within the church developed (such as the temple), or how the church was administered (by the priesthood). These practices evolved over time, of course, but in the beginning, in the early restoration, we must see how Smith quietly looked to one of the most important sources of religious thought and sacred protocol that he knew: the Book of Mormon.

1

The Formative Influence of the Book of Mormon

THE YEAR 1973 MARKED THE BEGINNING of a watershed period for Mormonism, though it seems to have passed completely unnoticed. In that year the Church of Jesus Christ of Latter-day Saints launched a dramatically new standardized teaching pedagogy—a revolutionary approach to teaching missionary lessons to new converts.[1] This approach was similar in structure to its predecessor program that had been in effect since 1961.[2] Missionaries then had memorized over one hundred biblical scriptural passages along with six lesson dialogues (the "Brother Brown" missionary discussions) designed to provide compelling *biblical* evidence that Mormonism was the restoration of the primitive church of Christ. In 1973 the new pedagogy upended all that, requiring missionaries to memorize a modified set of eighty-four scriptural passages and six new lesson dialogues. The scriptural basis for this new teaching focused less on the Bible and more on the Book of Mormon and modern revelation—offering distinctly Mormon perspectives on salvation, Christ, and the latter-day restoration of the church of Christ.

This does not suggest that the church had demoted the Bible, but in an unprecedented way it promoted the Book of Mormon as an acknowledged, accepted instrument alongside the Bible, even assigning it a primary role in missionary conversion. For missionaries this new direction was bold and breathtaking but at the same time paradoxical. Approaching truth seekers with broadly accepted scripture like the Bible made perfect sense, but how would they respond to unknown scriptural texts—like the Book of Mormon? The new direction of the 1973 discussions made a statement, asserting unequivocally that the Book of Mormon merited its own recognition as scripture, equivalent in stature to the Bible. The new missionary pedagogy established a fresh path for teaching and conversion: not a logically designed biblical persuasion as if in a courtroom proceeding, but instead a candid assertion that Mormonism held the answers to spiritual life. The wellspring for those answers was modern scripture—beginning with the Book of Mormon.

From its inception the church had used the Bible to convince the world that Mormonism was the restored church promised anciently. Early apostle Parley P. Pratt's *A Voice of Warning*,[3] first published in 1837 and considered the most influential Mormon missionary tract of the nineteenth century,[4] established a doctrinal blueprint for missionary teaching and conversion. According to Pratt, the restoration was the fulfillment of biblical prophecy from Old Testament prophets such as Isaiah, Jeremiah, and Ezekiel and from New Testament apostles such as Paul, Peter, and John. They prophesied of what Peter called the latter-day "times of restitution of all things, which God hath spoken by the mouth of all his holy prophets since the world began" (Acts 3:21).[5] Charles Bliss's 1890 popular Mormon missionary pamphlet, *Is Baptism Essential to Salvation?*,[6] exclusively quoted New Testament sources—Luke, Paul, John, Mark, and Peter—never once mentioning similar writings from Book of Mormon prophets Nephi, Alma, Mormon, or Moroni. John Morgan's 1881 pamphlet, *Plan of Salvation*,[7] justified the unique Mormon doctrines of premortal life, physical resurrection, and the premortal mission of Christ—all by quoting biblical passages, even though the Book of Mormon discusses the plan of salvation and the plan of redemption nineteen times. The New Testament never mentions these terms.[8]

Upon its arrival in nineteenth-century North America, the Book of Mormon was considered by Latter-day Saints to be scripture. Indeed, when the Book of Mormon first appeared in 1830, both believers and nonbelievers instantly framed it as another "Bible." "Martin Harris [early Book of Mormon scribe] referred to the [printer's] manuscript as the 'Mormon Bible' when he was negotiating with the printer," wrote American historian Richard Bushman. "Newspapers derisively called it the

'Gold Bible.' Eber D. Howe, the Painesville, Ohio, editor who took an interest in Mormonism, described the recovery of the *Book of Mormon* as a 'pretended discovery of a *new Bible,* in the bowels of the earth.'"[9] Alexander Campbell's scathing critique, released because "several hundred persons of different denominations believed in it," derisively called the Book of Mormon "the Bible of the Mormonites."[10] This early biblical framing of the Book of Mormon set a tall standard for acceptance and marked the beginning of an epoch struggle over what the book was and what it should become in the religious milieu of modern Christianity. The debate continues to the present day, with the most recent example being Broadway's parody and pillory in *The Book of Mormon* musical production.

Smith himself adopted this same biblical proclivity, as shown during his visit to Washington, DC, in 1840 seeking redress for grievances following the Mormon expulsion from Missouri. A journalist for the *New York Enquirer* reported on one of Smith's public meetings:

> He [Joseph Smith] then took up the Bible. "I believe," said he, "in this sacred volume. In it the 'Mormon' faith is to be found. We teach nothing but what the Bible teaches. We believe nothing, but what is to be found in this book." . . . He closed by referring to the Mormon Bible [the Book of Mormon], which he said, contained nothing inconsistent or conflicting with the Christian Bible, and he again repeated that all who would follow the precepts of the Bible, whether Mormon or not, would assuredly be saved.[11]

Another Washingtonian observed: "He quotes from the New Testament readily in his addresses. He took good care, as there was an intelligent congregation, including several members of congress, present, to say but little about the 'Book of Mormon.'"[12]

Smith's followers were likewise unsure of how to incorporate the Book of Mormon into their religious catechism. Later in his life Brigham Young confessed: "In all my teachings, I have taught the Gospel from the Old and New Testaments. I found therein every doctrine, and the proof of every doctrine, the Latter-day Saints believe in, as far as I know, therefore I do not refer to the Book of Mormon as often as I otherwise

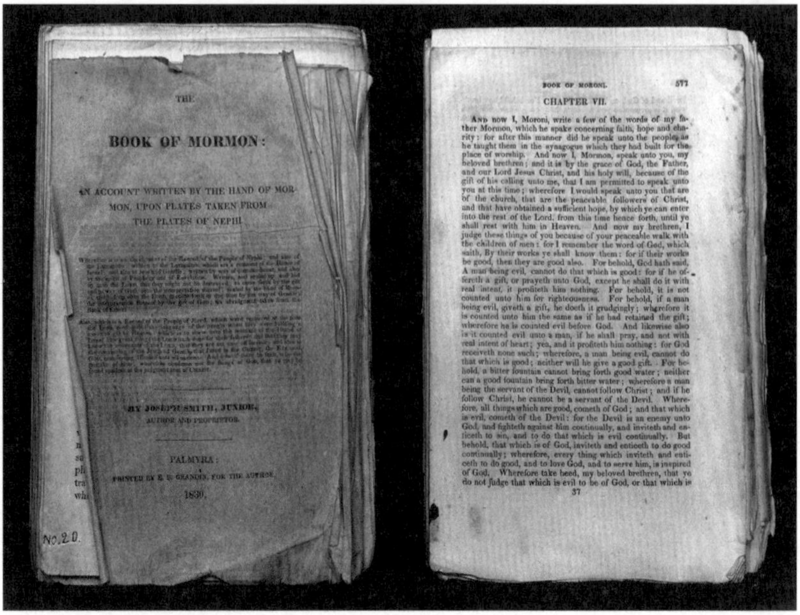

Fig. 1. The proofs of the first edition of the Book of Mormon include typeset signature marks and a copyright notice.

should."[13] Even Young's testing of the Book of Mormon's authenticity was based on the Bible:

> Christians, search the Scriptures of the Old and New Testament, for in them you think you have eternal life, and they are they that testify of the doctrine that we preach; . . . Here is the Book of Mormon. We believe it contains the history of the Aborigines of our continent, just as the Old Testament contains the history of the Jewish nation. In that book we learn that Jesus visited this continent, delivered his Gospel and ordained Twelve Apostles. We believe all this, but we do not ask you to believe it. What we do ask is that you will believe what is recorded in the Holy Bible concerning God and His revelations to the children of men. Do this in all honesty and sincerity, then you will know that the Book of Mormon is true.[14]

Grant Underwood suggested that neglect of the Book of Mormon among the faithful "was calculated to avoid Protestant antipathy to the 'new scripture.' . . . Yet no evidence exists for either a formal church directive or even an informal agreement not to use the Book of Mormon in the public ministry."[15] "Many early Mormon converts were steeped in the study of the Bible but had not 'opportunity for formal instruction or catechization in the Book of Mormon,'" concluded Mormon scholar Noel Reynolds. "Although the existence and truthfulness of the Book of Mormon was a crucial point of faith and touchstone of conversion for the early [Latter-day] Saints, it would take time and effort for the contents of that distinctive volume to come into widespread use."[16]

Still, the Book of Mormon was used during the early restoration simply because "until 1835 not much else had been printed in the Latter-day Saint library," said Mormon scholar John Welch. "Even if not cited nearly as often in ordinary Latter-day Saint religious discourse as was the Bible, it is evident that the Book of Mormon was seen as a record of ancient inhabitants of the Western Hemisphere, as a sign of the Restoration of the gospel and of Israel, and as a source for several religious teachings. Countering any perception that the Book of Mormon was rarely used or sidelined as a mere artifact, considerable evidence shows that the early Saints indeed made actual use of the Book of Mormon for many reasons, including administrative purposes."[17]

Nonetheless, the Bible remained the dominant document of scriptural discourse among Latter-day Saints, just as it was among all Christians—the lingua franca of religious discourse among nineteenth-century Christianity. To place the Book of Mormon alongside the Bible as new scripture from God—equal in stature—evoked an enormously provocative comparison that was on its face implausible. The Bible had thousands of years of scholarship, official sanction by religions and governments, and status as the unrivaled word of God by Christian and Jew alike; the Book of Mormon had none of this. To its critics, the mere proposition of new scripture in and of itself was reason enough to discredit the Book of Mormon, denigrate its publication, and vilify Smith, its perpetrator. Campbell blustered: "Smith, its real author, [is] ignorant

Fig. 2. Alexander Campbell (1788–1866) was a prominent American Restorationist Christian leader who led the development of nondenominational churches called Disciples of Christ.

and impudent a knave as ever wrote a book, . . . [it] is, without exaggeration, the meanest book in the English language. . . . It has not one good sentence in it, save the profanation of those sentences quoted from the Oracles of the living God [the Bible]."[18] Nonetheless, over the ensuing two centuries Campbell's protestations melted into history; the Book of Mormon quietly accumulated growing, if ambivalent, prominence in religion and American culture. William Tyndale's English Bible of 1526 was banned from England as treasonous and led to Tyndale's execution a decade later. Nevertheless, within a century the Tyndale Bible was broadly embraced and became the foundation for the King James Bible of 1611, one of the most influential early Bible translations.

Reframing the Book of Mormon: Derivative or formative role in the restoration

For 150 years the coming forth of the Book of Mormon became for Latter-day Saints a symbolic icon for conversion. Its sudden appearance on the stage of American religion was considered a modern miracle evoking parallels with ancient biblical miracles, yet its contents were rarely used in Mormon curricula, and its unique institutions and observances seldom scrutinized. By default the Book of Mormon was accorded secondary status as a book of scripture. A revelation recorded by Smith in 1832 chastised the Saints: "You have treated lightly the things you have received which vanity and unbelief hath brought the whole church under condemnation . . . and ~~shall~~ they shall remain under this condemnation until they repent and remember the new covenant even the Book of Mormon."[19]

The symbolic status of the Book of Mormon led to another subtle framing of the book as a derivative document, suggesting it was derived from Joseph Smith and therefore should be considered essentially as a defining expression of his modern theology. I mentioned the distinction between *derivative* and *formative* briefly in the introduction to this book, but let me explain more completely why the distinction is important. LDS missionaries frequently quote Jesus's New Testament test of a true prophet: "Every good tree bringeth forth good fruit; but a corrupt tree bringeth forth evil fruit. . . . Wherefore by their fruits ye shall know them" (Matthew 7:17, 20).[20] The coming forth of the Book of Mormon was the fruit of the restoration; it was the test of Joseph Smith's prophetic calling. Because he produced the Book of Mormon, then *if* it was true so was his divine mission as prophet.

Fig. 3. This oil portrait of Joseph Smith Jr., circa 1842, is attributed to David Rogers.

This test unnecessarily constrains our understanding of the Book of Mormon: it was not merely derivative from the Prophet but actually may have been formative in what he sensed to be his life's work to restore the modern church of Christ. If so, then the book must be examined through a different lens as an independent text. This distinction between viewing the book as derivative or formative is important because it affects how the Book of Mormon is framed, and framing is a powerful force in the arena of public discourse, persuasion, and conversion. The derivative view frames the Book of Mormon as a modern by-product of Joseph Smith: he is the book's producer and translator, and even though he changed the book's title page in the second edition (1837) to underscore the fact that he was the book's *translator* and not author, the distinction between those two roles is lost in common discourse. Still, to Mormons and non-Mormons alike, this seems a perfectly sensible way to approach the Book of Mormon. On the other hand, the derivative framing invites a series of unintended biases, for it unwittingly frames the Book of Mormon as a nineteenth-century document rather than an ancient document. In response to critics, for example, Mormons frequently recommend an implausible test: could an unschooled Joseph Smith have produced such an extraordinarily complex book of scripture in such a short time, in about two months?

This reasoning, however, has naturally invited scholars and theologians to consider a variety of potential hypotheses about the Book of Mormon's nineteenth-century appearance. Biographer Fawn Brodie proposed that Joseph Smith was a treasure seeker whose story line of golden plates eventually grew into a religious novel.[21] Although Yale scholar Harold Bloom considered Joseph Smith an imaginative genius, sufficient to create (fictional) history and great poetry, he dismissed the Book of Mormon as being unworthy of serious reading.[22] The problem with the derivative framing of the Book of Mormon is that it places Smith in the primary role of author and therefore deflects any reasonable notion that the book itself exerted a unique and independent influence on the Prophet himself and the development of the restoration.

Despite their scholarly orientation, the derivative hypotheses do not typically examine the depths of the Book of Mormon's historical and prophetic narrative, nor do they explain the subtleties and intricacies of the text itself as originating with an ancient lost people. This is an essential distinction. Of the religious works to emerge roughly contemporaneously to Joseph Smith in the eighteenth and nineteenth centuries, the Book of Mormon stood alone on one dimension: as a narrative history of an ancient people. The writings of Alexander Campbell, Barton

Fig. 4. Thomas Campbell, his son Alexander Campbell, Barton W. Stone, and Walter Scott formed the American Restoration Movement and sought a return to the pristine apostolic religion.

Stone, and Walter Scott of the Disciples and Restorationist movements (1823–66); the *Arcana Cœlestia*, by Emanuel Swedenborg (1749–56); *View of the Hebrews*, by pastor Ethan Smith (1825); *Evidence from Scripture and History of the Second Coming of Christ, about the Year 1843*, by William Miller of the Adventist movement (1841); and *Science and*

Health, with Key to the Scriptures, by Mary Baker Eddy (1889), were all interpretations of or commentaries on biblical scripture.

Nevertheless, the Book of Mormon clearly depicted historical narratives and sacred observances of an ancient people who, the book averred, had originated among the Jews of Jerusalem in the seventh century BC, migrated via an ocean voyage to a new land, and recorded over a thousand years of religious history. To outsiders, the very existence of such a fabulous sacred text provoked intense curiosity and skepticism. Nevertheless, to Smith and his transcribers, sifting word for word through the book's contents during the translation, the mere presence of this sacred ancient text in their midst in the months leading up to the church's formal organization stimulated thought, discussion, inquiry, revelation, and contemplation—all of which benefited the early organizing energies of the emerging restoration.

The formative view thus asks a fundamentally different question—how did the Book of Mormon influence Joseph Smith and the early restoration? This view implicitly frames the Book of Mormon as a divinely revealed original source text that inevitably influenced the unfolding restoration. In this view it matters less how the Book of Mormon came forth—how it was translated, transcribed, or produced (these important themes are well explored elsewhere)—but rather how it shaped or affected the doctrines, practices, and religion that would evolve into the modern Church of Jesus Christ of Latter-day Saints. The formative view focuses on the Book of Mormon—on its content, its people, its institutions, its history. What were the structures, the practices, and the rites and rituals of these ancient Book of Mormon peoples? Could their history be useful to the Prophet's mission at the birth of the restoration? For example, if Smith believed his modern mission had been to restore the church of Christ, could it be possible that he might have restored elements of a church of Christ that had existed anciently in the Americas? Was this ancient American church broadly consistent with the ancient Christian church recorded in the New Testament? If so, then using both biblical and Book of Mormon precedents, Smith had a broader palette to work with to complete his canvas, fill in gaps, and inform and shape the emerging and unfolding restoration.

Schooling the Prophet

Joseph Smith Sr. and Lucy Mack Smith tried to establish early the precedent of formal education for their three eldest children. Hyrum, at age eleven or twelve, attended Moor's Charity School, affiliated with Dartmouth College; Alvin, thirteen, and Sophronia, eight, attended a common public school in Lebanon, New Hampshire.[23] Just as Joseph Jr. would have come of age to attend school, the Smith children were plagued one by one by the typhoid fever epidemic of 1813. As a consequence, Joseph contracted severe osteomyelitis in his left leg, requiring expensive debilitating surgery and then rehabilitation in Salem, Massachusetts. Persistent indebtedness and three consecutive crop failures from 1814 to 1816 led the family to abandon New England entirely and move to western New York. There, in Palmyra, their lives became consumed earning a subsistence living. "Joseph Sr. and the older sons hired out for haying and harvesting in the peak seasons when every farmer needed extra hands," described Bushman, "and took on odd jobs like gardening and digging wells. . . . When the census taker came to the Smiths in 1820, Joseph Jr. was not listed, probably because he was living elsewhere earning during the growing season."[24] Joseph Jr. said he felt "doomed to the necessity of obtaining a scanty maintainance by his daily labor."[25]

These tumultuous years of 1813 through 1819, prime elementary years for learning, left Joseph with little opportunity for formal education, and the situation persisted through adolescence. "Suffice it to say I was mearly instructtid in reading and writing and the ground <rules> of Arithmatic which const[it]uted my whole literary acquirements,"[26] admitted Joseph in 1832. Mormon apostle John Widtsoe summarized Joseph's formal learning during his teenage and young adult years: "From the records extant, the conclusion is justifiable that from his fourteenth [1819] to his twenty-second year [1827] Joseph Smith received practically no school education, and did no extensive reading."[27]

The general notion that Joseph Smith was completely unlearned overstates the point, however. He certainly was literate and quite familiar with the Bible. According to his mother, by eighteen years of age Joseph "had never read the Bible through in his life; he seemed much less inclined to the perusal of books than any of the rest of our children, but far more given to meditation and deep study."[28] Yet she later quoted her son as boasting: "I can take my Bible, and go into the woods, and learn more in two hours, than you can learn at [church] meeting in two years, if you should go all the time."[29] Pomeroy Tucker, admittedly suspicious of Smith and the origins of Mormonism, claimed to be "well acquainted with 'Joe Smith' . . . and all the Smith family, since their removal to Palmyra from Vermont in 1816," and gave a self-described "truthful" assessment of Joseph Smith's early learning as related by neighbors and residents of Palmyra:

> Joseph, moreover, as he grew in years, had learned to read comprehensively, in which qualification he was far in advance of his elder brother [Hyrum], and even of his father; and this talent was assiduously devoted, as he quitted or modified his idle habits, to the perusal of works of fiction and records of criminality [crime novels], such for instance as would be classed with the 'dime novels' of the present day. . . . As he further advanced in reading and knowledge, he assumed a spiritual or religious turn of mind, and frequently perused the Bible, becoming quite familiar with portions thereof, both of the Old and New Testaments; selected texts from which he quoted and discussed with great assurance when in the presence of his superstitious acquaintances. The Prophecies and Revelations were his special forte.[30]

Early in Joseph's emerging career as church leader, his understanding of how the Bible would inform his work with the restoration was still quite undeveloped. When Parley P. Pratt, an early convert and self-taught preacher, spoke to the Latter-day Saints in September 1830, he

> brought forth from the prophecies of Isaiah, Jeremiah, Ezekiel and other prophets, abundant proofs concerning the work which the Lord had established through his servant Joseph[;] a great many of the Latter-day Saints were surprised that there were so many evidences existing in the Bible concerning this work. The church had then been organized some five months, but the members had never heard from any of the Elders these proofs and evidences

> which existed in the Bible. [Even scribe] Oliver Cowdery and the Prophet Joseph himself were surprised at the great amount of evidence there was in the Bible concerning these things.[31]

Still, Joseph's comfort with the Bible must have been an indispensable prerequisite for a learning phase in his young life that would immerse him in deep instruction of ancient scripture. Beginning with a vision in 1823, at age seventeen, he describes the commencement of an intense personal schooling by divine messenger Moroni, last of a line of ancient prophets to write in the ancient Book of Mormon record:

> He called me by name and said unto me that he was a messenger sent from the presence of God to me and that his name was [Moroni] That God had a work for me to do, and that my <name> should be had for good and evil among all nations kindreds and tongues. or that it should be both good and evil spoken of among all people. He said there was a book deposited written upon gold plates, giving an account of the former inhabitants of this continent and the source from whence they sprang. He also said that the fullness of the everlasting Gospel was contained in it as delivered by the Saviour to the ancient inhabitants.[32]

If Moroni's message seemed clear enough—this commission to recover an unusual buried book—he suddenly enveloped Joseph in a much more ambitious program of scriptural learning and exposition. For the remainder of the night vision, as reported by Smith, Moroni quoted, corrected, and commented on twenty-eight biblical passages, sixty-nine verses in total, from Old Testament prophets and New Testament apostles. Their themes were broad and prophetic, foretelling and retelling the future events predicted to transpire in the latter days. In spite of this, none of these scriptural passages seemed even remotely related to instructions on how to recover, interpret, or translate Moroni's yet-to-be discovered ancient record. Nearly one-third of Moroni's scriptural quotations were prophecies relating to the latter-day temple; almost one-half dealt with prophecies of the establishment of Zion in the last days; two-fifths prophesied of the latter-day gathering of Israel.[33]

Oliver Cowdery later intimated that Moroni's schooling visions were more than mere oral lectures and also included visual presentation to illuminate and elaborate on scriptural content:

> You will understand then, by this, that while those glorious things were being rehearsed, the vision was also opened, so that our brother [Joseph Smith] was permitted to see and understand much more full and perfect than I am able to communicate in writing. I know much may be conveyed to the understanding in writing, and many marvelous truths set forth with the pen, but after all it is but a shadow, compared to an open vision of seeing, hearing and realizing eternal things.[34]

Moroni's schooling vision was replicated annually over a four-year period, from 1823 to 1827, in advance of obtaining the actual Book of Mormon record. Increasingly, it must have been evident that God's "work for [Joseph] to do" portended a larger mission than merely unearthing the buried ancient record.[35] Moroni's instruction seemed intent on shaping and molding the expectations of the young prophet, schooling him in themes relating to the temple, the gathering of Israel, and a latter-day Zion that would precede the prophesied coming of the Messiah. In all, researchers have identified twenty-two visits from Moroni, ten during this preparatory four-year period and another twelve during the two-year translation period of the Book of Mormon, 1828 and 1829.[36]

September 1827 marked the completion of this early course of scriptural mentoring under Moroni, when Smith then received access to the plates. With plates in hand, he then embarked on the translation project itself, which constituted a new and more hands-on course of learning involving twenty-two months of immersion, from September 1827 to June 1829, in unusual and previously unknown ancient textual material. Like a modern-day graduate dissertation, this process involved setting up secure research locations, improvising translation protocols, organizing scribes as assistants, and even at one point seeking external verification with a scholar at Columbia College (today Columbia University) in New York City. Throughout the process there are hints that the research was revealing and stimulating, unfolding insights into who these ancient Book of Mormon peoples were. Joseph's mother, Lucy Mack Smith, recalled, "During our evening conversations, Joseph would occasionally give us some of the most amusing recitals that could be imagined. He would describe the ancient inhabitants of this continent, their dress, mode of traveling, and the animals upon which they rode; their cities, their buildings, with every particular; their mode of warfare; and also their religious worship. This he would do with as much ease, seemingly, as if he had spent his whole life among them."[37]

After translating, he spent eight months financing, proofing, printing, and publishing his translation project as a book—the Book of Mormon. For Joseph Smith, this alone was a signal accomplishment, reflecting grit, vision, and determination. Ralph Waldo Emerson, for example, published his first groundbreaking essay, "Nature," in 1836, ten years after leaving Harvard.[38] Richard Bushman and Dean Jessee summarized Smith's unique path of embarking on his religious career:

> In March 1830, Joseph Smith published the 584-page Book of Mormon, an unusual beginning for a life as a minister of the gospel. No other religious career in Smith's time began this way. Others of his generation claimed visions, but none published a "translation" or wrote a parallel Bible. Charles G. Finney, an apprentice lawyer in Adams, New York, claimed to see a vision of Christ at the time of his conversion in 1821, but Finney immediately began preaching; he went on to become the most influential evangelical preacher of his generation. Other budding religious reformers took the same path, moving from visionary to preacher. Joseph Smith, instead of communicating with the world through sermons, made his entrance onto the religious stage with the translation of a large book of ancient records. Though not widely read himself, he instinctively sensed the increasing potency of print in disseminating religious knowledge.[39]

Considering the influence of the Book of Mormon and the Bible

This background sets up a perplexing paradox: after the prodigious effort and signal achievement involved in publishing his life's work to that point, after the excitement among friends culminating in seven early revelations citing the Book of Mormon as a "marvelous work," did Joseph Smith subsequently ignore it for the rest of his life? Terryl Givens confirms that at least in the Prophet's public discourse this indeed seems to have been the case:

> Joseph was relentless and adamant in presenting the story of the Book of Mormon's reception and translation as the paramount sign of his prophethood, even as he distanced himself—and potential readers—from what lay between its covers. He never sermonized from it. He virtually never quoted from it. After its publication, he never demonstrated intimate knowledge of its content or story line or themes. It is as if, like a court stenographer, he felt the text flow through him without ever taking cognizance of it. There is no evidence that he studied the Book of Mormon, or even read it after its publication (except to make the most minor of grammatical changes for subsequent editions).[40]

Could it be that the young Smith sensed that self-citation would provoke criticism and ridicule? There is evidence that the extreme skepticism he received after going public with his first vision in 1820 led him to pull back and assimilate for a period into the Protestant religious milieu of upstate New York. It may be that he felt determined to let the Book of Mormon stand entirely on its own, similar to Moroni's concluding spiritual appeal before sealing up his record: "I would exhort you that ye would ask God, the Eternal Father, in the name of Christ, if these things are not true; and if ye shall ask with a sincere heart, with real intent, having faith in Christ, and he will manifest the truth of it unto you, by the power of the Holy Ghost" (see Moroni 10:4).[41] Or perhaps Smith's and Cowdery's time and focus were consumed in organizing a new church—establishing preaching and baptizing protocols, administering membership, settling disputes, organizing congregations; they might have looked to the Book of Mormon as a useful source for polity because those were the pressing concerns of the new restoration. Nevertheless, for everyday preaching and conversion it simply was easier for them—and their converts—to fall back on old familiar biblical narratives and passages.

Perhaps Smith's avoidance of public citation was merely one layer of evidence among other less visible layers pointing to a connection between the ancient source document, the Book of Mormon, and the modern institutional religious forms that would emerge during the church's early restoration. Could it be that in fact the Book of Mormon exerted more subtle tacit influences that never could have been discerned without exposing deeper patterns and underlying associations? In the world of scholarship, citation is clearly one measure of a work's influence, but certainly not the only one. Another is adoption, whether a body of work is adopted or adapted by others, either in whole or in part. Beethoven's innovative body of music was directly influential on subsequent music composers Brahms, Liszt, Chopin, Schubert, and Schumann. Sometimes they dedicated a musical work specifically to Beethoven—that is, they recognized his influence by citation—but often they simply adopted or adapted his ideas: the descending and rising harmonies of thirds and sixths and the extended symphonic form with delayed transition from the middle to the finale.[42]

The same is true of the Bible. Lord Melvyn Bragg argued substantively that the King James Bible, published in 1611, became the most influential book in the English-speaking world by providing the seedbed for the foundations of religion, law, government, culture, and nation empires:

> The King James Bible was the steel of will and belief that forged America and other British colonies. It has inspired missionaries around the globe and consoled the hopeless in their desperation. It was used by the enforcers of slavery and later by the liberators of slaves, and transformed into liberation theology by the slaves themselves. It became the bedding of gospel music and the spirituals which set in motion soul, blues, jazz and rock, the unique cultural gift of America to the world. It has defined and re-defined sexual attitudes. It has fortified and provoked philosophy. Followers of the King James Version—as it is known in America—provided the vocabulary, the seedbed and construction model for the early development of democracy. It was the consolidating voice of two world empires. . . . Its ferocious sense of mission transformed and sometimes destroyed native cultures. For centuries the King

> James Bible fed some of the finest thinkers and artists and men of science and politics; others it persecuted.[43]

Like the King James Bible, so also the religious expressions, institutions, and observances of the Book of Mormon peoples, chronicled by ancient prophets previously unknown to the world—Mormon, Nephi, Mosiah, Alma, Jacob, and Moroni, among many others—would have had a similar formative influence on Smith and the founders of the restoration of the early nineteenth century. The Book of Mormon provided its own vocabulary, seedbed, and liturgical models that were unique and distinct in ways that would effectively define Mormonism as a new religion, with new visions and distinctive theologies. Moreover, the Book of Mormon's models were immediately accessible because Smith and his associates had just spent the better part of the late 1820s translating and scrutinizing the book's text. Yet because the book was the uneven compilation of "more than a thousand years of history involving some two hundred named individuals and nearly a hundred distinct places . . . [based on accounts from] dozens of preexisting records,"[44] explained scholar Grant Hardy, its models were in many ways abstruse; they required careful study, reflection, deliberation, and time to distill the uneven textual narratives into cogent religious forms, meanings, expressions, and doctrinal distillations.

The influence of the translation process

There remains, however, another vital question: Did Joseph Smith learn from the translation process itself? Late in his life (in 1887), David Whitmer, one of three witnesses who claimed to have been shown the plates by Moroni, described the translation process in automatic terms: "One character at a time would appear, and under it was the interpretation in English. Brother Joseph would read off the English to Oliver Cowdery, who was his principal scribe, and when it was written down and repeated by Brother Joseph to see if it was correct, then it would disappear, and another character with the interpretation would

Fig. 5. These collaborators of the early restoration, designated as the Three Witnesses to the Book of Mormon, are Oliver Cowdery (1806–1850), David Whitmer (1805–1888), and Martin Harris (1783–1875).

appear."[45] Martin Harris, also one of the Three Witnesses and an early scribe, provided a similar description: "Sentences would appear and were read by the Prophet and written by Martin, and when finished he would say, 'Written,' and if correctly written, that sentence would disappear and another appear in its place, but if not written correctly it remained until corrected."[46]

Still, the Harris and Whitmer accounts may have been speculative, surmised Mormon scholar Stephen D. Ricks: "Neither David Whitmer nor Martin Harris had knowledge of the method of translation of the Book of Mormon from personal experience. . . . Their notions concerning the translation probably derive as much from the inerrantist preconceptions concerning Holy Writ which were common at the time."[47] Based on his pioneering research on the original Book of Mormon manuscript, linguistic scholar Royal Skousen commented: "It turns out that these kinds of claims are not supported by the evidence in the original manuscript. Of course, the witnesses themselves did not see what Joseph saw. For these kinds of claims, the witnesses were either offering their own conjectures or perhaps recalling what Joseph might have told them. Nonetheless, all seemed to believe that Joseph Smith actually saw words in English, and there is evidence in the original manuscript to support this idea."[48]

Skousen proposed a "tight control" explanation of the translation process—the translation was divinely received with some precision, a view that has received considerable recent scholarly support. For example, linguist Stanford Carmack shows that the Book of Mormon text does not loosely borrow from the English language forms of the King James Bible but appears to follow forms of Early Modern English of essentially the late 1500s: "Textual evidence and syntactic analysis argue strongly against 19th-century composition and an imitative effort based on King James English. Book of Mormon past-tense syntax could have been achieved only by following the use of largely inaccessible 16th-century writings,"[49] the Elizabethan era of English literature.

Skousen summarized his findings of tight control from his research:

> All witnesses of the translation stated that Joseph Smith dictated the text of the Book of Mormon. This claim is supported by certain errors in the original manuscript which clearly resulted from the scribe mishearing what Joseph had dictated. . . . Joseph [likely] had at least twenty words in view as he was dictating. . . . Joseph Smith sometimes spelled out names to the scribe. And we find evidence in the original manuscript in support of this process. . . . The specific evidence from the original manuscript is consistent with the claim that the scribe read back what had been written. In such a process, Joseph Smith would be checking what he was hearing from the scribe against what he was viewing in the interpreters. . . . There is substantial evidence within the text itself for tight control over specific words, phrases, and sentences of English.[50]

He concluded:

> All of this evidence (from the witnesses' statements, the original manuscript, the printer's manuscript, and from the text itself) is thus consistent with the hypothesis that Joseph Smith could actually see (whether in the interpreters themselves or in his mind's eye) the translated English text—word for word and letter for letter—and that he read off this revealed text to his scribe. Despite Joseph's

> reading off of the text, one should not assume that this process was automatic or easily done. Joseph had to prepare himself spiritually for this work. Yet the evidence suggests that Joseph was not the author of the Book of Mormon, not even its English language translation, although it was revealed spiritually through him and in his own language.[51]

There are additional explanations of the translation process. Attorney and Mormon philosopher Blake Ostler argued that Smith's translation was revelatory, that "the translation was not merely mechanical or 'automatic' but involved human thought and feelings as well as divine response . . . [and] was not merely from one language into another but was also a transformation from one thought-world to another that expands and explains the meaning of the original text in terms that Joseph Smith and his contemporaries would understand."[52] Brant Gardner, specialist in Mesoamerican studies, concluded that the vast majority of the Book of Mormon translation followed what he termed a more *functional* translation protocol that "adheres to the organization and structures of the original [ancient text] but is more flexible in the [modern] vocabulary. It allows the [modern] target language to use words that are not direct equivalents of the [ancient] source words, but which attempt to preserve the intent of the source text."[53] Thus, he notes that "the King James translation of the Bible frequently mentions 'candles' even though oil lamps provided light during both the Old and New Testaments. While 'candle' is an anachronism, it is an artifact of the translation, not the original text."[54] In the same way, it is surprising to "see the word 'money' in the English Book of Mormon, since Mesoamerican peoples, including those in the Book of Mormon, operated in a nonmonetary economy. Nevertheless, [the term] 'money' still operates as a functional equivalent. . . . Although not a literalist equivalent, 'money' nevertheless stands for a medium of exchange. The exchange existed, even though our concept of money did not."[55]

Emma Smith, Joseph's wife, who sometimes served as scribe and closely observed the translation project from start to finish, gave this description to her son Joseph III in 1879:

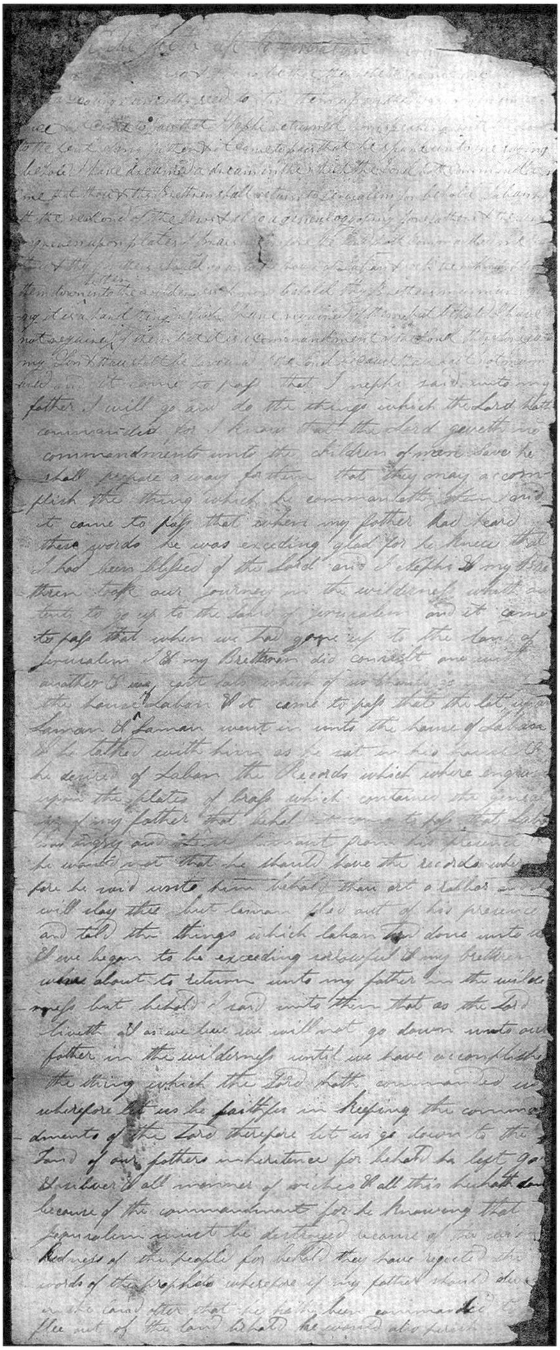

Fig. 6. Only about a quarter of the original manuscript of the Book of Mormon is extant. This portion is designated as "The First Book of Nephi: His Reign and Ministry" (1 Nephi 2:2b–3:18a).

> [Your father] had neither manuscript nor book to read from. If he had had anything of the kind he could not have concealed it from me. I was an active participant in the scenes that transpired, and was present during the translating of the plates, and had cognizance of things as they transpired, it is marvelous to me, "a marvel and a wonder," as much so as to anyone else. . . . My belief is that the Book of Mormon is of divine authenticity—I have not the slightest doubt of it. I am satisfied that no man could have dictated the writing of the manuscript unless he was inspired; for, when [I was] acting as his scribe, your father would dictate to me hour after hour; and when returning after meals, or after interruptions, he would at once begin where he had left off, without either seeing the manuscript or having any portion of it read to him.[56]

The early accounts reveal little evidence of difficulty or cognitive challenge. A late nineteenth-century church publication made the process appear effortless: "There were no delays over obscure passages, no difficulties over the choice of words, no stoppages from the ignorance of the translator; no time was wasted in the investigation or argument over the value, intent or meaning of certain characters, and there were no references to authorities. These difficulties to human work were removed. All was as simple as when a clerk writes from dictation."[57]

Still, Smith himself was never quite so definitive. In an 1842 publication he described the translation process in these terms: "Immediately after my arrival there I commenced copying the characters of ~~all~~ the plates. I copyed a considerable number of them and by means of the Urim and Thummin I translated some of them which I did between the time I arrived at the house of my wife's father in the month of December, and the February following."[58] Elsewhere he described the process simply as by the "gift and power of God."[59] With inquisitive literati during his visit to Washington, DC, in 1840, he was more oblique: "The Mormon Bible, he said, was communicated to him, *direct from heaven*. If there was such a thing on earth, as the author of it, then he (Smith) was the author; but the idea that he wished to impress was, that he had penned it as dictated by God."[60] At a conference in 1831 Joseph "said that it was not intended to tell the world all the particulars of the coming forth of the Book of Mormon, & also said that it was not expedient for him to relate these things."[61]

Why not be more definitive? Perhaps he simply couldn't. Even for a prophet working by inspiration, the process nonetheless may have been both complex and challenging, and at least difficult to articulate or to describe to others. His revelations describe his translation abilities as a gift: "He [Joseph] hath A gift to translate the book, & I [God] have commanded him that he ~~should~~ shall pretend to no other gift."[62] By contrast, scribe Cowdery assumed the translating process could be easily replicated and picked up with a few tries. He was surprised at how difficult the task was. A revelation corrected his misperceptions:

> Behold you have not understood you have Supposed that I would give it unto you when you took no thought save it was to ask me but Behold I say unto you that you must study it out in your mind then you must ask me if it be right & if it is right I will cause that your bosom shall burn within you therefore you shall feel that it is right but if it be not right you shall have no such feelings but you shall have stupor of thought that shall cause you to forget the thing which is wrong there-fore you cannot wriete that which is sacred save it be given unto you.[63]

Thus, apparently for Cowdery and, by inference, for Smith as well, translating involved deliberative effort, spiritual insight, and confirmation from God. There is, however, another stream of emerging evidence of Joseph's perceptive engagement while translating and making grammatical revisions to the Book of Mormon. This confirmation is found in a literary device used frequently in the Book of Mormon text—corrective conjunction phrases.[64] For example, in one Book of Mormon passage in the book of Mosiah, as the sons of Mosiah prepared to embark on separate missions to the Lamanites, the translated text describing Ammon's leadership role among them is as follows: "Now Ammon *being the chief among them, or rather he did administer unto them*; and he departed from them, after having blessed them according to their several stations, *having imparted the word of God unto them, or administered unto them* before his departure; and thus they took their several journeys throughout the land" (see Alma 17:18).[65] In the first half and again in the second half of this sentence, two thought phrases were linked by a corrective conjunction—*or rather* (in the first half) and *or* (in the second half)—to fully express the meaning of the original language in English.

One can easily observe in the Book of Mormon text many similar corrective conjunction phrases that stand out in the textual narrative as awkward, noticeable attempts to correct, clarify, or amplify a mistaken or incomplete thought or expression without going back and completely restating the initial idea from the beginning. Here is another example from the Book of Mormon: "And after the house of Israel should be scattered they should be gathered together again; *or, in fine*, after the Gentiles had received the fulness of the Gospel" (see 1 Nephi 10:14).[66] This type of corrective conjunction phrase occurs 163 times in the 1830 edition, averaging roughly one for every three pages. For any translator—whether Joseph Smith or ancient editors or translators like Mormon or Moroni who had no access to modern word-processing or textual correction capabilities—the usage of corrective conjunctions would have been a useful, if not indispensable, tool to progress through a literary work while making textual corrections and amendments extemporaneously.[67]

What is telling is how the Prophet treated these awkward corrective conjunction phrases, many of which seemingly could have, and indeed should have, been changed to improve the readability of the Book of Mormon text. The fact that Smith made many minor changes in subsequent Book of Mormon editions is well known, as shown in the 1837 Kirtland second edition and the 1840 Nauvoo third edition. "In his editing for the 1837 and 1840 editions, [Smith] made several thousand changes," explained Hardy, "virtually all grammatical or stylistic in nature, in an attempt to modernize the language."[68] Skousen provides a list of 719 important changes across all editions to the present day; simple inspection shows them to be essentially grammatical changes.[69] But how many corrective conjunction phrases were changed across successive editions? Remarkably I found no significant changes in corrective conjunction phrases across Book of Mormon editions. From the earliest text (Skousen's Yale edition), to the 1830 edition, to the 1837 edition, to the 1840 edition, the corrective conjunction phrases that I studied remained surprisingly constant over time. This was true even for corrective conjunction phrases that appeared to involve an apparent error or mistake. In other words, over time and across editions the Prophet chose to retain the original translation of corrective conjunction phrases, including seemingly obvious errors and mistakes. Here are a few examples from the 1830 edition where one might expect to have seen changes:

- Jarom 1:14 upon them the record of our wars are engraven, according to the writings of the kings, *or* those which they caused to be written.
- Mosiah 2:31 if ye shall keep the commandments of my son [Mosiah$_2$], *or* the commandments of God which shall be delivered unto you by him.
- Mosiah 7:8 they stood before the king [Limhi], and were permitted, *or rather* commanded, that they should answer the questions which he should ask them.
- Alma 1:15 and there he [Nehor] was caused, *or rather* did acknowledge, between the heavens and the earth, that what he had taught to the people was contrary to the word of God.
- Alma 11:46 And thus ended the words of Amulek, *or* this is all that I [Mormon?] have written.

Why the persistent refusal to tamper with these inelegant corrective conjunction phrases? Their persistence, virtually unchanged through time, versus the "thousands" of grammatical changes across successive Book of Mormon editions is very striking and suggests to me a dichotomy in Joseph Smith's mind. Grammar and stylistic syntax appear to have been treated as transitory and subject to change even as Joseph attempted "to modernize the language" in later editions.[70] Yet history, doctrine, theology, and liturgies of this ancient people—the canonical content contained in the corrective conjunction phrases—evidently were judged to be essentially unalterable and permanent. Smith seems to have been much less willing to tamper with this type of scriptural content. Why? Perhaps because he knew they were not entirely his own to tamper with—errors and all. They belonged to the ancient prophets, historians, editors, and writers of the original Book of Mormon texts—with all the mistakes and imperfections endemic to *their* writings, whether originating with principal engravers Mormon, Moroni, or Nephi or with other writers they had sourced for their written material.

Another intriguing possibility is that Joseph Smith understood that the translation of the entire Book of Mormon record was not his translation at all but instead was the translation of another ancient historian, editor, or redactor—he (Joseph) therefore would have been a transcriber of the anciently translated record. Mormon scholar Roger Terry studied archaic English pronouns (*thee*, *thou*, *ye*, *you*) in the English translation of the Book of Mormon and suggested this possibility. The Book of Mormon "is a human translation. And it shows all the signs of being just that. Someone wrestled with the words and phrases and did so very imperfectly. But who was the human translator? Joseph? I doubt this."[71] He proposes that the translator may have been ancient prophet Moroni, the final writer, editor, and redactor of the Book of Mormon, who then directed the Prophet's discovery and transcription of the original text plates during the successive visions of 1823 to 1829.

Conclusion

In conclusion, we can see evidence of the Prophet's engagement during and after the translation (dictating, sometimes spelling, reading back, and correcting), as well as in his judgment and decision making (what to change and what to retain) as he immersed himself into the detailed phrases, words, and meanings of the Book of Mormon text. He made many grammatical changes across editions but left all corrective conjunction phrases virtually intact—even though many of these phrases contained apparent errors and mistakes. These awkward corrective sentence forms were accorded much greater weight than the grammatical—they belonged to a higher critical realm of historical narrative, doctrine, theology, and liturgy. Significantly, these sentence forms were preserved—mistakes and all—for the world to see, signaling that this scriptural text was at once in the realm of the divine, with miraculous visions and revelations from God; yet the text itself clearly was imperfect, not only in presentation grammar (which Smith tried to perfect over time), but even in the substantive and canonical texts (which he clearly did not)—a truly revealing paradox. As with the Bible, we see evidence of the hand of God but also the imperfections of inexpert writers and translators, both ancient and modern, trying to carry out this commissioned work of God. It appears to be what it says it is—the writings of ancient prophets, writers, and teachers of God in their own words, that is, the writings of Mormon, and of Moroni, and of Nephi, and so on.

We must also consider the facilitating effect of Cowdery on Smith's learning throughout the translation project. Cowdery transcribed, reread, and edited, all the while carefully comparing the detailed texts of both the original manuscript and the printer's manuscript of the Book of Mormon for meaning and clarity. He seems to have been a catalyst to the Prophet, an especially inquisitive intellectual collaborator as main scribe in Joseph's dictation of the text. Oliver came from an accomplished literary family with four of six children becoming either doctors or lawyers.[72] A schoolteacher at the beginning of the translation project, Oliver later became a well-respected attorney in Ohio. William Lang, an apprentice in Cowdery's law office, later mayor of Tiffin, Ohio, and a member of the Ohio Senate, described Mr. Cowdery as "an able lawyer and a great advocate. His manners were easy and gentlemanly; he was polite, dignified, yet courteous. . . . His addresses to the court and jury were characterized by a high order of oratory, with brilliant and forensic force."[73]

Oliver appears particularly inquisitive while working with Joseph throughout the translation, asking questions or stimulating discussion between the two that led them to seek answers through further revelation. For example, Smith recorded: "During the month of April I continued to translate, and he [Oliver] to write with little cessation, during which time we received several revelations. A difference of opinion arising between us about the account of John the Apostle, mentioned in the new testament, John, twenty first chapter and twenty second verse, whether he died, or whether he continued [likely while translating 3 Nephi 28:6–7]; ~~We~~ we mutually agreed to settle <it> by the Urim and Thummin, and the following is the word which we received."[74] The answer is recorded in chapter six of the 1833 Book of Commandments [D&C 7]. On another occasion, Cowdery recorded, "After writing the account given of the Savior's ministry to the remnant of the seed of Jacob, upon this continent [3 Nephi 11–29 modern edition], . . . [o]n reflecting further, it was as easily to be seen . . . [that] none had authority from God to administer the ordinances of the gospel [baptism]."[75] Smith records they then "went into the woods to pray and inquire of the Lord respecting baptism for the remission of sins as we found mentioned in the translation of the plates. While we were thus employed praying and calling upon the Lord, a Messenger from heaven, descended in a cloud of light, and having laid his hands upon us, he [John the Baptist] ordained us."[76] The words to this revelation are recorded in section 13 of the modern LDS Doctrine and Covenants.

Of the handful of Book of Mormon scribes Joseph Smith worked with, the collaborative work that he did with Cowdery especially exhibits this beneficial learning pattern of translating, questioning, and discussing, followed by direct revelation. This joint effort was one of the great collaborations of the early restoration.

The point here is that even though Joseph Smith possessed a gift for translation, he still must have invested significant cognitive and revelatory effort in translating the ancient Book of Mormon writings before him—both during and after the completion of the translation. The numerous corrections in the printer's manuscript and subsequent editions, as well as his selective treatment of corrective conjunction phrases, suggest this involvement. Through this process, it seems clear that Smith and Cowdery would have learned and assimilated detailed contextual information from the Book of Mormon narrative that would eventually prove useful to the emerging designs of the early restoration.

If the Prophet and his associates learned, or were schooled, by the Book of Mormon translation process, then we turn our attention to the larger question of what it is that they learned. It would be relatively straightforward to show the adoption of various Book of Mormon religious forms and observances—we see this frequently in the early restoration in rites and ordinances, doctrinal nuances, priesthood structures and practices, and forms and patterns of temple development and temple worship. This schooling process consists of much more, which becomes evident as we scratch beneath the surface and explore more deeply these various spheres. We are interested not merely in what was taught, but especially in how this schooling appears to have taken place, the ways in which it influenced the unfolding restoration. Let us now explore these ideas more deeply and see how the Book of Mormon influenced the early restoration.

2

Influences on Doctrine and Theology

From its beginnings in the early nineteenth century, Mormonism's doctrines and beliefs became a source of contention and controversy with competing Christian orthodoxy. Among other things, Joseph Smith taught that Zion would be restored to America; the fall of Adam was a fortunate fall with the promise of eternal progression; the Trinity consists of three separate Gods: the Father, Son, and the Holy Ghost; God is embodied, not a spirit; and Satan existed in premortality as a son of God. Terryl Givens commented on Smith's interpretation of Adam's fall as a "fortunate fall." According to creedal Christianity, "the fall is divinely mitigated disaster, but it is first and foremost a disaster." Givens elaborated, "Not so in Mormonism, which rewrites the expression to deny the catastrophe altogether. The fall itself is fortunate, insofar as it unleashes not the triple specter of sin, death, and depravity but the possibilities of human incarnation and the educative processes of mortality."[1]

Where did these distinct doctrines come from, and what was the Book of Mormon's role in the emergence of this unique theology? In this chapter we examine how Book of Mormon theology helped frame Mormonism's distinctive theology as Smith established a unique model for doctrinal development based on modern scripture. We begin with interpretations of God.

Interpreting the first vision of God and Christ

In 1829, even before the organization of the formal church in 1830, the name embraced for Smith's new religion was the Church of Christ, consistent with the name of a Book of Mormon "church of Christ" documented as existing in the ancient Americas for perhaps half a millennium—beginning with Alma's new church of Christ organized in the second century BC (Mosiah 18:17), acknowledged again at the appearance of Christ in the Americas (3 Nephi 27:5–10), and mentioned later in editor Mormon's record as still extant in the early third century AD (4 Nephi 1:29). David Whitmer, who left Mormonism after the collapse of the financial institution called the Kirtland Safety Society during the economic panic of 1837, detailed the history of the name of the church: "In June, 1829, the Lord gave us the name by which we must call the church, being the same as He gave the Nephites. We obeyed His commandment, and called it The Church of Christ until 1834, when, through the influence of Sydney Rigdon, the name of the church was changed to 'The Church of the Latter Day Saints,' dropping out the name of Christ entirely, and which Christ by His own lips makes so plain."[2] Rigdon was a former reformed Baptist preacher and previously affiliated with Alexander Campbell's movement that also named its various local churches the "Church of Christ." Finally, in 1838 Joseph Smith recorded by formal revelation the official name for the new religion, reflecting essential identities of both Christ and modern Saints: "For thus shall my Church be called in the Last days even the Church of Jesus Christ of Latter Day Saints."[3]

From its earliest beginnings the name of the church seemed designed to place a stake in the soil of American religion that this new religion was Christian. For example, in Smith's earliest vision, which later came to be known as the "first vision," he described seeing "two personages, (whose brightness and glory dify all description,) standing above [me] in the air. One of them called me by name, [and] said (pointing to the other,) this is my beloved son, hear him."[4] During Smith's life, and throughout Mormonism, this was considered the defining modern vision of God and Jesus Christ, the seminal moment of the boy prophet's early career. Still, his earliest account suggests that he perceived the first vision to be more intimate and personal than theological: "I saw the Lord and he spake unto me saying Joseph <my son> thy sins are forgiven thee. go thy <way> walk in my statutes and keep my commandments."[5] Yet it must have been clear from his first encounter with the divine that the God of his vision differed substantially from the Trinitarian conception of the God of orthodox Christianity. The Methodist *Book of Discipline* of 1808 spoke of "one living and true God, everlasting, without body or parts, of infinite power, wisdom, and good . . . three persons, of one substance, power, and eternity—the Father, the Son, and the Holy Ghost."[6] Still, at age fourteen Joseph was struck by the forgiveness he achieved in his initial vision; an 1830 revelation confirmed that after "<it> truly was manifested unto this first Elder [Joseph] that he had Received a remission of his sins he was entangeled again in the vanities of the world but after truly Repenting God ministered unto him by an Holy Angel."[7] In other words, even a decade after the first vision, the Prophet looked back in reflection on the early years of the 1820s and defined this spiritual experience in terms of his personal worthiness before God—his sins, repentance, and remission of sin.[8]

One reason for Smith's introspection was the sudden and surprising backlash he encountered when he initially shared his first vision. One preacher "treated my communication not only lightly but with great contempt, saying it was all of the Devil, that there was no such thing as visions or revelations in these days, that all such things had ceased with the apostles."[9] Joseph described "a hot persecution, and this was common <among> all the sects: all united to persecute me."[10] Though his 1838 historical account recalled feelings of an epoch struggle in confronting his adversaries—"I felt much like ~~as~~ Paul ~~did~~ when he made his defence before King Aggrippa and related the account of the Vision he had when ~~t~~he saw a light and heard a voice"[11]—the Prophet quietly reconsidered the public impact of his vision. His earliest 1832 recorded account of the first vision left this final humble coda: "My soul was filled with love and for many days I could rejoice with great Joy and the Lord was with me but could find none that would believe the hevnly vision nevertheless I pondered these things in my heart."[12]

In fact, the religious criticism appeared to have had a restraining effect, causing Joseph to assimilate back into the surrounding Protestant milieu. "There is no contemporary evidence (that is, documents from the 1820s) to show that Joseph Smith told his story very widely in 1820; and it is not clear, even from his own accounts, how long he continued to tell it," commented Mormon scholars James Allen and John Welch. "With the reception he apparently received, it was probably not very long."[13] In the next section I want to paint a contrasting before/after picture of the Prophet's religious life in the years prior to the beginning of the Book of Mormon project in 1827 and then compare it to a similar portrait of the period immediately after. The difference is striking and revealing, showing the quite sudden transformation from young school-age adolescent to young prophet—pivoting on the moment the Book of Mormon translation got under way.

Smith's religious beginnings in the 1820s and his emergent prophetic awakening

Throughout the early and middle years of the 1820s, rather than challenge the established religions of the so-called "burned-over district" of upstate New York, Joseph, and indeed the entire Smith family, lived a life of diffident truth seeking, looking for answers and even solace from their various Protestant coreligionists, sometimes working alongside them, attending meetings, and worshipping with them. For example, Joseph maintained a continuing on-and-off association with Methodism through 1828, even after taking possession of the Book of Mormon plates. "My mind became somewhat partial to the Methodist sect, and I felt some desire to be united with them,"[14] he recounted, speaking of his early life prior to 1820. Orsamus Turner, Palmyra contemporary to Smith until summer 1822, recorded: "After catching a spark of Methodism in the camp meeting, away down in the woods, on the Vienna road, he [Joseph] was a very passable exhorter in evening meetings."[15] Pomeroy Tucker, another Palmyra contemporary to Smith, described the Prophet's association with the Methodists: "At one time [Joseph] joined the probationary class of the Methodist church in Palmyra, and made some active demonstrations of engagedness, though his assumed convictions were insufficiently grounded or abiding to carry him along to the saving point of conversion, and he soon withdrew from the class."[16]

According to Presbyterian scholar John Matzko, "a childhood acquaintance, Lorenzo Saunders, recalled that the first time he ever attended Sabbath School he went with 'young Joe Smith at the old Presbyterian Church.'"[17] "At some unspecified date," noted Richard Bushman, "Lucy [Mack Smith, Joseph's mother] finally overcame her reservations and joined the Western Presbyterian Church in Palmyra, probably the best established church in the village and before 1823 the only one with a building of its own. Hyrum, Sophronia, and Samuel joined with her."[18]

At the sudden death of Joseph's brother Alvin in November 1823, Presbyterian Reverend Benjamin B. Stockton officiated at the funeral; he later led a Palmyra religious revival of 1824–25 (similar to the religious revival of 1819 prior to Smith's first vision).[19] According to Lucy Mack Smith, "About this time [1824] there was a great revival in religion and the whole neighborhood was very much aroused to the subject and we among the rest flocked to the meeting house to see if there was a word of comfort for us that might relieve our overcharged feelings."[20] Joseph himself, however, remained aloof from Presbyterianism, according to his mother Lucy's account:

> Shortly after the death of Alvin [Smith], a man came into the neighborhood, and commenced laboring to effect a union of the different churches, in order that all might be agreed, and thus worship God with one heart and with one mind. This seemed about right to me, and I felt much inclined to join in with them: in fact, the most of the family appeared quite disposed to unite with the rest in the general union; but Joseph from the first utterly refused, even to attend their meetings; saying, "mother, I do not wish to prevent you from going to meeting; or any of the rest of the family, or even your joining any church you please; but do not ask me to join them. [He] would say: that it would do us no injury to join them; for, if we did ~~should~~, we would not continue with them long, for we were mistaken in them.[21]

METHODIST ITINERANT SYSTEM

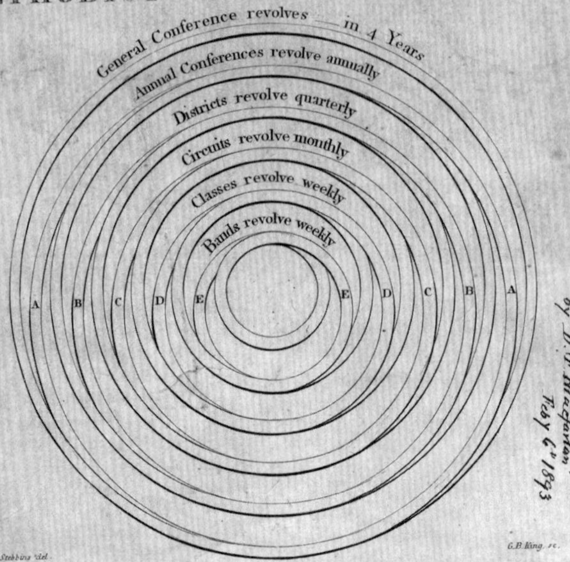

Presented to the Methodist Historical Society by D. T. Macfarlan Feby 6th 1893

It is here seen that the Methodist Connexion in America, is represented under the notion of an orbit within an orbit, or a wheel within a wheel, and is very analogous to the revolving order of the Planets. By the gradation of the circles one within another, and the ligaments, A. B. C. D. E. connecting them together, are beautifully represented the corporating genius of the Methodist Connexion.

The divisions and sub-divisions of the Church are recognized by the following names and functions:

General Conference—Bishops in charge.
Annual Conferences—Subject to the General Conference—Bishops in charge.
Districts—Subject to the Annual Conferences—Presiding Elders in charge.
Circuits—Subject to the Districts—Elders in charge.
Classes—Subject to the Circuits—Class-Leaders in charge.
Bands—Subject to the Elders—Band-Leaders in charge.

There is 1 General Conference in America.
12 Annual Conferences.
70 Districts.
545 Circuits.
Classes consist of 12, or more members, each.
Bands consist of 4, or more members, each.

For their respective time of setting, or period of revolving, see Plate above.

Those who never put their intellectual eye upon the full glories and beauties of the Methodist System, have here the whole field mechanically delineated before them, the object of which is, completely to explain the System at one glance.

The merit of this object involves, both the interest and entertainment of our friends.

John C. Totten, Printer, New-York.

Nonetheless, Joseph continued an intermittent association with his Protestant contemporaries. Emma Hale, Joseph's wife, had grown up a Methodist, and her uncle was a lay minister of the local Methodist Episcopal church in Harmony, Pennsylvania. In 1828 Joseph and Emma were living on her parents' farm in Harmony near Emma's extended family. On June 15, 1828, Emma's first pregnancy ended with the death of their child, who lived only three hours; Emma hovered near death for two weeks while Joseph kept a vigil at her bedside.[22] "Sometime [just before] this dark period," said Bushman, "Joseph attended Methodist meetings with Emma, probably to placate her family."[23] And, Matzko added, "Smith briefly joined a Methodist class meeting that convened at the home of Emma's uncle, the Reverend Nathaniel Lewis."[24]

Beginning in April 1828, all this coy ambivalence between the Smiths and their neighboring Protestants seems to have changed dramatically and definitively as Joseph developed new confidence in his emerging role as a prophet. This was precisely the moment when the Book of Mormon translation project had gained real momentum with the translation of the first 116 manuscript pages of the Book of Mormon. These pages, which were promptly lost by scribe Martin Harris, are today known as the lost book of Lehi. Receiving the ancient records at the hand of Moroni in 1827 would have been momentous, to be sure. Yet what made the experience life changing for the young prophet occurred not in 1827, but in the following year, from April 12 through June 14, 1828, as he immersed himself in the content inscribed on the scripture's plated leaves and pages.[25] Here finally, and perhaps for the first time, he found written, documented corroboration of the doctrines and prophecies he had been taught over the last four years during the visits from Moroni.

Fig. 7. The concentric circles represent the organizational structure of the Methodist itinerant system. Joseph Smith would have been exposed to various levels during the 1820s: classes in Palmyra, New York, and Harmony, Pennsylvania; possibly a general or annual conference in Vienna, New York, in 1819; and likely regular local visits of the circuit rider.

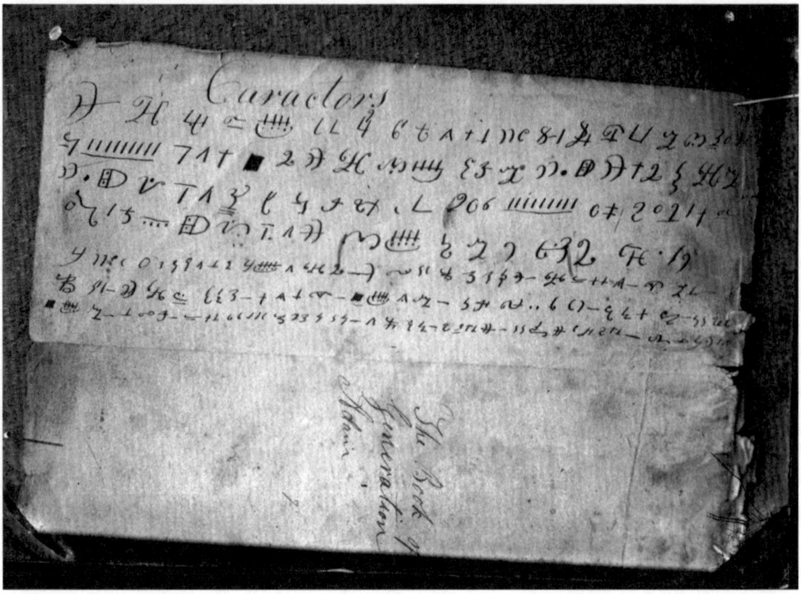

Fig. 8. Martin Harris took a copy of the original Book of Mormon plate characters to New York City to seek a scholarly opinion of the translation. The "Caractors" document is also known as the Anthon Transcript.

It was then that Joseph received his first written revelation from God, recorded with this original entry: "July one Thousand Eighthundred & Twenty Eight Given to Joseph the Seer after he had lost certan writ=ings [the book of Lehi] which he has Translated by the gift & Power of God." The revelation was in God's voice and spoke of "my [God's] People the Nephiti{s\es} & the Jacobites & the Josephites & the <Zorumites> ~~Lamanites <& the Lemuelites~~ [that would] come to the ~~Lamanites~~ knowledge of the Lamanites, & the ~~Lamanites~~ <Lemuelites> & the Ishmaelites which dwindeled in unbelief because of the iniquities of their Fathers."[26] The revelation was grounded in Book of Mormon history, places, and themes.

According to Bushman, "Eighteen twenty-eight was a turning point in Joseph Smith's development. It was the year when he found his prophetic voice. Not two years earlier, he was entangled with the money-diggers and struggling to scrape together rent money for his family. In 1828, he dictated 116 pages of the *Book of Mormon* and received a revelation spoken in God's voice."[27] Joseph's spiritual confidence provided an opening for the rest of the Smith family. Lucy and her children drifted away from attending the Western Presbyterian Church in Palmyra, and the church began formal disfellowshipment proceedings in September 1828; they were finally disfellowshipped eighteen months later on March 10, 1830.[28]

Book of Mormon influences on early Mormon doctrine

No longer solely reliant on the Bible, Joseph leaned tacitly, though not exclusively, on the Book of Mormon to inform his newly developing theology. Nowhere is this more evident than in the 1829 "Articles of the Church of Christ" and also in its successor document, the 1830 "Articles and Covenants of the Church of Christ." In fall 1829, as Smith and Cowdery contemplated the launch of the forthcoming Church of Christ, Cowdery prepared a document, the "Articles of the Church of Christ," to define and document the early protocols for the new church's religious ordinances and observances—for example, sacrament, baptism, and ordination. Oliver asked the Prophet what to include in this document and received the following answer in a revelation: "Behold I [God] have manifested unto you [Oliver], by my Spirit in many instances, that the things which you have written are true," prompting him to use the Book of Mormon text as his first source.[29]

"The great inspiration of this text, received as a revelation by Oliver, perhaps with encouragement if not direction from Joseph, was to gather out of the mass of about 608 original Book of Mormon manuscript pages the basic instructions and guidelines upon which the Church should be organized and administered. That selection process alone would have been a daunting task unless aided by the guidance of the Holy Ghost to help him remember where in that sheaf of papers these administrative provisions were to be found," said John W. Welch.[30] "More than half of Oliver's document, known as the 'Articles of the Church of Christ,' consisted of either direct quotations or close paraphrases from the Book of Mormon."[31] The 1829 Articles were superseded the following spring by the 1830 "Articles and Covenants of the Church of Christ," which eventually became section 20 of the modern Doctrine and Covenants. Also known as the "Constitution of the Church," it was published in the *Painesville (OH) Telegraph* on April 19, 1831, under the title "The Mormon Creed." Robert Woodford reported that the 1830 Articles and Covenants was "read aloud at the first conference of the Church in June 1830 . . . [and] became the first revelation of this dispensation canonized by the Church."[32]

The 1830 Articles and Covenants contained the church's first formal articulation of Mormon theology, including a 284-word statement of the foundational doctrines of the new church, quoted only in part here (see also D&C 20:17–28):

> Wherefore by these things we know that there is a God in Heaven who is infinite & Eternal from everlasting to everlasting the same unchangeable God the Maker of Heaven & Earth & all things that in them is & that he created man male & female & after his own Image & in his likeness created he them. . . . Wherefore the almighty God gave his only begotten Son as it is Written . . . that he was crusified died & rose again the third day & that he ascended into Heaven to sit down on the right hand of the Father . . . believe in the gifts & callings of God by the Holy Ghost which beareth Record of the Father & of the Son which Father & Son ~~is~~ & the Holy Ghost is one God Infinite & eternal without end amen=.[33]

Beneath the surface of this 1830 declaration are simply worded scriptural imprints of the church's theological DNA and textual motifs, the majority of which show decisive influence from the Book of Mormon. For example, the opening declaration is a Book of Mormon phrase—"there is a God in Heaven"—which appears twelve times word for word in the Book of Mormon and twice in the Old Testament. God is "infinite and eternal" is a Book of Mormon phrase, not appearing elsewhere in biblical scripture. Many scriptural references speak of Christ sitting down on the right hand of God (four in the Old Testament, seventeen in the New Testament, two in the Book of Mormon), but only one, a Book of Mormon passage, contains essentially the entire 1830 Articles phrase "ascended into Heaven to sit down on the right hand of the Father" (see Moroni 7:27, modern edition).[34] The core phrase identifying the Godhead as "Father and Son and the Holy Ghost" is mentioned twelve times in the Book of Mormon and once in the New Testament. According to the 1830 Articles, God is an "unchangeable God," another phrase uniquely derived from the Book of Mormon. Mormons have interpreted the phrase literally to mean that if God revealed his word to prophets anciently, he should do so again in the modern day. Moroni declared: "For I know that God is not a partial God, neither a changeable being; but he is unchangeable from all eternity to all eternity" (see Moroni 8:18).[35] Overall, nearly two-thirds of the phrases in this revealed statement of Mormon theology in the 1830 Articles and Covenants correspond to Book of Mormon phrases either exactly or closely.[36]

This 1830 statement of Mormon theology is striking in its confident simplicity and unique in its theological focus: "We know that there is a God in Heaven, who is infinite and eternal." Surprisingly, it begins with a declaration of the existence of God, as if this new religion had not even noticed the religious fervor of the Protestant burned-over district of New York. Missing too are signs of carefully crafted, painstaking workmanship from the scholarly labors of many contributors, seen for instance in the copiously footnoted Westminster Confession of Faith: "There is but one only[a] living, and true God,[b] who is infinite in being and perfection,[c] a most pure spirit,[d] invisible,[e] without body, parts,[f] or passions.[g]"[37] Note too that the Westminster Confession begins not with the existence of God, but with the Trinitarian essence of God; it is a document arising amid the English Protestant Reformation of the seventeenth century, like the Augsburg Confession of the Lutherans of AD 1530 "concerning the unity of the divine essence and of the three persons [the Trinity]."[38]

Yet the 1830 Articles and Covenants also reflected the new Mormon theology's reliance on an expanded scriptural canon, including the Old Testament. For example, the phrase "he [God] created man male and female, after his own image, and in his own likeness created he them" corresponds with Genesis 1:26–27. Similarly, "Wherefore, the Almighty God gave his only begotten Son, as it is written in those Scriptures, which hath been given of him" appears in the New Testament (John 3:16).

Another New Testament phrase—Christ "was crucified, died, and rose again the third day"—appears in New Testament passages sixteen times, compared to one in the Book of Mormon.

Still, the Book of Mormon became a defining point of reference that framed the intersection of theology within the newly emerging scriptural canon of Bible and Book of Mormon. However, it did so in an unusual way. The Book of Mormon rarely conveyed in any one section, chapter, or verse an authoritative, succinct articulation of a doctrine or principle, as might have been found, say, in the Methodists' *Book of Discipline.* The Book of Mormon was not a book of discipline, but appeared in the form of native scriptural history like the Old Testament: jagged, uneven, disjointed, with raw and indigenous-appearing, early-period narratives. Teachings, doctrines, and theologies appeared in various places within the text from different priests, prophets, and writers in disparate social settings who were dealing with diverse religious challenges at different moments in time.

Mormon Christology and Book of Mormon influences

The Book of Mormon shaped Mormon Christology through stories and narratives of prophets and believers as they experienced Christ in vision and revelation, interacted with him personally during his post-resurrection visit to the New World, and recorded their observations in the scriptural record. In a very early Book of Mormon narrative (two millennia before Christ), the brother of Jared received a visitation from the premortal Christ offering a unique interpretation on the nature of Christ that again countered prevailing orthodoxy. According to this Book of Mormon passage, before his birth Christ not only lived as a premortal spirit but also had a spirit body as well:

> And the veil was taken from off the eyes of the brother of Jared, and he saw the finger of the Lord; and it was as the finger of a man, like unto flesh and blood. . . . Behold, I am he which was prepared from the foundation of the world, to redeem my people. Behold,

> I am Jesus Christ. I am the Father and the Son. . . . Behold, this body, which ye now behold, is the body of my spirit; and man have I created after the body of my spirit; and even as I appear unto thee to be in the spirit, will I appear unto my people in the flesh. (See Ether 3:6, 14, 16.)[39]

When Christ appeared to the Nephites at Bountiful following his resurrection in the Old World, the Nephite congregation witnessed a conversational interaction between God the Father and his Son, revealing yet another divine familial dimension of Christ. "Behold, my beloved Son, in whom I am well pleased, in whom I have glorified my name, hear ye him" (3 Nephi 11:7).[40] They then saw the Son "descending out of Heaven; and he was clothed in a white robe, and he came down and stood in the midst of them . . . and spake unto the people, saying: Behold I am Jesus Christ . . . and have glorified the Father in taking upon me the sins of the world, in the which I have suffered the will of the Father in all things, from the beginning" (see 3 Nephi 11:10–11).[41] Jesus invited each in the congregation to physically "thrust your hands into my side, and also that ye may feel the prints of the nails in my hands, and in my feet, that ye may know that I am the God of Israel, and the God of the whole earth, and have been slain for the sins of the world" (see 3 Nephi 11:14).[42]

Taken together, these Book of Mormon narratives were the Prophet's first scriptural evidence of the divine nature of God and Christ outside the Bible. Here in 1828 and 1829, nearly a decade after the first vision, the Book of Mormon translation amplified the experiential impressions of the first vision of 1820 and at once expanded the meaning of God beyond the widely disputed Christian interpretations in the biblical canon on seven dimensions: (1) Christ lived in a premortal state as a spirit with a spirit body, and by implication so did others who were created: "Yea, even all men were created in the beginning, after mine [Christ's] own image" (see Ether 3:15).[43] (2) God is a personal God who appears and speaks to man dialogically—especially to others beyond the biblical canon. (3) Christ is a resurrected, embodied being, and by implication so is God. (4) God and Christ are physically distinct and separate beings, existing in a divine familial relationship defined by terms such as *my*

Son and *my Father*. (5) Christ was the creator of the world and father by adoption of his "sons and . . . daughters" who "shall believe on my name." (6) Christ was the God of redemption, the son of the Father who suffered for the sins of the world. Finally, (7) the Father, Son, and Holy Ghost are one in divine purpose, affirming Christ's prayer of divine oneness in the book of John, "that they may be one, even as we are one" (John 17:22).[44]

Later in his life, in 1841, Joseph taught that "there is no other God in heaven but that God who has flesh and bones,"[45] then considered a radical assertion. Joseph, however, recognized this much earlier in his life, almost certainly by 1830 when the Book of Mormon was published. Indeed, the "Book of Mormon, translated by Joseph Smith in 1829 and first published in 1830, provides early revelatory data affirming divine embodiment," said Mormon scholar David Paulsen while researching Smith's Bible retranslation project of 1830. "While some 283 passages in the Book of Mormon text refer directly to [God's body], three passages recording divine appearances are especially explicit. The first two confirm that God the son (or Jesus Christ) was embodied in humanlike form in both his premortal and his postmortal (resurrected) states, and the third apparently affirms that the Holy Ghost is also ["in the form of a man" (1 Nephi 11:11)]."[46] Paulsen concluded that "it appears clear that in 1830 [Joseph] understood that both the Father and Son are embodied and that man's body was made in their image. Moreover, Joseph's revisions cohere tightly with [similar] passages from the Book of Mormon already discussed. Taken together, they show that Joseph understood the doctrine of divine embodiment at least as early as 1830."[47]

According to Givens, "years before the Nauvoo era [1839–44], Smith's followers were focusing on Christianity's bodiless God as a hallmark of their apostate condition. Warren Cowdery criticized the Methodists for believing in a deity 'without body or parts' in an 1836 church article. While Cowdery wrote in a Mormon periodical for a Mormon audience, others seem to have been listening; in that same year, a Presbyterian minister from Kirtland wrote that Mormons believed in a 'material being, composed of body and parts.'"[48]

Book of Mormon influences on soteriology and doctrines of salvation

The Book of Mormon provided an early theological foundation for an important thought pattern that became prominent in Mormon theology—the plan of salvation, or plan of redemption. Alma described this plan: "Now if it had not been for the *plan of redemption*, which was *laid from the foundation of the world*, there could have been no resurrection of the dead; but there was a *plan of redemption laid*, which shall bring to pass the resurrection of the dead, of which has been spoken. And now behold, if it were possible that our first parents could have went forth and partaken of the tree of life, they would have been forever miserable, having no preparatory state; and thus the *plan of redemption would have been frustrated*" (see Alma 12:25–26).[49] This thought pattern pertaining to the plan of salvation, or redemption, was incorporated into the diaries and teachings of the early restoration, as seen in this letter from Oliver Cowdery to W. W. Phelps, published in the church periodical *Messenger and Advocate*:

> The great *plan of redemption being prepared before the fall of man*, and the salvation of the human family being as precious in the sight of the Lord at one time as at another, before the Messiah came in the flesh and was crucified, as after the gospel was preached, and many were found obedient to the same. This gospel being the same from the beginning, its ordinances were also unchangeable . . . because through that sacrifice they looked for a remission of their sins, and for their redemption. Had it not been for this *plan of salvation*, which God devised before the fall, man must have remained miserable forever.[50]

The Book of Mormon was the only scriptural record that laid out the plan of salvation per se; the phrase is never mentioned in the Bible. Still, the idea of a "gospel plan of salvation" certainly was widespread in antebellum Christian discourse and earlier, with varying views. Adam Clarke, a Methodist theologian, commented on Romans 3:23–25 in the New Testament: "[This passage] contains a fine and striking synopsis of the whole Christian system . . . and the plan of salvation . . . the Catechism of Christian Righteousness. . . . To whom are these blessings actually communicated? To all who repent, turn from their sin, and believe on the Lord Jesus."[51] For Presbyterians, the plan of salvation was founded upon the core Calvinistic constructs of total depravity, unconditional election, and limited atonement: "God once established by his eternal and unchangeable plan," wrote Calvin, "those whom he long before determined once for all to receive into salvation, and those whom, on the other hand, he would devote to destruction. We assert that, with respect to the elect, this plan was founded upon his freely given mercy."[52]

Walter Scott, a Christian evangelist, considered clarity in defining the gospel plan of salvation his chief contribution to the fledgling early nineteenth-century Christian restorationist movement. He formally published these ideas in 1836 as a six-point précis:

> In other words, brethren, to make us see the beauty and perfection of the gospel theory as devised by God; *faith* is to destroy the love of sin, *repentance* to destroy the practice of it, *baptism* the state of it, *remission* the guilt of it, the *Spirit* the power of it, and the *resurrection* to destroy the punishment of sin; so that the last enemy, death, will be destroyed.[53]

In these Protestant views, God's plan of salvation was selective, effectively a limited atonement intended for some who repent and believe on Jesus, but not all. Terryl and Fiona Givens commented on the dilemma that this imposed when considering all those—non-Christians, infants, those living before Christ—who died without any exposure to the gospel of Christ:

> The larger problem, however, is that vastly more people have lived, and will always live, outside the orbit of Christianity, never hearing a sermon, seeing a missionary, or reading a Bible, than have died in infancy. The multitudes that covered the earth before Christianity made its appearance, all the inhabitants of nations past, present, and future where Christianity is virtually unknown, the countless children reared in secular homes—the numbers of these

> uncatechized throngs dwarf the number of children who have died unbaptized. The largest portion of humanity would still fall outside the gospel's reach.[54]

In contrast, the Book of Mormon spoke of a different paradigm that sowed the seeds for an emerging and radical formulation that at once distinguished Mormon salvation theology from its nineteenth-century contemporaries. The genesis of this theology began with a victory over physical death (the first death) through a physical embodied resurrection, a gift through the atonement of Christ that was universal and unconditional, applicable to the entire human family. Book of Mormon prophet Alma explained that "the spirit and the body shall be re-united again, in its perfect form; both limb and joint shall be restored to its proper frame, even as we now are at this time. . . . *Now this restoration shall come to all*, both old and young, both bond and free, both male and female, both the wicked and the righteous" (see Alma 11:40–41).[55] Still, according to Alma and other Book of Mormon prophets, the nonpenitent would suffer a spiritual death (the second death): "And he [Christ] shall take upon him the transgressions of those who believe on his name; and these are they that shall have eternal life, and salvation cometh to none else" (see Alma 11:40).[56]

Throughout his life Joseph Smith had been preoccupied by a quest to overcome death. "Afflicted during an epidemic of typhoid fever (Salmonella blood poisoning) that began in 1812, Joseph found himself near death twice," reported scholar Samuel Morris Brown. "A limp reminded Joseph ever after of his childhood encounter with possible amputation and death, but the battle with typhoid was only the beginning of the Mormon prophet's brushes with death."[57] "Joseph's mother, Lucy Mack Smith (1775–1856), lost seven of her eleven children, while in the next generation Joseph Jr. lost six of his eleven before dying himself in his late thirties, a death rate higher than the already significant nineteenth-century average," noted Brown.[58] Joseph was especially affected by the loss of his older brother Alvin—described as "dutiful, pious, and tender-hearted in his family's memory"—in 1823.[59]

Fig. 9. Joseph Smith Jr. mourned the premature passing of his older brother Alvin in 1823 at the age of 25.

> Coming of age in the culture of holy dying, the Mormon prophet never fully recovered from Alvin's death. Though it would be overly simplistic to attribute all of Smith's religious activity to Alvin, this death cast a long shadow over Joseph Jr.'s career. Joseph soon confronted the similar death of his father in 1840 from consumption; Alvin was the angel that carried Joseph Sr. home. In constant negotiation with the inevitability of death, the intensity of human revulsion toward it, and the inscrutability of God's Providential will, Smith made his way through the founding of a new religion.[60]

Of course, as the Book of Mormon plainly articulates, the peril of death was dual natured, consisting not just of physical death but of spiritual death as well. If the Book of Mormon clearly conveyed the universal triumph over physical death, then somehow the plan of salvation must address in like manner spiritual death. Smith expounded his thoughts in an 1843 sermon: "Salvation is nothing more or less than to triumph over all our enemies & put them under our feet & . . . to triumph over all evil spirits in the world to come then we are saved as in the case of Jesus . . . & the last enemy was death Perhaps there [is a] principle here that few men have thought of. No ~~power~~ person can have this Salvation except through a tabernacle."[61]

Joseph was captivated by this idea that eternal salvation required a physical "tabernacle"—that is, a mortal body. The Book of Mormon had taught that one's physical body was essential not only to the resurrection, but to eternal life and the salvation of the eternal soul as well. The physical body had provided the vehicle in mortality for living, learning, and experiencing life, and in the eternities to come the perfection of the body would be forever associated with the perfection of the soul itself. Thus all men would have, as Jacob taught in the Book of Mormon, a "perfect knowledge like unto us in the flesh, save it be that our knowledge [in the eternal world] shall be perfect. Wherefore, we shall have a perfect knowledge of all our guilt, and our uncleanness, and our nakedness; and the righteous shall have a perfect knowledge of their enjoyment, and their righteousness, being clothed with purity, yea, even with the robe of righteousness . . . they shall inherit the kingdom of God, which was prepared for them from the foundation of the world, and their joy shall be full forever" (2 Nephi 9:13–14, 18).[62]

Early in the restoration Smith took these universal Book of Mormon ideas and expanded upon them, asserting that over time, even in the eternities beyond death, the saving power of Christ's atonement eventually would redeem nearly all of God's children, not only from physical death but from spiritual death as well. The month the Book of Mormon was published, March 1830, Smith penned a revelation stating that God's punishment for sin did not mean "that there shall be no end to this torment" but instead that this torment would eventually end with the "destroying of Satan and his works at the end of the world, and the last great day of judgement."[63]

Then on February 16, 1832, the expansive revelation (D&C 76) known as "The Vision" was received; this revelation states that true damnation was the fate of only a very few—the sons of perdition; they were "the only ones <on> whom the second death shall have any power yea verily the only ones who shall not be redeemed in the due time of the Lord. . . . [But] through him all [others] might be saved whom the father had put unto his power & made by him who glorifieth the father & saveth all the work of his hands except those sons of perdition who denyeth the son after the father hath revealed him."[64]

The revelation spoke of a diverse afterlife with gradations of glory depending on one's faithfulness, divided into three eventual kingdoms: the celestial, terrestrial, and telestial. Another revelation received later in the year, December 27, 1832, given the name "Olive Leaf" (D&C 88), elaborated on these new ideas: "for he that is not able to abide the law of a celestial kingdom cannot abide a celestial glory . . . and they who are not sanctified, through the law which I have given unto you; even the law of Christ, must inherit another kingdom even that of a Terestrial kingdom, or that of a telestial kingdom."[65] Above all, virtually the entire human family would inherit one of the three kingdoms of glory in the divine afterlife. Bushman explained, "The doctrine recast life after death. The traditional division of heaven and hell made religious life arbitrary. One received grace or one went to hell. In Joseph's afterlife, the issue was degrees of glory. A permanent hell threatened very few. The question was not escape from hell but closeness to God. God scaled the rewards to each person's capacity."[66]

Later, the Prophet looked back with delight on the universal themes of the Vision revelation:

> Nothing could be more pleasing to the Saint[s], upon the order of the kingdom of the Lord, than the light which burst upon the world, through the foregoing vision. Every law, every commandment, every promise, every truth, and every point, touching the destiny of man, from Genesis to Revelation, where the purity of either remains unsullied from the wisdom of men, goes to shew the perfection of the theory, and witnesses the fact that that document is a transcript from the Records of the eternal world. The sublimity of the ideas; the purity of the language; the scope for action; the continued duration for completion, in order that the heirs of salvation, may confess the Lord and bow the knee; The rewards for faithfulnes & the punishments for sins, are so much beyond the narrow mindedness of men, that every honest man is constrained to exclaim; It came from God.[67]

So radical were Smith's universalist ideas to his followers that some left the church in protestation. According to Brigham Young,

> When God revealed to Joseph Smith and Sidney Rigdon that there was a place prepared for all, according to the light they had received and their rejection of evil and practice of good, it was a great trial to many, and some apostatized because God was not going to send to everlasting punishment heathens and infants, but had a place of salvation, in due time, for all, and would bless the honest and virtuous and truthful, whether they ever belonged to any church or not. It was a new doctrine to this generation, and many stumbled at it.[68]

Joseph's grandfather, Asael Smith, had helped found a Universalist society in Vermont in 1797 (the remainder of his family never followed in his paths),[69] but various Book of Mormon narratives nonetheless denounced universal salvation. For example, one Nephite antagonist, Nehor, was castigated for teaching that "the Lord had created all men, and had also redeemed all men; and in the end, all men should have eternal life" (see Alma 1:4).[70] Nonetheless, in the spirit of Universalism, Joseph taught in the Vision revelation (D&C 76) a more nuanced, more just, and more merciful plan of salvation. Bushman clarified the doctrines in the Vision:

> "The Vision" did not actually endorse universal salvation any more than the *Book of Mormon* did. It imposed permanent penalties for sinning, rewarded righteousness with higher degrees of glory, and assigned the sons of perdition to permanent outer darkness. But "The Vision" also eliminated the injustices of heaven-and-hell theology. . . . [It focused] on the exalted condition of humans in the celestial heavens. They enjoy godly power, dominion, and rank. . . . No blessing, power, or glory of God would be withheld from worthy humans. . . . In "The Vision" the workings of heaven were made intelligible, and the law became less a set of forbidding commandments than of instructions on how to reach heaven. The laws were helpful and informative rather than distancing. Knowledge made heaven accessible.[71]

Fig. 10. Sidney Rigdon (1793–1876), early pastor and follower of Alexander Campbell, converted to Mormonism in Kirtland along with others of his congregation.

Communal salvific sealing with those we love

Yet Smith's salvific development was not complete, for what mattered still in his quest was to deny the power of death to destroy the filial bonds of mortality—to preserve forever the familial relationships of those we love in the eternities to come. "What [Smith] called 'the orders of Heaven,' [would transform] the enemy death—'annihilation'—into a blessed state of heavenly community he termed 'exaltation,'"[72] observed Brown. The Book of Mormon had described a prophetic power to seal, implying that this sealing power could effect not only individual salvation, but communal and filial salvation as well. God informed a later prophet Nephi, "I give unto you power, that whatsoever ye shall seal on earth, shall be sealed in heaven" (see Helaman 10:7).[73] Mormon's editorial hand preserved a very lengthy passage that he must have deemed exceptionally important (longer than the entire book of Moroni and longer than Mormon's personal writings in his own internal text, the book of Mormon).[74] In it he recorded the events of Mosiah$_2$'s coronation by his father, King Benjamin, at the Zarahemla temple. The entire passage contains profound spiritual insights that seem to culminate in Mosiah 5–6 when the aging King Benjamin establishes a salvific covenant community among his people—with a *sealing blessing*. His communal covenantal ceremony included a ritual purification (Mosiah 4:2), a new name taken collectively as a people (5:7), an oath made in the presence of ordained priests and the prophet-king himself (6:3), and a formal recording of the names of those received into the covenant community (6:1).

Significantly, during King Benjamin's coronation ceremony for his son Mosiah$_2$, the aging king appears to invoke ancient enthronement rituals, covenants, symbols and sealing, but then applies them to all members of his covenant community. According to Mormon scholar Matthew Bowen,

> It is the application of royal coronation/enthronement texts to the people themselves—making them all potentially kings and queens, sons and daughters at the right hand—that makes Benjamin's speech so revolutionary. In Israelite thought, Benjamin [whose name means "son of the right hand"] was already a royal son who was already at the right hand of God, as [his son] Mosiah soon would be. Benjamin [extends] this idea, teaching the people about the truly royal and divine Son [Christ] and how this Son's atonement made it possible for all of them, through covenant obedience, to become his sons and daughters and to be enthroned with this Son at God's right hand.[75]

Thus, for example, one expects that the new king Mosiah will take upon him a new name—a throne name (such as *Benjamin*, or *Nephi*, used historically in Nephite coronations; see Jacob 1:9–11). But Benjamin extends this symbolic rite to all his people: "The name of Christ, rather than Benjamin's own name, is given to all his people as a new name—a 'throne' name."[76] After placing his people under covenant, Benjamin quotes a long-established ancient royal formula: "And now, because of the covenant which ye have made, ye shall be called the children of Christ, his sons, and his daughters: for behold, this day he hath spiritually begotten you" (see Mosiah 5:7).[77] According to Bowen, "he is evidently quoting the royal rebirth formula (sometimes called an adoption formula) of Psalm 2:7: 'Thou art my Son [Hebrew, *bĕnî ʾattâ*]; this day have I begotten thee.' . . . Earlier in Psalm 2:2, the royal addressee is called the Lord's 'anointed' (*mĕšîḥô*, his 'messiah' or 'Christ'; LXX christos). The newly enthroned Judahite king took upon himself the name-title 'anointed' (*māšîaḥ*). King Benjamin probably likened this psalm to his people so that they too might take upon themselves or 'bear' this name (see Mosiah 26:18)."[78] John Welch noted the chiastic structure of King Benjamin's discourse in which Mormon attempted to accentuate the unique creation of "a well-ordered covenant community based on individual righteousness and generosity . . . [and] the jubilee laws of Leviticus 25–56."[79]

King Benjamin finally left this benedictory sealing blessing on his faithful covenant people:

> Therefore, I would that ye should be steadfast and immovable, always abounding in good works, that Christ, the Lord God Omnipotent, *may seal you his, that you may be brought to Heaven, that ye may have everlasting salvation and eternal life*, through the wisdom, and power, and justice, and mercy of Him, who created all things, in Heaven and in Earth, who is God above all. Amen. (See Mosiah 5:15.)[80]

In Benjamin's covenant community salvation was personal but also communal—as a people of God they would be "brought to Heaven" and sealed with "everlasting salvation and eternal life." In their communal covenant making, "all cried with one voice" (Mosiah 5:2; also 4:2), affirming with a 195-word oath (5:2–5) centered in the covenantal words: "We are willing to enter into a covenant with our God, to do his will, and to be obedient to his commandments in all things, that he shall command us, all the remainder of our days" (5:5). Scholars David Bokovoy and John Tvedtnes established that "the idea of covenant creating a familial relationship appears throughout the Book of Mormon [and] Benjamin clearly recognized that [this] covenant created a familial relationship."[81] Note "King Benjamin's descriptions of divine rebirth, enthronement at the right hand of God, and the sealing of sons and daughters to him, all . . . mark the [royal] capstone of his marvelous sermon," said Bowen.[82] In sum, salvation for *this* people of God was covenantal, communal for those remaining faithful, and sacramental—suffused with priesthood, ritual, royal and temple symbolism, and filial heavenly relationships as sons and daughters of Christ, formally adopted and recorded with a royal throne name, that is, Christ (5:7).

Salvific covenant communities had been missing or marginalized from Protestant North America since the earlier memory of the Separatist Pilgrims of Plymouth, the Puritans of New England, or the Shakers. Exclusive and sectarian, they sought salvation in pure and separated congregations and were most concerned "about the Lord's Supper and the importance of worthy communicants," according to James White.[83] They disregarded set worship forms, believed in free worship and free prayer—even the Eucharist was led without notes or text by the minister. The Puritans believed "that authority could come only from God's word. Human inventions could not be tolerated in worship."[84] The Shakers likewise disavowed oath taking and anti-Christian ideas such as "priests, the Church, [and] the pope"[85] and embraced universal celibacy—denouncing "the sexual relationship originating with Adam and Eve . . . [and the] corrupt, passionate animal life of the world [so] that we may be resurrected in pure and angelic societies."[86] By contrast, Smith embraced a much more palpable paradigm of salvific covenant community that was much closer to the Book of Mormon ideal portrayed in the lengthy presentation of King Benjamin. First, Smith's paradigm was grounded in priesthood and ritual to formally seal believers into communal covenant relationships. Brown described that "Smith sacramentalized adoption, first with patriarchal blessings and baptism for the dead, complementary impulses of connection and salvation, then with family sealings [with an oath] within the Nauvoo Temple."[87]

We see these impulses emerging early in the restoration. In December 1830 Joseph recorded the prophecy of Enoch describing in detail the filial bonds of communal covenant relationships in Enoch's ancient city of Zion, representative of the filial relationships of heaven itself and echoing the Benjamin narratives of a covenant community brought to heaven with everlasting salvation and eternal life:

> And the Lord said unto Enoch, then shalt thou and all thy city meet them there, and we will receive them into our bosom, and they shall see us; and we will fall upon their necks, and they shall fall upon our necks, and we will kiss each other; and there shall be mine abode, and it shall be Zion. . . . And Enoch <all> his people walked with God, and he dwelt in the midst of Zion: And it came to pass that Zion was not, for God reeceived it up into his own bosom.[88]

Enoch's communal covenant relationships were so sublime that the city itself, with its inhabitants, was taken to heaven. In Smith's heaven, "the work of the universe was the creation of relationships, connections he framed within a notion of the family that encompassed all of humanity, indeed the entire cosmos."[89] We will discuss Zion in detail in the next chapter.

In 1834 the Prophet's father, Joseph Smith Sr., was ordained a patriarch to the church, a new office instituted to provide personal blessings of comfort, wisdom, and promises of personal destiny—but also to spiritually and ritually adopt the believer into the communal family of God, which meant, as the office evolved, adoption into the house of Israel with promises of eternal blessings flowing from the ancient biblical covenant of Abraham, Isaac, and Jacob. On July 22, 1837, for example, John Pack received his patriarchal blessing, which began: "Brother Pack In the name of Jesus Christ the Son of God I lay my hands on thy head [to] Seal and Confirm on the[e] blessings that Shal never be taken. . . . Thou art of the blo[o]d of Isaral through the Loins of Joseph the Son of Jacob."[90] The blessing continued with promises and spiritual direction. What was significant here was the adoption itself—into the lineage of Joseph and biblical patriarch Jacob: It was literal, "sealed and confirmed" by priesthood ritual, promising a communal place with heavenly blessings of the prophetic destiny of the house of Israel, in God's eternal family for this life and for all eternity—blessings that never would be taken away.

In Nauvoo in 1842 Smith's vision of filial salvation finally came to fruition by institutionalizing the sealing power as part of the Nauvoo temple ordinances—sealing families, converts, and ancestors. Joseph Smith's sealed "genealogical chain extended from church members to their file leaders to the Prophet himself, then through the biblical patriarchs, ultimately to Adam."[91] By the time of his death in 1844, Smith's unique plan of salvation had laid out a concrete, ritualistic path to eternal salvation based on the twin pillars of the Book of Mormon's plan of salvation theology, with the promised gift of a physical resurrection for all, but also with eternally sealed relationships that would continue as part of the covenantal communal family of God. Brown provided this conclusion:

> Smith's divine anthropology broadcast human relationships onto the cosmos, establishing their permanence in both time and space. This divine anthropology became Smith's ritual and theological swan song, the culminating volley in his battle against death. In this anthropology, supported by a distinctively Mormon *imitatio Christi*, the Latter-day Saints saw their own safe passage to a heaven so inseparable from the good things of earth as to deny completely the power of death.[92]

The Book of Mormon influences on Nauvoo temple theology

On the surface Joseph Smith's theological development of the early restoration, in both New York and Kirtland in the 1820s and early 1830s, appeared to differ from that of the later Nauvoo era, from 1839 through

TEMPLE AT NAUVOO.

Fig. 11. The complete temple worship was introduced in Nauvoo. Although the Saints dedicated the Nauvoo Temple in 1846, they were forced to abandon the city shortly thereafter.

1844. In Nauvoo Smith introduced the temple endowment, the theosis of man, and sealing ordinances, all well removed from the more traditional Christian doctrines of the early restoration. Sociologist Rodney Stark explained that "it was in Nauvoo that Smith revealed the full scope of his revelations thus giving final form to a Mormon theology that clearly made it a new religion. The Book of Mormon, first published in 1830, may not have added enough doctrinal novelty to the Christian tradition to have made Mormonism more than a Protestant sect. The doctrines revealed in Nauvoo, however, added as much novelty to Christianity as it, in turn, had added to Judaism."[93] This assumption, that Nauvoo doctrines and theologies were distinctly later-period revelations to the Prophet emerging spontaneously in the Nauvoo era, is widely held among both Mormons and non-Mormons, but is incorrect.

As we have seen in this chapter and will see later in this book, rarely did the Prophet articulate a doctrine, principle, or practice ex nihilo, without a tangible connection to a previously known scriptural or historical precedent. Above all, the Prophet saw his role as a restorer of lost or corrupted truths; Bible scholar Margaret Barker similarly maintains that Jesus was more a restorer of truth than a deliver of new truth.[94] Speaking of Joseph's role as restorer, Givens recounted: "Sometime between 1829 and 1835, Joseph enthusiastically embraced this version of restoration, as a reassemblage of a scattered—rather than abandoned—church [lost] in the wilderness."[95] This of course raises the question, Where were the scattered lost ancient doctrines and practices that were the genesis for the restored doctrines of the Nauvoo era, many of them relating to the Nauvoo Temple? Recent research on the Wisdom tradition of ancient Hebrew scripture—parts preserved in the Hebrew Bible, or Old Testament, and other parts in noncanonical texts such as the book of *Enoch*, the Dead Sea Scrolls found at Qumran, and Jewish oral tradition (the Midrash)—provides insights into what these doctrines and practices may have been and where they had been observed in antiquity. Especially relevant to the Nauvoo era was the First Temple theology of Solomon's temple and the Wisdom tradition of the preexilic era (before the Babylonian exile of the sixth century BC).

Some religious scholars have increasingly focused on the deeper religious dimensions of the Wisdom tradition originally found in ancient Israelite temple worship, which is often misunderstood as Solomon's great secular wisdom of the first millennium BC. This ancient religious *Wisdom*—recorded in the Writings of the Hebrew Bible (for example, in Job, Psalms, and Proverbs)—was sacred and often secret knowledge believed to be so rare and treasured that only faithful religious initiates were considered worthy to possess it. Sublime and deeply personal, this sacred knowledge centered on knowledge of God as king of the universe, of his creations, and of man's divine relationship within the cosmos as a royal scion of God. Interwoven into the ancient Israelite temple, evidence of this ancient Israelite Wisdom can be found among the architects, architecture, hymns, and poetic literature of the First Temple (the Temple of Solomon) and the tabernacle of Moses.

Barker, whose research at the leading edge of Wisdom scholarship is controversial with some scholars, provides a brief definition of the ancient Wisdom and a starting point for understanding it. Anciently, "Wisdom was the secrets of creation, learned in heaven and brought to earth, the recurring theme of the apocalypses. There must have been some way in which the king, and the wise men, 'went' to heaven like the prophets in order to learn these secrets by listening in the council of God."[96] She emphasizes the symbolic elements that were present in First Temple theology or should have been present and were lost or corrupted through time:

> It cannot be coincidence that amongst the few scraps of information we can glean about the first Temple [from the Hebrew Bible and noncanonical sources], we discover trees, cherubim [angels], the throne of God, a mountain cult, life-giving waters, a serpent, and a blurring of the distinction between earth and heaven in the sacred space of the sanctuary. [But] from the [biblical] Deuteronomic account alone there [should be but] is no emphasis upon the supernatural or Eden motifs; . . . there is no mention of the divine throne, nor of the living waters, the mountain setting nor the role of the cherubim. There is no tree of life, no Menorah. . . . The ancient Temple was Eden, the mountain of the gods, in which there was the divine throne, and in which judgement took place.[97]

Throughout the Book of Mormon narrative are passages that seem to conform to this Wisdom literature pattern and evoke comparisons to First Temple theology. From the book's outset, prophet Lehi seems intent on establishing his identity as being familiar with—even a faithful participant in—the myths, stories, and beliefs of an ancient religious tradition that shares symbolic markers resembling the ancient Israelite Wisdom tradition. Only five paragraphs into the entire Book of Mormon narrative, the text unfolds a vision in which Lehi was taken to the heavens, to the divine council with God sitting on his throne surrounded by angels (alternatively called Sons of God in the Wisdom literature):

> And being thus overcome with the spirit, he was carried away in a vision, even that he saw the Heavens open; and he thought he saw God sitting upon his throne, surrounded with numberless concourses of angels in the attitude of singing and praising their God. And it came to pass that he saw one descending out of the midst of Heaven, and he beheld that his lustre was above that of the sun at noon-day; and he also saw twelve others following him, and their brightness did exceed that of the stars in the firmament. (See 1 Nephi 1:8–10.)[98]

"Specific [Wisdom] elements in Lehi's initial visions (1 Nephi 1:7–14)," according to scholar Kevin Christensen, "include the anthropomorphic nature of God, the throne, the numberless angelic hosts, the 'One' like the sun at noonday, the twelve others like 'stars,' the heavenly book (1 Nephi 1:11), and the judgment (1 Nephi 1:13)."[99]

Thirteen pages further into the Book of Mormon narrative, the text details another prophetic vision of Lehi in which he saw the tree of life; the tree itself is a focal symbol of the Eden narrative, also a core part of the ancient Wisdom tradition. In Barker's surprising discovery of the tree of life vision in the Book of Mormon narrative, she finds its description unexpectedly similar to other tree of life findings previously discovered by Wisdom researchers:

> The tree of life made one happy, according to the Book of Proverbs, but for detailed descriptions of the tree we have to rely on the noncanonical texts. Enoch described it as perfumed, with fruit like grapes, and a text discovered in Egypt in 1945 described the tree as beautiful, fiery, and with fruit like white grapes. I do not know of any other source that describes the fruit as *white* grapes. Imagine my surprise when I read the account of Lehi's vision of the tree whose *white fruit* made one happy, and the interpretation that the Virgin in Nazareth was the mother of the Son of God after the manner of the flesh. . . . This revelation to Joseph was the ancient Wisdom symbolism, intact, and almost certainly as it was known in 600 BCE.[100]

At the end of Lehi's life he gave counsel and a final blessing to each of his children; in so doing he left a lasting imprint of the legacy of his ancient religious tradition. Significantly, these blessings were preserved for a thousand years of Book of Mormon history and finally selected for inclusion in Mormon's edited sacred text. In one of these final blessings, Lehi chose to suffuse his blessing on son Jacob with the symbols of the Eden narrative—core to the ancient Israelite Wisdom tradition. Many of these symbols are contained in the Genesis account of the Hebrew Bible, but in Lehi's weaving of this ancient story into his deathbed blessing, the symbols and actors of Eden were curiously cast as part of an ascension narrative of the meaning of life and the journey of man back to the presence of God. Note the symbols woven into Lehi's blessing (italicized in the text below) and their semblance to core elements of the ancient Israelite Wisdom literature that describe the purpose of life in terms of the *ascension* narrative of Adam and Eve:

> There is a *God*, and he hath *created all things, both the heavens and the earth*, and all things that in them is . . . [and] there was an opposition; even *the forbidden fruit* in opposition to *the tree of life*; the one being sweet and the other bitter. . . . [*A*]*n angel of God* . . . had *fallen from Heaven*; wherefore, he became a Devil, having sought that which was evil before God. . . . And after that Adam and Eve had partaken of the forbidden fruit they were driven out of the garden of Eden. . . . And now, behold, if Adam had not transgressed he would not have fallen; but he would have remained in the garden of Eden. . . . And they would have had no children; wherefore they would have remained in a state of innocence, having no joy, for they knew no misery: doing no good, for they knew no sin. But behold, all things have been done in the wisdom of Him who knoweth all things. *Adam fell, that men might be; and men are, that they might have joy*. And *the Messiah cometh in the fulness of time, that he might redeem the children of men from the fall*. And because that they are redeemed from the fall, *they have become free forever*. (See 2 Nephi 2:14–27.)[101]

To Joseph, this view of Adam and Eve must have seemed far removed from the old nineteenth-century Christian orthodoxies that taught of Adam's responsibility for the introduction of sin and evil into the world. Matthew Henry, eighteenth-century Presbyterian minister, left a vivid statement of his dour view:

> Adam therefore sinning and falling, the nature became guilty and corrupt, and is so derived. Thus in him all have sinned. Death by sin, for death is the wages of sin. Sin, when it is finished, brings forth death. When sin came, of course death came with it. . . . If Adam had not sinned, he had not died; the threatening was, In the day thou eatest thou shall surely die, Gen. 2:17. So death passed, that is, a sentence of death was passed, as upon a criminal, *dielthen*—passed through all men, as an infectious disease passes through a town, so that none escape it. . . . Now all this we may thank Adam for; from him sin and death descend. . . . O Adam! what hast thou done? . . . [D]eath [even] reigned over those that had not sinned any actual sin, that had . . . never sinned in their own persons as Adam did—which is to be understood of infants . . . because Adam's sin was imputed to them.[102]

The Book of Mormon conversely had transported Smith into a dramatically different understanding of the Eden narrative as part of an ancient Wisdom-like tradition. The text from the brother of Jared, cited earlier in this chapter, provided a "temple-mount" account that was grounded in the fall of man motif, with vivid Wisdom-like markers when the brother of Jared took sixteen clear white stones up to Mount Shelem and asked God to touch them to give light to his ships. Similar to the Wisdom-like vision of Lehi (in 1 Nephi 1:6–14 and that of Isaiah in Isaiah 6:1–12), God "showed unto the brother of Jared all the inhabitants of the earth which had been, and also all that would be; and he withheld them not from his sight, even unto the ends of the earth" (Ether 3:25). Then like Moses on Sinai, he conversed with God face-to-face:

> The Lord shewed himself unto him, and said, Because thou knowest these things, ye are redeemed from the fall; therefore ye are brought back into my presence; therefore I shew myself unto you. Behold, I am he which was prepared from the foundation of the world, to redeem my people. Behold, I am Jesus Christ. I am the

> Father and the Son. . . . And never hath I shewed myself unto man whom I have created, for never hath man believed in me as thou hast. Seest thou that ye are created after mine own image? Yea, even all men were created, in the beginning, after mine own image. (See Ether 3:13–15.)[103]

After incorporating this text into the Book of Mormon record, Moroni added a prophetic coda, one that would not have been lost on the Prophet: "And in that day that they [the Gentiles] shall exercise faith in me, saith the Lord, even as the brother of Jared did, that they may become sanctified in me, then will I manifest unto them the things which the brother of Jared saw, even to the unfolding unto them all my revelations, saith Jesus Christ, the Son of God, the Father of the heavens and of the earth, and all things that in them is" (see Ether 4:7).[104] Even the Gentiles eventually could have access to the timeless knowledge and secrets of the grand cosmos of God preserved in the Book of Mormon's Wisdom-like tradition for those who were worthy.

Still, in order to substantiate a connection between Book of Mormon temple theology and Smith's Nauvoo temple theological innovations, we need to ascertain whether these Israelite-like Wisdom narratives, preserved among the Nephite peoples for centuries of Book of Mormon history, were in some way associated with the Nephite temple institution itself and then became early seeds for the Prophet's later Nauvoo temple theology. Evidently this was so.

Eden ascension narratives in Book of Mormon temple texts and the Nauvoo Temple

Four hundred years after Lehi lived, another Book of Mormon narrative tells of prophet Alma and Amulek in the community of Ammonihah, which had by then apostatized from the Nephite religion but still searched for the lost meaning of the Eden narrative and its distinctive theology of Adam.[105] Amulek, a citizen of Ammonihah, first cites his own temple lineage as a sign of his social standing: "I am Amulek . . . a descendant of Aminadi; and it was the same Aminadi who interpreted the writing which was upon the wall of the temple, which was written by the finger of God" (see Alma 10:2).[106] The memorable temple wall, with writings by the finger of God (like God's writings on stone tablets on Sinai in the Hebrew Bible), and the religious figure Aminadi (probably a priest), who successfully interpreted these sacred writings (implying a larger focus within the community on sacred temple texts), are all telling signs that this once was, and still may have been, a vibrant religious temple community.

Consequently, Alma speaks to this temple community using the language and themes of their ancient temple traditions. In Alma 12 he describes his teachings as deeply sacred, "the mysteries of God," and selectively secret, "under a strict command that they shall not impart only according to the portion of his word which he doth grant." He acknowledges that access to these mysteries is granted only to the faithful, based on their "heed and diligence . . . until it is given unto [them] to know the mysteries of God until [they] know them in full" (see Alma 12:9–10).[107] In this narrative the chief ruler, Antionah, spontaneously evokes the Eden narrative and betrays his fascination with the symbolic tree of life, a central symbol in Lehi's earlier Israelite-like Wisdom tradition: "What does the scripture mean, which saith that God placed cherubim and a flaming sword on the east of the garden of Eden, lest our first parents should enter and partake of the fruit of the tree of life, and live forever?" (see Alma 12:21).[108] Alma responds as if his Ammonihah audience had once been temple initiates, well steeped in the Wisdom-like teachings of the Eden ascension narrative: "I say unto you that if it had been possible for Adam to have partaken of the fruit of the tree of life at that time, there would have been no death. . . . And now behold, if it were possible that our first parents could have gone forth and partaken of the tree of life they would have been forever miserable, having no preparatory state" (see Alma 12:23, 26).[109]

In all, Alma's discourses to this ancient temple community identify sixteen core symbols or themes that evoke meanings similar to the ancient Israelite Wisdom tradition: (1) the tree of life and the desirable fruit, (2) the forbidden fruit (from the other tree), (3) a plan of redemption prepared, (4) the creation of the world, (5) man becoming as God, (6) the knowledge of God and knowing good from evil, (7) Eden as the abode (temple) of God, (8) the fortunate fall of Adam as prelude to a spiritual ascension to God, (9) God conversing with man, (10) angels conversing with man, (11) a premortal event (council of God?) in which the faithful were called with a holy (priesthood) calling, (12) an order of high priests after the order of the Son of God at the center of their temple community, (13) who in some way had been sanctified, (14) having garments symbolically washed white through the blood of the Lamb, (15) with reference to ancient holy king Melchizedek, and finally (16) "enter[ing] into the rest of the Lord their God."[110] Twelve of these sixteen themes are present also in Lehi's visions and blessings.[111]

Of course, with a casual reading it is easy to miss many of these Wisdom-like symbols and themes, and because they are also present in the Eden narrative of Genesis in the Hebrew Bible, it is easy to mistake them as mere elaborations of the biblical Genesis narratives, with perhaps the addition of a savior theme. It might be argued too that by making the fall of Adam a temple theme the fall acquires a more positive value. Yet we encounter similar issues when some view the Writings of the Hebrew Bible—for example, the books of Psalms, Proverbs, or Job—merely as collections of valuable and worthwhile sayings. It is often overlooked, however, that various psalms were likely temple hymns containing hidden remnants of ancient Israelite temple worship or that the books of Proverbs or Job were repositories of ancient sacred stories and theological narratives that over time became obscured and distorted. The original meanings of the sacred motifs, patterns, symbols, and myths of the ancient Israelite Wisdom tradition contained in the First Temple religion were lost.

The connections between the Book of Mormon's evident temple theology, the ancient Wisdom tradition discovered in the Old Testament First Temple religion, and Smith's temple theology of the Nauvoo era now become more apparent. For example, when the Prophet introduced temple theology in Nauvoo on May 4–5, 1842, he used the large upper room of an old brick store building to improvise a makeshift temple with props and decorations designed to represent the creation narrative. Scholar Andrew Ehat quotes from Lucius N. Scoville's diary, one of a handful of men asked to assist:

> We therefore went to work making the necessary preparations, and everything was arranged representing the interior of a temple as much as the circumstances would permit, he [Joseph Smith] being with us dictating everything. . . . Those men busily cut canvas for dividing the room into subrooms, built at least one altar, and brought in potted plants, shrubs and small trees to furnish the "Garden" room—the section of the room that represented the Garden of Eden. . . . What they brought in as additional furnishings to organize the other subrooms (representing the Creation, the World, the Terrestrial and the Celestial orders of progression) [we] are not informed; we do know that they worked under the Prophet's detailed and total supervision, finishing by midday. They were then dismissed.[112]

Evolution from early temple impulses to Nauvoo temple theology

The idea of orienting Nauvoo temple theology in 1842 around the creation narratives may have seemed novel and audacious and seemingly appeared on the American religious scene completely without precedent or explanation. These ideas, though, were forming for well over a decade, much earlier than the Kirtland Temple of 1836, going back to the early days of the church's formation, possibly before and certainly after the publication of the Book of Mormon.

Don Bradley suggests that as early as 1828 Joseph Smith may have been exposed to temple texts in the lost book of Lehi, the earliest translated Book of Mormon text. Bradley relates an account from Smith's father, Joseph Smith Sr., recorded by another contemporary, Fayette Lapham, in which the father tells of some of the content of the early translation of the book of Lehi:

> Sometime after [Lehi's clan] arrived in the New World, they're traveling and they're [led] to this strange object, and the guy who finds it doesn't know what it is. So they [had] a tabernacle . . . when they first arrived in the New World and had not yet built a temple. . . . He brings this object into the tabernacle and immediately

> the voice of the Lord asks him a question, presumably from behind the veil covering the Holy of Holies where the Lord's presence was understood to dwell. And the voice asks him, "What is that in your hand?" And Lapham says the man responded that "he did not know but that he had come to inquire"—those are Lapham's exact words. So the Lord tells the man to take this object and put it on his face, and then to cover his face with animal skins. And when he does, he's able to see anything supernaturally, it's the interpreters.[113]

"The story is loaded with biblical freight," explains Bradley. "The question—'What is that in your hand?'—is actually in Exodus 4, where Moses is at the burning bush on Sinai, when he's first called as a prophet, and the thing in his hand is his staff. This is his experience of first entering the presence of God. The veiling of his face is related to Moses coming down from Sinai after the giving of the Ten Commandments, and his face is glowing from the presence of God. And so he veils his face so that the others won't encounter that glory that's reflected from him."[114] The mention of animal skins in the Lapham account is quite similar to biblical references to animal skins—probably meaning "fine leather"[115]—used to handle the most sacred objects of the tabernacle of Moses. For example, the New Revised Standard Version of Numbers 4:5–15 speaks of using "a covering of fine leather" to handle the ark of the covenant of the holy of holies, and the table of shewbread, the menorah, the golden incense altar, and "all the utensils of the service that are used in the sanctuary" (Numbers 4:12 NRSV). Bradley concludes:

> The lost 116 pages are actually the earliest scripture of the Restoration; . . . when we look and see some of the clues to what was in [the book of Lehi], it is already anticipating things that some people, including previously myself, considered to be a later development in Nauvoo-era Mormonism and thus not present in the Book of Mormon. And yet what we see from the clues is that "Nauvoo Mormonism," "temple Mormonism," is original and literal Mormonism—it's the very faith propounded by Mormon in his book, beginning with its lost opening, the Book of Lehi.[116]

In June 1830, the same month the Book of Mormon copyright was secured, the Prophet immediately turned again to his passion and gift of translation, now focused on making corrections and revisions to the Bible text itself. Before making progress with the Genesis text, he first recorded by revelation a preface to the book of Genesis, the Visions of Moses (Moses 1 in the LDS Pearl of Great Price). Significantly, the Visions opens with Moses witnessing the grand creation of the world—suggesting that the Wisdom-like narratives of the Book of Mormon must have remained in the Prophet's consciousness since the completion of the translation a year earlier in June 1829. The new Moses creation narratives also contained the imprints of the Wisdom and First Temple narratives, much like the Book of Mormon temple creation narratives: Moses is taken to a high mountain (symbolic of the temple) and sees God, his creations (the world and its inhabitants, which God created by the power of his Only Begotten Son), and Satan, who is also a son of God. Perhaps the most convincing detail is that the vision of Moses interprets the fall of Adam as a fortunate fall that facilitates joy and begins man's ascension to the presence of God—all reflecting closely the Wisdom-like patterns of Lehi's final blessing on his son Jacob. This section of Moses's vision was recorded in December 1830:

> & in that day Adam blessed God . . . saying Blessed be the name of God for my transgression for in this life I shall have joy & again in my flesh I shall see God & Eve his wife heard all these things & was glad saying were it not for our transgression we should never had seed & should never had known good & evil & the joy of our redemption & the eternal life which God giveth unto all the obediant.[117]

In September 1830 the Prophet recorded another revelation, published in the Book of Commandments and later in the Doctrine and Covenants (section 29), that began to expand and flesh out the meanings of the Eden narrative, again evoking the unique Wisdom-like patterns of Lehi's final blessing on Jacob. Note in this revelation that Satan's identity as a fallen angel is expanded from Lehi's deathbed blessing on his son Jacob (in 2 Nephi 2).

> & it came to pass that Adam being tempted of the Devil for Behold the Devil was before Adam for he rebelled against me saying give me thine honour which is my Power & also a third part of the host of Heaven turned he away from me Because of their agency & they were thrust down & thus came the Devil & his Angels . . . the Devil tempted Adam & he partook of the forbiden fruit & transgressed the commandment wherein he became subject to the will of the Devil Because he yielded unto temptation.[118]

In December 1830 Smith added new revelation to the Visions of Moses, the "Extracts from the Prophecy of Enoch." Once again, the new Enoch text brings to mind the themes of Lehi's final blessing on Jacob and the temple themes of Alma's discourse at Ammonihah (italicized in this passage):

> and it came to pass that I turned and went *upon the [temple] mount* . . . and *I was clothed upon with glory* and *I saw the Lord* . . . and *he talked with me* even as a man talketh one with another *face to face* and he saith unto me look and I will shew unto thee the world for the space of many genarations . . . and *Enoch beheld Angles decending out of heaven* bearing testimony of the father and Son and the Holy Ghost fell on many . . . and were it possable that man could number the particles of the earth yea and milions of earths like this it would not be a begining to *the number of thy creations* . . . but peace justice and truth is the habitation of *thy throne* . . . and *I gave unto them their knowledge in the day I created them* and in the garden of Eden gave I unto man his agency.[119]

Over the ensuing decade these grand spiritual themes continued to mature into a complete temple theology that was introduced as the endowment in Nauvoo in May 1842. For example, in the 1832 Vision revelation (D&C 76), Smith and Rigdon saw the ultimate destiny of the faithful: "They are they who are Priests & Kings who having received of his fullness & of his Glory are Priests of the most high after the order of Melchisidec which was after the order of Enoch which was after the order of the only begotten Son wherefore as it is written they are Gods even the Sons of God wherefore all things are theirs."[120] The revelation evoked themes from Alma's temple discourse at Ammonihah, of priests after the order of Melchizedek, "which were made pure, and entered into the rest of the Lord their God" (Alma 13:12).[121] Inspired by the Enoch revelation of 1830, Smith's theology evolved ever more toward the theosis of man—of man becoming as God. Givens provided details about this doctrine: "Mormons often consider theosis a late development in Smith's thought associated with King Follett theology, but here it is in the Enoch text, years earlier. . . . Just days after the Enoch revelation, Smith had pronounced in God's voice that 'I [will] give unto as many as will receive me, power to become my sons' . . . [and] Enoch's rather surprising assertion that he makes to God, 'thou hast made me, and given me a right to thy throne.'"[122]

Putting this all together, we can see how the Book of Mormon provided foundational groundwork beneath an evolution—from Book of Mormon temple theology texts, to the ascension theology of Adam in the earliest days of the restoration, eventually to more ritualistic expressions of theosis in the Kirtland period (discussed in chapter 4), to full temple theology in the Nauvoo era. At the center of this evolution were the creation and Eden ascension narratives that seemed reminiscent of the ancient Wisdom and First Temple theology that only recently has been brought to light by biblical scholarship.

Harold Bloom remarked on Joseph Smith's introduction of these ancient lost theologies: "I can only attribute to his genius or daemons his uncanny recovery of elements in ancient Jewish theurgy that had ceased to be available either to Judaism or to Christianity, and that had survived only in esoteric traditions unlikely to have touched Smith directly."[123]

Rather than persisting with the prevailing notion that the fall of Adam was the origin of evil and death, the Book of Mormon reframed Adam as a divine son of God, showing the faithful the ascension path to return to the presence of God through symbols, rituals, and narratives that appeared similar to the earliest Wisdom traditions enshrined anciently in the Israelite temple. In this the Book of Mormon completely bypassed traditional nineteenth-century theologies, pointing Joseph Smith toward a different path to doctrinal development that ultimately was enshrined in the theology of the Mormon temple.

3

Sacred Rituals, Symbols, and Narratives of Sacrament, Baptism, and Zion

Rituals, rites, and ordinances are the repository of religion's spiritual identity. They embody sacred actions and narratives that involve the believer experientially in the re-creation of conative or enacted religious meaning. Their symbols evoke, inspire, and remind the believer of the essence of sacred truths. In nineteenth-century religion, there were differences in how rites and rituals were viewed. For some, such as Catholics or Methodists, rites and rituals were actual vehicles of grace, having true salvific value. John Wesley, for example, insisted that the divinely ordained means of grace, or salvation, were the sacraments, or ordinances of God, such as the Lord's Supper, prayer, and fasting or abstinence.[1] For others, such as Presbyterians, Baptists, or Mennonites, rites and rituals were only symbolic outward expressions of an inward commitment or faith. Saving grace was a gift from God based purely on a profession of faith in Jesus Christ.[2]

In 1820, within only an eight-mile radius of Palmyra, New York, nineteen competing Christian congregations offered variations of ritualistic meaning, including three Presbyterian churches, one Methodist church plus other Methodist classes, four Society of Friends (Quaker) congregations, and three mainline Baptist churches. Additionally, separate congregations of Freewill Baptists, Calvinist Baptists, Seventh-day Baptists, Episcopalians, Congregationalists, Eastern Christians, Universalists, and a nondenominational church in Junius, New York, were

Fig. 12. Religious revivals similar to this Methodist camp meeting of March 1, 1819, had an influence on Joseph Smith Jr.'s determination to independently seek religion.

nearby.[3] In this burned-over district, religious competition had a frontier flavor, as seen in James White's description of camp meetings, which were at the time central venues for Protestant revivalism:

> Camp meetings were genuinely ecumenical events, with Methodists, Presbyterians, Baptists, and Disciples [of Christ] collaborating in sponsoring the meeting and preaching at different places on the same grounds. For the closing sacramental services, however, the faithful and the new converts regrouped along denominational lines. . . . Even obdurate and unrepentant sinners might be worn down by four days of incessant singing, praying, and preaching. Indeed, many did catch religion through these strange new forms of [frontier] worship, and those who were converted were sure to return the next year and bring their friends.[4]

Of these camp meetings, Joseph Smith especially remembered "a scene of great confusion . . . [with p]riest contending against priest, and convert against convert so that all their good feelings one for another (if they ever had any) were entirely lost in a strife of words and a contest about opinions."[5] Scholars often point out that the fertile setting of the religious burned-over district in upstate New York provided the impetus for the appearance of Smith's new American religion. However, this intensely competitive milieu posed a daunting task as well: to create a religion that could actually survive, one with rites, rituals, and ordinances that distinguished the religion in a compelling way from that of competitive religionists. As a new Christian religion, Smith's church would incorporate rites, rituals, and symbols of the New Testament, similar to other Christian religions. Then again, in the burned-over district this would hardly be distinctive. As we see in this chapter, the differential meanings associated with Mormonism's rites and rituals, while embracing a New Testament heritage, were deeply influenced by their presentation in the Book of Mormon.

The Eucharist, or sacrament of the Lord's Supper

To better understand the meaning of the sacrament (the Lord's Supper, the Eucharist, or Communion)[6] in the early restoration, it is helpful to contrast it with sacramental observances in other Christian faith traditions. For two thousand years Christian religion assiduously evolved sacramental worship into a deep and intricate eucharistic tradition that defined the essence of symbolic Christian meaning. From Christ's first simple observance of the sacrament of the last supper portending the events of Calvary, over time the sacrament ritual became enveloped within early Catholicism as the central element of the larger liturgical service, the Mass. "The Mass is the complex of prayers and ceremonies, that make up the service of the Eucharist in the Latin rites,"[7] explains the *Catholic Encyclopedia*.

First let us examine the early Mormon sacrament. In the early restoration the sacrament was observed with a simple protocol of blessing

Fig. 13. Below the prominent ascending west pulpits in the Kirtland Temple lower court was a sacrament table for the preparation, blessing, and distribution of the sacrament during Sunday services and Thursday evening sacrament meetings.

the sacramental emblems (bread and wine until water replaced the latter officially in 1892)[8] and distributing to those present. Lacking elaborate structure or intricate ceremony, the sacrament usually was observed as a customary coda, or sometimes introduction, to a larger sacrament meeting, conference, or even informal gathering. It was observed usually weekly, sometimes more frequently. Congregants received the sacrament while sitting in the congregation. In the Prophet's history we find record of a conference with simple administration of the sacrament before routine confirmations and ordinations, all preceding the larger body of the meeting:

> On the first day of June 1830, we held our first ~~conference as an~~ conference as an organized Church. Our numbers were about thirty, beside<s> whom, many assembled with us, who were either believers or anxious to learn. Having opened by singing and

> prayer, we partook together of the emblems of the body and blood of our Lord Jesus Christ, we then ~~called~~ proceeded to confirm several who had lately been baptized; after which we called out and ordained severals to the various offices of the Priesthood. Much exhortation and instruction was given; and the Holy Ghost was poured out upon us in a miraculous manner many of our number prophecied, whilst others had the Heavens opened to their view.[9]

A conference held August 4, 1831, included song, prayer, exhortation by Edward Partridge, remarks by Sidney Rigdon, confession of Ziba Peterson, and exhortation by Joseph Smith. According to the minutes, the meeting closed with: "Thirty-one members present, who, with the Elders partook of the sacrament Closed by prayer by Oliver Cowdery."[10] Heber C. Kimball recorded a similar simple protocol with the Baptist church before his conversion to Mormonism: "I concluded to put myself under the watch care of the Baptist church; . . . the next day I went with my wife and we were baptized by [Baptist] Elder Elijah Weaver, and we partook of the sacrament[11] on that day for the first and also last time with them."[12] What appeared to matter most in the administration of the sacrament in the early restoration was its plain symbolism of spiritual communion with the Lord and the sacred unity of the communicants with each other. Its protocol was understated and informal. Smith even recorded in his history being instructed by a heavenly messenger to substitute water for wine as a sacrament emblem if necessary so as "not [to] purchase wine, neither strong drink of your enemies."[13] The context of the incident itself reveals the informality of Smith's sacramental protocol.

> Early in the month of August, Newel Knight and his wife paid us a visit, at my place at Harmony, Penn; and as neither his wife nor mine had been as yet confirmed, ~~and~~ it was proposed that we should confirm them, and partake together of the sacrament, before he and his wife should leave us.— In order to prepare for this; I set out to go to procure some wine for the occasion, but had gone ~~but~~ <only> a short distance when I was met by a heavenly messenger, and received the following revelation. . . . I say unto

> you, that it mattereth not what ye shall eat, or what you shall drink, when ye partake of the sacrament if it so be that ye do it with an eye single to my glory; remembering unto the Father my body which was laid down for you, and my blood which was shed for the remission of your sins."[14]

Consequently, Smith continued,

> In obedience to the above commandment we prepared some wine of our own make, and held our meeting, consisting only of five viz: Newel Knight and wife, myself and my wife, and John Whitmer. We partook together of the sacrament, after which we confirmed these two sisters into the church, and spent the evening in a glorious manner. The Spirit of the Lord was poured out upon us, we praised the Lord God, and rejoiced exceedingly.[15]

The eucharistic observances in the Roman Catholic Mass, or even in higher forms of Methodist, Presbyterian, or Lutheran worship, were considerably more formal and elaborate, with much greater prominence given to the Eucharist itself in time, focus, and setting within the service. The entire service was scripted to elevate the Eucharist as the very climax of the service. In fact, Joseph Smith was likely exposed to frontier versions of these worship services, which we discuss in more detail below. What I want to show at this point is a contrast in expression, meaning, and protocol of the Mormon sacrament service itself compared to other Christian Eucharist services and the possible role of the Book of Mormon as an influence on sacramental worship.

The contrast of the simple protocol of the sacrament for Latter-day Saints is perhaps most vivid in comparison to the High Church worship forms of the Roman Catholic Mass, for example, in which the Eucharist service occupies two-thirds of the Mass in a much longer and more elaborately drawn-out ceremony.[16] During the nineteenth century, Catholicism followed the worship protocol of the Tridentine Mass, observed from 1570 to 1962. Here the Eucharist service itself flowed with thematic crescendo through sequential recited rituals and prayers in three successive sections: Offertory, Consecration, and Communion.[17]

The Offertory introduced the sacramental emblems at the altar with a prayer to the Most Holy Trinity that "my sacrifice and yours may be acceptable to God the Father almighty." The Consecration, the climactic center of the service, offered eucharistic and intercession prayers, and then the culmination of the Eucharist—the moment of consecration, or transubstantiation—when the sacramental bread and wine were converted into the body and blood of Christ with the sacred Words of Institution (cited below) that effected transubstantiation. During the Communion, the priest distributed the sacramental emblems to the congregation with an invitation to come to the altar rail and finally gave each congregant the body and blood of the Lord—all framed by the sign of the cross.[18]

One comes away from the eucharistic service with awe and reverence, having witnessed in detail a dramatic spiritual representation of the events leading to the crucifixion. Even the Words of Institution that effected transubstantiation, which came from the New Testament narrative of the last supper, anticipated this final sacrifice by Christ.

> Take this, all of you, and eat it:
>   this is my body which will be given up for you.
> Take this, all of you, and drink from it:
>   this is the cup of my blood,
>   the blood of the new and everlasting covenant.
> It will be shed for you and for all
>   so that sins may be forgiven.
> Do this in memory of me.[19]

The early Methodist celebration of the Holy Eucharist observed with Wesley in England would have been comparable in form to the Catholic Eucharist, with sequential recited prayers by the elder leading up to corresponding Words of Institution, though Methodists did not accept transubstantiation but instead believed that the Lord was present at that moment.[20] In North America, even on the frontier, Joseph Smith probably experienced some of the formal elements of the Methodist Eucharist during the quarterly visits of the circuit rider, when an ordained elder formally administered the sacraments. White explained that when converts would respond to the altar call to come forward and receive the emblems of the Eucharist, these were considered red-letter days.[21]

Still, the frontier forms of Methodism or other Protestant worship forms that Smith might have witnessed on a weekly basis would have been less formal. In Methodism, for instance, "local [non-ordained] preachers were appointed and began to hold weekly preaching services, leaving it to the circuit rider to administer the sacraments on his next visit."[22] After Wesley's death in 1791, his detailed *Book of Discipline* was quietly set aside in favor of the much shorter "Sacramental Services, &c.," which retained only the second half of the full Eucharist service along with baptism and various other rites, according to White.[23] The Palmyra-area "camp meetings and other services conducted by Methodists [Sunday services, class meetings, midweek prayer services] were held so frequently at the time of the first vision that notices of such gatherings seldom appeared in the local newspapers."[24] So Smith witnessed, and even experienced, forms of the Methodist Eucharist frequently during his young life; he certainly would have been familiar with its practice.

Book of Mormon influences on the Mormon sacrament

Yet despite his considerable exposure to Protestant celebrations of the Eucharist, Smith quietly chose to set aside these long-established communion rites and instead embraced a different sacramental model. The Mormon sacrament ordinance that emerged was in contrast remarkably modest with no reference to a re-presentation drama of the crucifixion, no thematic crescendo, only two simple recited prayers, no climactic moment of transubstantiation or ritually defined moment of the presence of Christ, no suffusive symbol of the cross, and a sacrament table instead of an altar.[25] The singular part of the sacrament service that *was* formally prescribed was the sacramental prayers, thematically similar to the traditional Christian Eucharist, but nonetheless distinctly different.

> O God, the Eternal Father, we ask thee in the name of thy Son Jesus Christ, to bless and sanctify this bread to the souls of all those who partake of it, that they may eat in remembrance of the

SACRAMENTAL SCENE IN A WESTERN FOREST.

Fig. 14. This large frontier Presbyterian congregation is assembled for a sacramental service. "It was a common adage . . . that during the Joseph Smith years 'Mormonism flourished best out of doors'" (William Hartley, *Ensign*, January 1978).

> body of thy Son, and witness unto thee, O God the Eternal Father, that they are willing to take upon them the name of thy Son, and always remember him, and keep his commandments which he hath given them, that they may always have his spirit to be with them. Amen.[26]

> O God, the Eternal Father, we ask thee, in the name of thy Son Jesus Christ, to bless and sanctify this wine to the souls of all those who drink of it, that they may do it in remembrance of the blood of thy Son, which was shed for them, that they may witness unto thee, O God the Eternal Father, that they do always remember him, that they may have his spirit to be with them. Amen.[27]

The recitation of these prayers was the most important moment of personal symbolic covenant making of the Mormon sacrament service—their words were administered perfectly, word for word. These words, however, were not derived directly from the New Testament, like the similarly meaningful Words of Institution of the Catholic Mass or Methodist Communion Service. Instead these sacrament prayers were taken word for word from the Book of Mormon and then later confirmed by revelation to Smith at the time of the formal founding of the new church in April 1830. Scott Faulring and Robert Woodford separately traced the derivation of the sacrament prayers from the Book of Mormon.[28] The setting of the Book of Mormon sacrament prayers is especially interesting, revealing a Nephite sacramental tradition that extended back centuries to the actual visit of Christ to the ancient Americas, as recorded in 3 Nephi.

The Book of Mormon documents Christ's seminal visitation to the Bountiful temple in the ancient Americas in meticulous detail, a visit comparable in significance to the risen Christ's appearance to his disciples on the road to Emmaus or in the Upper Room in Jerusalem. On the first day of his visitation in the ancient Americas, Jesus "took of the bread, and blessed it; and he gave unto the [ordained twelve] disciples, and commanded that they should eat. And when they had eat, and were filled, he commanded that they should give unto the multitude [the congregation]" (see 3 Nephi 18:3–4).[29] He repeated this procedure again with the wine; first blessing, then giving to the ordained priesthood officiators, and then commanding that they give to the congregation. The text of these historic sacramental prayers was formally codified into Nephite sacrament observance; these may have been the very words pronounced by the risen Christ during his first sacrament service in the Americas. They were preserved by Moroni and then translated into the Book of Mormon text currently found in Moroni 4–5.

Christ set his symbolic protocol in this ancient American setting. The sacrament was first given to Christ's priesthood servants and then to the congregation—signifying symbolically the ordained priesthood officiants' sacred example to first reconcile their own sins with God and then be filled. They then offered the sacramental emblems to those they serve, the congregants, so they likewise can then reconcile their sins and also be filled. In 1946 the church's First Presidency and Quorum of the Twelve Apostles sent a letter to all church members stating that "the sacrament should be first given to the presiding authority in the meeting. This may be the bishop, perhaps one of the stake presidency, or one of the visiting General Authorities . . . [so that] members of the Aaronic Priesthood officiating will have a lesson in Church government."[30] Still, this protocol was established millennia earlier as part of Christ's first sacrament service at the temple at Bountiful.

The Book of Mormon also set a precedent for informal and frequent sacramental observance in the ancient Americas. Late in the first day of his visitation among the Nephite congregation at Bountiful, "Jesus commanded his disciples that they should bring forth some bread and wine unto him" (see 3 Nephi 18:1),[31] a seemingly spontaneous moment in which he introduced the sacrament of the Lord's Supper to this ancient American congregation for the first time. The next day, the second day of his visitation, Jesus again administered the sacrament to the Nephite congregation as a consummation to a great spiritual outpouring (discussed in detail in chapter 4), following the same simple procedural protocol of the first day. After these two sacramental events, editor Mormon further documented that "the Lord [Jesus] truly did teach the people, for the space of three days; and after that, he did shew himself unto them oft, and did break bread oft, and bless it, and gave it unto them" (see 3 Nephi 26:13).[32] The Book of Mormon's final writer, Moroni, documented that in the period following Christ's visit to the Americas, "the church did meet together oft . . . to partake of the bread and wine, in remembrance of the Lord Jesus" (see Moroni 6:6).[33] This pattern seems to suggest that in the ancient Americas the sacramental observance was simple, informal, and designed to occur regularly on the Sabbath, although it sometimes occurred spontaneously as well.

The New Testament hints at similar informal communion patterns, but they are more obscure. Indeed, during the early nineteenth century only two New Testament passages were believed by theologians to have documented actual sacramental, or eucharistic, observances.[34] The first was Jesus's administration of the last supper in the Upper Room in Jerusalem on the eve of Passover (Luke 22:19–20). The second occurred later, "upon the first day of the week [the Sabbath], when the disciples came together to break bread, Paul preached unto them, ready to depart on the morrow; and continued his speech until midnight" (Acts 20:7).[35]

The first sacramental narrative at the last supper, of course, had a defining impact on the meaning of the sacrament. Subsequent New Testament allusions to sacramental occurrences were less definitive, leaving considerable latitude for interpretation of sacramental protocols.

In the eighteenth century, Wesley had stressed that the Eucharist should be taken frequently; he "received communion on 'an average of once every four or five days' throughout his lifetime."[36] However, by the nineteenth century things had changed. White reported that "Methodists had lost weekly communion after the death of Wesley [in 1791], Roman Catholics were not to achieve it as general practice for most laity until the twentieth century, and Anglicans were only slowly to restore the practice after 1833. But within a year or two after 1830, the Christian Church [Disciples of Christ], the Mormons in America, and the Plymouth Brethren in England, achieved and retained weekly communion for everyone."[37] The simple informal sacrament protocol that Smith instituted in 1829 was likely influenced at least in part by the Book of Mormon.

The idea that sacrament protocol and prayers used by the Prophet in the early restoration were the same as those recorded anciently in the Book of Mormon challenges belief, as if Smith had written them into the Book of Mormon translation for his own use in the modern day. Yet this is precisely the paradox asserted by the Book of Mormon and its translation. While translating the book's textual storyline narrative, Smith simultaneously recorded liturgical innovations that defined precisely how ordinances, in this case the sacrament, should be observed, word for word. Then, once written, these ritual innovations were set in place, regardless of competing sacramental claims and theologies, and continued uninterrupted and virtually without modification from 1830 to the present day. The entire process suggests that Smith had unusual confidence in the substance and correctness of these innovations, trusting their forms, expressions, and meanings as stemming from a vetted, reliable source—in this case ancient scripture similar to the Bible, but written by the hand of Mormon, Nephi, or Moroni. Smith was so confident of these ritual innovations that he instructed his scribes and assistants to use them verbatim in the emerging liturgy of the new church.

Another explanation adds to a fuller understanding of the symbolic meaning of the sacrament. The Book of Mormon text implies that the sacrament was as much about the resurrection of Christ as it was about his death. When Jesus instituted the sacrament in the ancient Americas, he charged the Nephite congregation: "And this shall ye do in remembrance of my holy body, *which I have shewn unto you*" (see 3 Nephi 18:7)[38]—they had personally witnessed the healed wounds of the resurrected Christ. To the New Testament disciples he declared, "This is my body which is *given for you*: this do in remembrance of me" (Luke 22:19, emphasis added).[39] Of course, this simple difference in texts, *shown unto you* and *given for you*, reflects the two essential sacramental premises: Christ gave his life in death to sacrifice for the sins of the world and again took up his life—overcame death—so that all would live again. John Welch elaborated on these subtle differences in the meaning of the sacrament.

> The prayers that we administer, the sacrament that we participate in, is really the sacrament of the Lord's appearance, because it is from the Book of Mormon that we know those prayers. We don't know those from the New Testament or from anything in early Christianity. The way in which the priests administer the sacrament is explained in the Book of Mormon and follows this prototype. . . . We usually think of the Last Supper, the Upper Room—the events that preceded the crucifixion and resurrection of Jesus. It seems to me that we should add to that an effort to try to spiritually place ourselves into the context of the Sermon at the Temple—that we should try to see ourselves as having experienced the same thing that these Nephites did.[40]

This passage demonstrates the essence of the Book of Mormon's formative influence on the restoration. It is not so much whether the Book of Mormon was influential—it was. Instead, it is *how* it was influential that matters—it was formative in nascent, remarkably subtle ways that even today few believers perceive. Yet even here it would be tempting to be satisfied with the notion that the Book of Mormon merely provided useful protocols for the early builders of the restoration, like an instruction manual for a new building project. This view, however, misjudges the influence of the Book of Mormon, for this view neglects history and provenance. It overlooks meaning, intent, and symbolism flowing from the original, ancient historic context that imbues ritual with validity and authenticity.

For the Christian world the Eucharist has deep historical authenticity from its New Testament origins, which gives sacred and symbolic meaning to all Christian believers today. Yet the sacrament of Mormonism also has deep historical authenticity from its Book of Mormon origins, which suggest previously unexplored symbolic meanings to believers. In Mormonism, the meaning of the sacrament traces to the Upper Room in Jerusalem and the last supper, as with all Christians. And it also traces to the temple at Bountiful in the ancient Americas—to the visitation of Christ and his personal initiation of this sacred observance. Christians have celebrated the eucharistic meaning of the last supper for millennia. The Book of Mormon peoples similarly must have celebrated the sacramental meaning of the Bountiful temple sacrament service for centuries after Christ, but then the ordinance was lost—until its recovery in 1829 with the translation of the Book of Mormon. Today Mormons celebrate the sacramental meanings of both settings—of the last supper from the New Testament and of the sacramental service at Bountiful from 3 Nephi. This is possible only because of the formative influence of the Book of Mormon.

A related question frequently arises: what about the absence of the cross or crucifix in Mormonism as a visible emblem of sacramental worship? In fact, during the nineteenth century the cross was broadly viewed as a Catholic symbol and was avoided by North American Protestants. During the Protestant Reformation the cross and other sacred relics were viewed as idolatrous and were rejected from worship. Michael Reed discussed the symbolism of the cross in the early nineteenth century:

> To Protestant Americans, the cross was perceived to be a strictly Catholic symbol. . . . [I]n 1847 a Presbyterian magazine insists that the cross is "not a symbol of redemption through the blessed Savior, but a perverted abused symbol of a great system of superstition

> and imposture." Protestants were unwilling to risk the threat of mob violence and internal dissent, and so they generally avoided crosses that would have otherwise made their churches appear Catholic. Most protestant denominations, "including the Methodists, Congregationalists, Episcopalians, Presbyterians, and Baptists, rigorously avoided any use of 'Catholic art.'"[41]

Early Mormon attitudes about the cross were much less prejudiced; indeed, Reed explained, "the condemnation of the cross is noticeably absent in the early years of Mormonism."[42] Brigham Young discussed the use of the cross:

> Protestants accuse the Roman Catholic Church of worshipping idols. It is the practice of its members to carry a cross with them to worship the Virgin Mary. They have paintings and images in their chapels and other places of worship. . . . But those representations were introduced in the same way that a father would show his children that Jesus Christ is actually a man like their father, by showing them a figure representing Jesus as extended upon the cross, and saying, "This gives you, my children, an idea that he was a man."[43]

Still, though spurned by nineteenth-century Protestants, the cross itself was central to the theology of the Eucharist for all Christians. Thus Martin Luther spoke famous words of eucharistic meaning: "The cross alone is our theology."[44] Over time Protestant attitudes shifted and became more accommodating to public expressions of the cross until its presentation became as commonplace for Protestants as it was for Catholics, yet Latter-day Saints seemed to have bypassed the controversy entirely. They had had unbiased attitudes toward the cross during the long era of North American Catholic discrimination, and their attitudes remained essentially unaffected well into the twentieth century. What could explain this diverging attention to the cross between Protestants and Mormons?

One reason is that from the outset sacramental theology for the Mormons had been established on not one scriptural sacramental narrative but two—the Bible and the Book of Mormon. These two sacramental or eucharistic narratives focused on the same pivotal historical episode, the death and resurrection of Christ, except that the events they described—occurring in the Old World in one account and in the New World in the other—led to dramatically different perspectives on this seminal moment in Christian history.

Not surprisingly, in the centuries following the death and resurrection of Christ, the early Christian religion in Rome, Catholicism, accentuated the cross in worship. The New Testament, the only sacramental scripture available to the Old World, chronicled in meticulous detail the events of the crucifixion at Jerusalem: the last supper, carrying the cross to Golgotha, Jesus being nailed to the cross, the vigil of the women at the foot of the cross, the words spoken by Jesus while on the cross, his final death on the cross, and Joseph of Arimathea claiming his body from the cross for burial. The New Testament writers left a substantial body of evidence, over 12,000 words in total (560 verses),[45] documenting definitively the events of Christ's crucifixion, beginning with the last supper. John Dominic Crossan proclaimed: "That [Jesus] was crucified is as sure as anything historical can ever be."[46]

The Book of Mormon peoples in the New World witnessed none of this. To be sure, when Jesus appeared to the congregation at the temple in Bountiful, he physically showed them evidence of his crucifixion: "And it came to pass that the multitude went forth, and thrust their hands into [Jesus's] side, and did feel the prints of the nails in his hands and in his feet; and this they did do, going forth one by one, until they had all gone forth, and did see with their eyes, and did feel with their hands, and did know of a surety, and did bear record" (see 3 Nephi 11:15).[47] Their witness, nevertheless, was of the resurrected Jesus, triumphant over death. Jesus gave these ancient Americans only a brief précis of the gruesome events of the crucifixion, saying only: "I have drank out of the bitter cup which the Father hath given me, and have glorified the Father in taking upon me the sins of the world" (see 3 Nephi 11:11).[48]

The Book of Mormon, however, carefully documented the words and acts of the risen Christ among these ancient people—over 17,000 words in total (511 verses)[49] of postresurrection doctrine, instruction, prayer, miracles, and sacramental worship. The New Testament writers had left roughly 3,600 words (158 verses)[50] documenting the events of the resurrected Christ. In the ancient Americas the cross as a defining symbol appears not to have been present; Jesus mentioned it only once—briefly at the final conclusion of his New World ministry: "My Father sent me that I might be lifted up upon the cross; and after that I have been lifted up upon the cross, I might draw all men unto me" (see 3 Nephi 27:14).[51]

Joseph Smith, of course, was quite familiar with both scriptural sacramental settings—the Old World setting through the New Testament and his experience with the Eucharist while attending Protestant services, and the New World setting through his immersion in the sacramental narratives of 3 Nephi and Moroni during the Book of Mormon translation. Which setting influenced his institution of the sacrament at the beginning of the restoration? In fact, both. The meaning of the sacrament for early Latter-day Saints originated clearly from the New Testament narratives of the atonement of Christ as well as from the 3 Nephi narratives of the resurrection of Christ. However, the administration of the Mormon sacrament appeared to derive unmistakably from the New World sacramental setting of the Book of Mormon.

To this day LDS chapels leave an open space where a defining religious insignia might be placed—inviting one to personally place a symbol there. However, if the symbol of Christ's death, the cross, is tangibly real, the symbol of his resurrection is perfectly opposite—intangibly ethereal. What should be the most appropriate symbol of the resurrection: the vacant tomb of the New Testament account, the risen Christ descending from the clouds of the Book of Mormon account? By design, the absence of defining religious symbols in Mormon chapels seems to invite the questioner to envision the answer. Perhaps the pulpit, the most prominent point in the chapel proper, frames one possible defining symbol of Latter-day Saint worship: the personal witnesses of those who speak there. Gordon B. Hinckley, then a modern LDS apostle, gave his answer: "The lives of our people must become the only meaningful expression of our faith and, in fact, therefore, the symbol of our worship."[52]

Baptism

Conversion and baptism were at the very center of the religious controversy enveloping the entire region of upstate New York, from Canada into central Pennsylvania; historians have designated the area as the "burned-over district." The June 7, 1820, issue of the *Palmyra Register* newspaper "carried a brief report of 'Great Revivals in Religion' in the eastern part of the state . . . [and] announced that 'the face of the country has been wonderfully changed of late.'"[53] William Smith, younger brother of the Prophet, described "this extraordinary excitement," which "prevailed not only in our neighborhood but throughout the whole country. Great numbers were converted. It extended from the Methodists to the Baptists, from them to the Presbyterians; and so on until finally, almost all the sects became engaged in it; and it became quite a fashion to 'get religion.'"[54]

In 1819, a year before Smith's first vision, "the national increase in Presbyterian Church membership was approximately 6,500, and the increase in New York state alone was 2,250, representing 35 percent of the national total," observed Milton Backman. "But what is most significant here is the fact that more than 67 percent or 1,513 of the 2,250 New York converts came from the burned-over district. This is 23 percent of the national total."[55]

The religious commotion among the various camp meetings and revivals led to ambivalence among the Smith family members about conversion, baptism, and joining a Protestant church, partly because of the complexity of the conversion process. "One was baptized upon conversion at the camp meeting, but one was received into the church by [later] being united to a specific local congregation of faithful people, usually after a period of ethical scrutiny," explained White. "Joining a congregation [was] an act quite distinct from joining the universal church through baptism."[56] Thus, Smith's mother, Lucy Mack Smith, sought out Presbyterianism, but still kept her distance: "I considered it my duty to be baptized, and, finding a minister who was willing to baptize me, and leave me free in regard to joining any religious denomination, I stepped forward and yielded obedience to this ordinance."[57]

Joseph Smith Sr. remained aloof and "would not subscribe to any particular system of faith."[58]

Later Lucy and three of her children—Hyrum, Samuel, and Sophronia—joined the Western Presbyterian Church, the most prestigious church in Palmyra village (the only one with a building).[59] Presbyterians embraced "believer's baptism," based essentially on an affirmation of faith in Jesus Christ. Founder John Calvin had stressed: "How much evil has been caused by the dogma, ill expounded, that baptism is necessary to salvation. . . . For when the opinion prevails that all are lost who happen not to be dipped in water, our condition becomes worse than that of God's ancient people, as if his grace were more restrained than under the Law [of Moses]."[60]

Smith reported that his "mind became somewhat partial to the Methodist sect [and he] felt some desire to be united with them,"[61] though his brother William noted that "he was 'not brought out,' as the phrase was."[62] Oliver Cowdery noted that Joseph had been "awakened" during a sermon by Methodist minister George Lane,[63] "celebrated throughout the country as a 'great revival preacher.'"[64] In 1819 Lane had visited nearby Vienna (now Phelps, 15 miles from the Smith farm) for the Genesee Conference meetings, July 1–8, that year's largest Methodist meeting in the region, attended by some 110 ministers and the region's bishop.[65] Methodists taught that baptism was a sacramental means to grace, the door to enter Christ's church and that "in baptism God initiates a covenant with us, announced with the words, 'The Holy Spirit works within you, that being born through water and the Spirit, you may be a faithful disciple of Jesus Christ.' This is followed by the sign-act of laying hands on the head, or the signing of the cross on the forehead with oil."[66] Wesley, however, clarified, "Christ no where, as far as I can find, requires *dipping*, but only *baptizing*: which word, many most eminent for learning and piety have declared, signifies to *pour on*, or *sprinkle*, as well as to *dip*."[67] Still, though he favored Methodism, Smith never went so far as to be baptized a Methodist.

Baptists, similar to Presbyterians, embraced "believer's baptism" by declaring one's faith in Christ. Nonetheless, they taught that if one chose baptism it should be by submersion, but only for those who had

Fig. 15. During the Great Awakening of the nineteenth century, Baptists practiced baptism by immersion.

experienced a spiritual conversion; infants were therefore excluded from baptism, which generated considerable controversy. Methodists and Presbyterians both embraced, but did not require, infant baptism.[68] An 1834 article in the Mormon periodical the *Evening and the Morning Star* summarized these contending positions:

> For instance, the Presbyterian, the Episcopalian, the Methodist, and the Catholic god, with the god of some other sects, requires them, (or at least they think he does,) to sprinkle their children, while the Baptist, the Christian, (so called,) and the Campbellite god, or gods, are greatly offended with it, and considers it an insult to him for them to perform such a thing in his name; but reqires [requires] them to immerse only. . . . [T]he Episcopalian god reqires [requires] the children of his worshipers to be sprinkled, that their sins may be remitted, as also the Catholic god; but the Methodist god considers the children of his worshipers all fit for heaven without sprinkling, as he considers them without sin: the Baptist and the Presbyterian god have elect and non elect among the children of their worshipers, as well as among the adults.[69]

The evident confusion over baptism appears to have been a crucial issue for Smith and his associates at the beginning of the restoration.

The mode of baptism was uncertain—even the necessity of baptism itself for conversion was equivocal. Not surprising, one of the earliest questions Smith and Cowdery posed to God while translating the Book of Mormon record related to baptism. By mid-May 1829, the translation project had progressed to the point of 3 Nephi's record of Christ's visit to the Nephites of ancient America. According to Cowdery, "After writing the account given of the Savior's ministry to the remnant of the seed of Jacob, upon this continent [3 Nephi 11–29], . . . it was easily to be seen, as the prophet said would be, that . . . none had authority from God to administer the ordinances of the gospel [baptism]."[70]

Smith records that he and Cowdery "went into the woods to pray and inquire of the Lord respecting baptism for the remission of sins as we found mentioned in the translation of the plates. While we were thus employed praying and calling upon the Lord, a Messenger from heaven, descended in a cloud of light, and having laid his hands upon us, he ordained us. . . . [He] said that his name was John, the same that is called John the Baptist in the new Testament."[71] The heavenly messenger, though, gave limited instruction about the nature of baptism, saying only, "Upon you my fellow servants in the name of Messiah I confer the priesthood of Aaron, which holds the keys of the ministring of angels and of the gospel of repentance, and of baptism by immersion for the remission of sins."[72] Then "he commanded us to go and be baptized, and gave us directions that I should baptize Oliver Cowdery, and afterward that he should baptize me. ~~and that I should be called the first elder of the Church and he the second.~~ Accordingly we went and were baptized, I baptized him first, and afterwards he baptized me."[73]

Given the various competing Christian orthodoxies of conversion and baptism in the burned-over district, this first Mormon baptism seems to have proceeded remarkably routinely for Smith and Cowdery, as if they had been doing baptisms for years. They posed no questions about how to baptize, what words to say, how to perform the ordinance—should it be preceded by a profession of faith like that of the Baptists or laying hands on the head or the signing of the cross on the forehead like that of the Methodists? In Smith's account, the messenger identified "baptism by immersion" in his ordination prayer—clearly dismissing other forms of baptism such as pouring water over the head or sprinkling on the forehead. He indicated that one should baptize the other—that is, one should not baptize oneself; but there is no record that he clarified, elaborated, or gave any further detail on precisely how baptism should occur.

Book of Mormon influences on baptism and baptismal meaning

Yet this was not the first time Smith and Cowdery had been exposed to doctrinal protocol regarding baptism. Only days earlier they had translated a Book of Mormon text recording the visitation of the newly risen Christ in the ancient Americas. It must have impressed them that Christ's very first doctrinal discourse among these people addressed baptism, baptismal authority, and qualifications for baptism—with no mention of a profession of faith—including how the baptismal ritual was to have been performed anciently in the New World, together with the words of the baptismal prayer. All this was preserved by Mormon.

> And he gave unto them power to baptize. And he saith unto them, On this wise shall ye baptize. . . . Behold, ye shall go down and stand in the water, and in my name shall ye baptize them. And now behold, these are the words which ye shall say, calling them by name, saying: Having authority given me of Jesus Christ, I baptize you in the name of the Father, and of the Son, and of the Holy Ghost. Amen. And then shall ye immerse them in the water, and come forth again out of the water. (See 3 Nephi 11:22–26.)[74]

Just as with the sacrament, these Nephite baptismal protocols became tacit precedent for the development of early restoration baptismal instructions. Under the Prophet's direction, when Cowdery compiled the church's first procedural regulations in 1829, the "Articles of the Church of Christ," he quoted directly from this Book of Mormon baptismal text word for word. Later Smith made further slight revisions to Oliver's draft as part of revelation that was published in the 1830 edition of the "Articles and Covenants of the Church of Christ" (see D&C 20). Faulring noted one significant change: "The baptismal prayer in the 1829 Articles

Fig. 16. This wood engraving from 1882 features a photographer ready to document a Mormon baptism of a North American Indian.

and in the 1830 Articles and Covenants begins with the phrase *Having authority given me of Jesus Christ* (3 Nephi 11:25) rather than *Having been commissioned of Jesus Christ,* as it reads today in Doctrine and Covenants 20:73. The prophet Joseph Smith revised the earlier wording in that verse when he published the Articles and Covenants in the first edition of the Doctrine and Covenants in 1835. Before the organization of the church in 1830, the Articles and Covenants used the Book of Mormon's phrase *Having authority*."[75] The point is that the provenance of the church's modern baptismal ordinance traces back directly to the Book of Mormon baptismal text of 3 Nephi.

Another more subtle influence, just as significant yet much less obvious on the surface, is how the Book of Mormon influenced Mormonism's unique interpretation of the *theology* of baptism and its meaning to believers. To illustrate, in 2001 the Roman Catholic Church published a papal directive stating that differences between Mormon and Catholic doctrine invalidated Mormon baptism and the person being so baptized.[76] Practically speaking, this meant that Latter-day Saints converting to Catholicism must be rebaptized as a Catholic. However, those converting to Catholicism from a Protestant religion need not be rebaptized; their original Protestant baptisms would be fully recognized by the Catholic Church. Methodists, Lutherans, and Presbyterians all adopted policies similar to the Catholics, rejecting Mormon baptism based on the logic that "the LDS Church is not a part of the historic, apostolic tradition of the Christian faith."[77] Latter-day Saints might take exception to this idea, pointing to Mormonism's claim to be a restoration of the pure apostolic tradition of the original church of Christ. Then again, Latter-day Saints rebaptize all persons converting to Mormonism, so some Mormons might be surprised that other Christian religions actually recognize baptisms performed in the convert's previous religion. According to the Vatican, "This validity is possible because Christ is the true minister of the sacrament [of baptism]: Christ is the one who truly baptizes, whether it is Peter or Paul or Judas who baptizes."[78]

Still, why do Protestants and Catholics view Mormon baptism so differently? One attending a Baptist baptism, for example, would see baptism by immersion that is quite similar in form to Latter-day Saint baptism. The first reason has to do with the origin of baptism: Catholics and Protestants believe that baptism began uniquely with Christ's baptism by John the Baptist at the meridian of time, whereas Mormons believe that baptism is much older. The Vatican explained further:

> In their [Mormon] understanding *Baptism was not instituted by Christ but by God and began with Adam* (cf. Book of Moses 6:64). Christ simply commanded the practice of this rite; but this was not an innovation. . . . According to the New Testament, there is an essential difference between the Baptism of John and Christian Baptism. The Baptism of the Church of Jesus Christ of Latter-day Saints, *which originated not in Christ but already at the beginning of creation*, is not Christian Baptism; indeed, it denies its newness.[79]

Few Mormons would quibble with this interpretation of a belief in pre-Christian baptism, but where did this idea come from? Certainly none of Smith's religious exposure to Methodists, Presbyterians, or Baptists in the 1820s prompted this view. Yet somewhere amid the conversion furor of the burned-over district, he introduced an innovative insight about the theological meaning of baptism—*baptism was timeless*, going back millennia into ancient Israelite history, indeed to the beginning of time. Did Moroni, Smith's divine messenger and mentor throughout the Book of Mormon translation, provide this explanation in his visions? Perhaps. Still, the Book of Mormon record had documented the practice of pre-Christian baptism in ancient America for many centuries prior to Christ. Moreover, the fact that these ancient American peoples had originally emigrated from ancient Palestine just prior to the destruction of Jerusalem in about 600 BC raises the question of whether some form of baptism might have been observed among the Israelite Jews of ancient Jerusalem.

For example, in the sixth century BC, Book of Mormon priest Jacob taught of baptism as a distinctly ancient Israelite, even Jewish, practice associated with the Messiah. "And now, my beloved brethren, I have read these things [to you] that ye might know concerning the covenants of the Lord; that he hath covenanted with all the House of Israel; that he hath spoken unto the Jews, by the mouth of his holy prophets, even from the beginning. . . . And he commandeth all men that they must repent, and be baptised in his name, having perfect faith in the Holy One of Israel" (see 2 Nephi 9:1–2, 23).[80] In the second century BC, after a period of apostasy, Alma restored baptism as the way to enter his newly organized church of Christ. These were the words of his ancient baptismal ritual:

> I baptize thee, having authority from the Almighty God, as a testimony that ye have entered into a covenant to serve him until you are dead, as to the mortal body; and may the spirit of the Lord be poured out upon you; and may he grant unto you eternal life, through the redemption of Christ, which he hath prepared from the foundation of the world. And after Alma had said these words,

> both Alma [the officiator] and Helam [the convert] were buried in the water.[81]

The Book of Mormon makes sixty references to baptism prior to the advent of Christ, including many references to being baptized in the name of Christ. Nephi quoted a passage from the biblical prophecy of Isaiah 48 that in Nephi's version (1 Nephi 20) was later revised in 1840 by Joseph Smith to reflect the centrality of baptism in ancient Israelite religion: "Hearken and hear this, O house of Jacob, who are called by the name of Israel, and are come forth out of the waters of Judah, (*or out of the waters of baptism,*) who swear by the name of the Lord, and make mention of the God of Israel."[82]

The phrase "or out of the waters of baptism" was not included in the original 1830 Palmyra edition or the 1837 Kirtland edition of the Book of Mormon[83] but was added parenthetically in the 1840 Nauvoo edition.[84] Significantly, by adding this parenthetical phrase, the Prophet gave us a clue of his evolving baptismal theology. The original 1829 Book of Mormon translation had piqued Smith's curiosity of baptism in ancient pre-Christian religion; just a year later, in December 1830, during his biblical retranslation project of the book of Genesis, the Prophet recorded a revelation of an ancient text, "an extract from the words of Enoch." The Enoch revelation tells of God teaching Adam of the principles and ordinances of Christian religion: "Hearken unto my voice, and believe, and repent of all thy transgressions, and be *baptized even by water,* in the name of mine only begotten Son, which is full of grace and truth, which is Jesus Christ, the only name which shall be given under heaven, whereby salvation shall come unto the children of men."[85]

Note that the simple expression of the Enoch revelation, *baptized even by water,* had precedent almost word for word in the Book of Mormon in Nephi's treatise on the universal necessity of baptism: "And now, if the Lamb of God, he being holy, should have need to be *baptized by water,* to fulfil righteousness, O then, how much more need have we, being unholy, to be *baptized, yea, even by water*" (see 2 Nephi 31:5).[86] Smith's newly revealed Enoch text had extended the scriptural precedent for pre-Christian baptismal theology beyond the earliest Book of Mormon peoples to the very beginning of time, to Adam. "& it came to pass when the Lord had spoken with Adam our father that Adam cried unto the Lord & he was caught away by the spirit of the Lord & was caried down into the water & was laid under the water & was brought forth out of the water & thus he was baptized."[87]

Significantly, the Prophet's insertion in Nephi's quotation of Isaiah 48:1, *or out of the waters of baptism*, was added to the 1840 Nauvoo edition of the Book of Mormon and not the 1837 Kirtland edition. On August 15, 1840, while speaking at the funeral of Seymour Brunson in Nauvoo, Smith introduced for the first time the doctrine of proxy baptisms for one's deceased ancestors, so the idea of timeless baptism was very much on his mind. Eyewitness at Smith's discourse, Simon Baker recorded:

> He [Joseph Smith] read the greater part of the 15th chapter of Corinthians and remarked that the Gospel of Jesus Christ brought glad tidings of great joy, and then remarked that he saw a widow in that congregation that had a son who died without being baptized, and this widow in reading the sayings of Jesus "except a man be born of water and of the spirit he cannot enter the kingdom of heaven," and that not one jot nor tittle of the Savior's words should pass away, but all should be fulfilled. He then said that this widow should have glad tidings in that thing. He also said the apostle [Paul] was talking to a people who understood baptism for the dead, for it was practiced among them. He went on to say that people could now act for their friends who had departed this life, and that the plan of salvation was calculated to save all who were willing to obey the requirements of the law of God.[88]

For Smith the timelessness of baptism was thus complete, and baptism's documentation throughout scripture was complete as well: in the Book of Mormon, in the New Testament, in Isaiah of the Old Testament (through 1 Nephi in the Book of Mormon), and in Genesis of the Old Testament (through the Enoch revelation recorded in the Book of Moses). For Mormons of the early restoration the timeless gospel was an exhilarating idea. An early church editorial articulated:

> Perhaps, our friends will say, that the gospel and its ordinances were not known till the days of John [the Baptist] the son of Zecharias. . . . For our own part, we cannot believe, that the ancients in all ages were so ignorant of the system of heaven as many suppose, since all that were ever saved, were saved through the power of this great plan of redemption, as much so before the coming of Christ as since.[89]

The evolving theology of timeless Christian baptism takes us back to John the Baptist's 1829 visitation to Smith and Cowdery. Here, according to Smith's 1838 history, the Baptist specifically referred to baptism as a ritual ordinance belonging to the priesthood of Aaron and to the sons of Levi of the ancient Israelite and Jewish priesthood:

> Upon you my fellow servants in the name of Messiah I confer the priesthood of Aaron, which holds the keys of the ministring of angels and of the gospel of repentance, and of baptism by immersion for the remission of sins, and this shall never be taken again from the earth, untill the sons of Levi do offer again an offering unto the Lord in righteousness.[90]

Ancient biblical forms of baptism and washings for purity and conversion

Did baptism in fact originate in the New Testament, or is there evidence of its practice earlier in time, consistent with Book of Mormon protocol and consistent with John the Baptist's visitation in which he connected baptism to the rites of the Aaronic Priesthood in the Old Testament? The word *baptism* clearly originated scripturally in the New Testament, where it appears 83 times; it is never mentioned in the Hebrew canon of Old Testament scripture. Remember, however, that the New Testament was originally written in common Koine Greek,[91] the lingua franca of the Hellenistic Western world following Alexander the Great. Hence the word *baptism* derived from the Greek noun βάπτισμα (*baptisma*), meaning "immersion or submersion," itself derived from βαπτισμός (*baptismos*), meaning a "washing."[92] Could it be that similar immersion washing rituals in Old Testament theology were somehow related to, or had become early precedent for, New Testament Christian baptism?

In fact, the Old Testament describes at least three clear forms of Israelite washings, one of which was an early form of washing for remission of sins. These forms of ritual washing were indeed extant throughout much of Old Testament history, certainly the First and Second Temple periods, and at least one form was similar to the baptismal washings administered to Jesus by John the Baptist at the beginning of Christ's ministry. These baptismal washings likely continued in some form in the New Testament church, even as, with the advent of Christ, they had become figuratively "new in Christ."

For example, the book of Psalms contains a temple hymn addressed to the chief temple musician in which King David seeks a washing for a cleansing of his sins (with Bathsheba), consistent with the meaning of New Testament baptism: "Have mercy upon me, O God, according to thy lovingkindness: according unto the multitude of thy tender mercies blot out my transgressions. Wash me throughly from mine iniquity, and cleanse me from my sin. . . . Purge me with hyssop, and I shall be clean: wash me, and I shall be whiter than snow" (Psalm 51:1–2, 7).[93] This washing in David's psalm sounds curiously akin to the washing mentioned in the New Testament when the Lord in vision commanded the Jewish convert, Saul of Tarsus (Paul after his conversion) not to delay but to "get up, be baptized, and have your sins washed away, calling on his name" (Acts 22:16 NRSV).[94]

The Old Testament speaks of other forms of Israelite ritual washings for priests officiating in the temple, such as washing the priest's hands and feet with water from the temple lavers (ritual washing basins) before officiating in the temple (Exodus 30), or washing and anointing newly ordained priests to serve in the temple (Exodus 40:12–15). The Temple of Solomon had a large "sea" of brass placed on the backs of twelve brazen oxen, which, according to Chronicles, "was for the priests to wash in" (2 Chronicles 4:2–6).[95] A third form of washings included Israelite ritual washings for purification intended for persons with physical issues, including washings for leprosy (Leviticus 14–15), bodily emissions (Leviticus 15), and handling the dead (Numbers 19).

Fig. 17. *Miqva'ot,* like this one at Qumran, were ancient ritual washing pools used for various Jewish religious rites, including conversion.

Archaeology and Jewish textual scholarship provide further evidence of washings through ritual immersion quite similar in form to baptism in ancient Israelite culture, including washings for conversion and initiation into Judaism. The writings of Josephus and Philo of Alexandria and the Dead Sea Scrolls contain detailed accounts and instructions of ritual washings that were part of ancient Jewish observances. Biblical scholar Jonathan Lawrence comprehensively documents the use of *miqva'ot,* ritual immersion pools or cisterns, during the Second Temple period centuries before Christ. Usually these miqva'ot cisterns were rectangular shaped and plastered and had steps leading down into the pool. They were located near distinctly Jewish religious sites such as the temple, synagogues, and cemeteries. According to Lawrence, "many archaeologists and other scholars have linked Second Temple [ritual] bathing practices to an origin with the Tabernacle [of Moses] . . . as if they were part of one continuous tradition. . . . [Scholar] Aryeh Kaplan traces the practice of immersion back to Abraham (Gen. 18:4), placing the *origins* of immersion even further back in history."[96] The *Jewish Encyclopedia* documents the practice of baptism as a key ritual in Jewish conversions:

> According to rabbinical teachings, which dominated even during the existence of the Temple (Pes. viii. 8), Baptism, next to circumcision and sacrifice, was an absolutely necessary condition to be fulfilled by a proselyte to Judaism (Yeb. 46b, 47b; Ker. 9a; 'Ab. Zarah 57a; Shab. 135a; Yer. Kid. iii. 14, 64d). Circumcision, however, was much more important, and, like baptism, was called a "seal" (Schlatter, "Die Kirche Jerusalems," 1898, p. 70). But as circumcision was discarded by Christianity, and the [temple] sacrifices had ceased, Baptism remained the sole condition for initiation into religious life. . . . The Baptism of the proselyte has for its purpose his cleansing from the impurity of idolatry, and the restoration to the purity of a new-born man.[97]

In further reference to ancient Jewish baptismal tradition, the *Jewish Encyclopedia* placed a form of baptism in the Garden of Eden narrative of Genesis: "Baptism was practised in ancient (Ḥasidic or Essene) Judaism, first as a means of penitence, as is learned from the story of Adam and Eve, who, in order to atone for their sin, stood up to the neck in the water, fasting and doing penance—Adam in the Jordan for forty days, Eve in the Tigris for thirty-seven days (*Vita Adæ et Evæ*, i. 5–8). According to *Pirḳe R. El.* xx., Adam stood for forty-nine days up to his neck in the River Gihon."[98] These references point quite definitively to ancient Jewish observances of baptism consistent with Book of Mormon baptismal observances, although the Jewish observances seem to have been lost in time.

Today the miqva, or mikvah, continues to be an active part of Orthodox Jewish religious life. For example, the National Capital Mikvah near the Kesher Israel Congregation synagogue in Washington DC provides a mikvah bath center for ritual purification—others are found throughout the world. Appointments can be made at the mikvah for conversion to Judaism, for a groom on his wedding day, or for an annual visit before Yom Kippur, the Day of Atonement. The most general usage of the mikvah is for purification by menstruant women who come to the mikvah after the seventh day following the end of their menstrual cycles, preceded by a requisite cleansing. "The immersion is valid only when the waters of the mikvah envelop each and every part of the body and, indeed, each hair. To this end, the woman bathes, shampoos, combs her hair, and removes from her body anything that might impede her total immersion," according to Rivkah Slonim at the Chabad Center for Jewish Student Life at Binghamton University.[99]

Baptism and the Trinity

The second defining objection of Catholics and Protestants to Mormon baptism is the Mormon rejection of the doctrine of the Trinity. The Vatican, in its 2001 papal directive, instructed: "There is not a true invocation of the Trinity because the Father, the Son and the Holy Spirit, according to the Church of Jesus Christ of Latter-day Saints, are not the three persons in which subsists the one Godhead, but three gods who form one divinity. One is different from the other, even though they exist in perfect harmony. . . . [The] firstborn is Jesus Christ, equal to all men, who has acquired his divinity in a pre-mortal existence."[100] In other words, though Latter-day Saints may be comfortable that they and all Christians worship Christ, the Vatican nonetheless maintained that the Trinitarian Christ that Catholics worship is very different from the corporeal Christ that Latter-day Saints worship. This essentially meant that Mormon baptism was theologically different from Catholic baptism.

The Vatican summed up its view of Mormon Christology: "The differences are so great that one cannot even consider that this [Mormon] doctrine is a heresy which emerged out of a false understanding of the Christian doctrine [of the Trinity]. The teaching of the Mormons has a completely different matrix."[101] At the epicenter of this theological divide is Smith's first vision in 1820 of God and Christ. Of this vision, Smith recorded: "I saw two personages (whose brightness and glory defy all description) standing above me in the air. One of <them> spake unto me calling me by name and said (pointing to the other) "This is my beloved Son, Hear him."[102] Over the ensuing decade, from 1820 to 1830 (when he was between ages fourteen and twenty-four), Smith fleshed out a comprehensive theology of the doctrinal identity of Christ that varied significantly from that of his Christian contemporaries—especially regarding Christ's premortal existence, his role as creator of the world, and his role as the God of ancient scripture (in the Old Testament and the Book of Mormon) before his (Christ's) own birth.

Chapter 2 points out that these fundamental aspects about the character of Christ were clearly documented in the Book of Mormon, providing a rich body of literature for precedent and theological meaning. For example, Nephi in the sixth century BC spoke of the imperative of a pre-Christian baptism anchored in Christ, but also in the oneness of the Father, Son, and Holy Ghost.

> Wherefore, my beloved brethren, can we follow Jesus, save we shall be willing to keep the commandments of the Father? And the Father saith, Repent ye, repent ye, and be baptized in the name of my beloved Son. And also, the voice of the Son came unto me saying, He that is baptized in my name, to him will the Father give the Holy Ghost. . . . And now, behold, this is the doctrine of Christ, and the only true doctrine of the Father, and of the Son, and of the Holy Ghost, which is in God, without end. Amen. (See 2 Nephi 31:5, 10–13, 21.)[103]

Nephi refers both to the voice of the Father and then to the voice of the Son as separate voices from separate beings (this division occurs in other instances in the Book of Mormon as well), and yet he concludes with this affirmation: "And now, behold, this is the doctrine of Christ, and the only and true doctrine of the Father, and of the Son, and of the Holy Ghost, which is one God, without end." The paradox is obvious: They are simultaneously separate voices, and yet they are inseparably "one God, without end." Similarly, for Nephi baptism is at once "the doctrine of Christ" alone, yet it is also "the only and true doctrine of the Father, and of the Son, and of the Holy Ghost." Nephi never tries to resolve this tension, as if to underscore the point that in his spiritual experience both tenets are perfectly real and consistent: For

Nephi, Christ was corporeally separate and distinct from the Father and the Holy Ghost—they were different voices from separate entities. Yet Christ's baptismal doctrines, principles, and canons were the doctrines, principles, and canons of all three—the Father, Son, and Holy Ghost; in that sense they were one.

Surprisingly, Mormonism's early embrace of pre-Christian baptism as taught in Book of Mormon baptismal theology went unnoticed by official mainstream Catholic and Protestant policy for 170 years, until 2000.[104] The Book of Mormon affirmed not only that baptism was an ancient pre-Christian ritual extending back centuries before the coming of Christ, but that Christ himself was the focus of worship by the ancient Nephites as the central theological foundation for baptism. They looked forward prophetically, ritually, and symbolically to his ministry, death, and resurrection at the meridian of time. In the competitive milieu of nineteenth-century Christianity, these Mormon doctrines and rituals not only appealed to potential Christian converts, whose heritage was biblical, but also distinguished Mormonism from other Christian religions precisely because its teachings originated in the Book of Mormon.

Zion in America, the New Jerusalem

Among Mormonism's most influential founding beliefs was the doctrine of a latter-day American Zion. By 1830 the building of a literal Zion had become a dominant focus of the new church, and even today remains a still-to-be-fulfilled prophecy. When Joseph Smith originally penned the Articles of Faith, the tenth article asserted: "We believe in the literal gathering of Israel and in the restoration of the Ten Tribes. That Zion will be built upon this [American] continent. That Christ will reign personally upon the earth, and that the earth will be renewed and receive its paradasaic glory."[105] Though written in 1842, this idea of Zion was fairly clear in Joseph's mind thirteen years earlier when at age twenty-three he was translating the Book of Mormon text.

Especially influential on the Prophet were two Book of Mormon prophecies of Zion as the promised land (the Americas), on which would be built a future New Jerusalem (3 Nephi 21 and Ether 13). Grant Underwood found that 3 Nephi 21 was the most frequently cited Book of Mormon chapter in early Mormon literature and that "Ether 13:4–8, more than any other passage," was responsible for key Zion-related concepts relating to the gathering and restoration of Israel in the Americas.[106] From these ideas sprang the impulse of the early Latter-day Saints not only to look forward to the coming of a New Jerusalem, but to literally find the place where they would build it—in Zion, Jackson County, Missouri.

"In the fall of 1830, while his identity as prophet was still damp in the mold," wrote Richard Bushman, "Joseph unfolded the first of the Church's missions, a massive program combining the biblical ideas of New Jerusalem, millennium, and gathering."[107] According to an early revelation received by the Prophet, "Behold I say unto you that it is not Revealed & no man knoweth where the City shall be built But it shall be given hereafter Behold I say unto you that it shall be among the Lamanites,"[108] generally understood to be "the western edge of Missouri, to which the federal government was forcibly removing the eastern states' Indians."[109]

Ezra Booth, a Methodist cleric and early convert to Mormonism who soon left the church, wrote a public letter published in the *Ohio Star* on December 8, 1831, linking together the Book of Mormon, the gathering of Native Americans as a branch of the house of Israel, the city New Jerusalem, and the temple in the midst of the city.

> The Book of Mormon, which I hold in my hand, is a divine revelation, and the very thing we need, to burst the cloud and remove the darkness, which has long surrounded the mysterious and degraded aborigines. We now know that the natives who inhabit the forests of America, are a "branch of the House of Israel;" and by means of this blessed book, they are soon, even in this generation, to be restored to the knowledge, and the true worship of the God of Israel.—Among them is to be built, the "glorious city of the New Jerusalem." In the midst of which is to stand, the splendid and magnificent temple, dedicated to the Most High God, and "Oliver

> [Cowdery] being called and commanded of the Lord God, to go forth among the Lamanites, to proclaim glad tidings of great joy unto them, by presenting unto them, the fullness of the gospel of the only begotten son of God," &c.[110]

Where did Joseph Smith conceive of the doctrine of a New Jerusalem in America? The sole biblical reference, found in the book of Revelation, pointed prophetically to a New Jerusalem but gave no detail about where or what it would be: "And I John saw the holy city, new Jerusalem, coming down from God out of heaven, prepared as a bride adorned for her husband" (Revelation 21:2).[111] The seventeenth-century New England Puritans John Cotton, William Bradford, Roger Williams, and various others believed that New England would become the latter-day New Jerusalem.[112] Samuel Sewall, a judge in Massachusetts, argued in 1697 that since "the aboriginal Natives of *America* are of *Jacob's* Posterity. . . . Why may not [America] be the place of New-Jerusalem?"[113] Yet Emanuel Swedenborg's New Jerusalem was a spiritual state of being, lacking physical attributes.[114] Alexander Campbell's view was that New Jerusalem had already come with the death of Christ and was now manifest daily in the people of the church.[115] Ellen G. White, a cofounder of the Seventh-day Adventist Church, asserted that Christ would not come again until he had been married in heaven to the New Jerusalem—obfuscating an already-complex prophecy.[116]

By contrast, Smith's understanding of the New Jerusalem prophecy was marked by extraordinary clarity about the location and size of the city, as well as the presence of a temple—even a temple complex with architectural detail comparable to Ezekiel's millennial temple vision in the Hebrew Bible. Once again, Smith's understanding developed quickly, within about a three-year period beginning in 1829. The foundational source for the Prophet's schooling on New Jerusalem was the Book of Mormon. If we track closely the chronology of 1829, it is clearly evident that the Book of Mormon texts dealing with New Jerusalem were translated at almost precisely the same time as the revelations the Prophet received on Zion and New Jerusalem. There appears to be a pattern in which the Book of Mormon translation led to inquiry, which led to revelation, which informed the Prophet's developing vision of Zion and New Jerusalem.

To illustrate, as the Book of Mormon translation project resumed in early 1829 (following a suspension of translating in summer 1828), several of Smith's closest associates "desired to learn from the Prophet how they could assist in the work committed to Joseph Smith."[117] He received revelations directed to each of them, revealing a distinct evolution in the meaning of Zion: First, to Smith's father in February 1829 the Lord frames Joseph's translation project as a "marvelous work," evoking Isaiah's prophetic imagery of "a marvelous work and wonder" (Isaiah 29:11–14), but never mentions Zion. At this point fewer than sixteen additional pages had been translated (starting with Mosiah) since Martin Harris had lost the first 116 pages of translation the previous summer of 1828. Then in April 1829 Smith received a revelation for Cowdery, quite similar to the first revelation to Joseph Smith Sr., except that now the concept of Zion is introduced for the first time:

> A Great and marvelous work is about to come forth unto the children of men: behold I am God. . . . Therefore give heed unto my words. . . . [S]eek to bring forth and establish the cause of Zion.[118]

By this time Smith and Cowdery were making steady progress translating and would have encountered the concept of Zion first in Mosiah (chapters 12 and 15) when the priests of King Noah quoted Isaiah's prophecy (Isaiah 52):[119] "How beautiful upon the mountains are the feet of Him that bringeth good tidings; that publisheth peace; that bringeth good tidings of good; that publisheth salvation; that sayeth unto *Zion, Thy God reigneth* . . . for they shall see eye to eye, when the Lord *shall bring again Zion*" (see Mosiah 12:21–23).[120]

Then came two additional revelations in May 1829, each with the admonition to "seek to bring forth and establish the cause of Zion": first to Smith's brother Hyrum (D&C 11) and then to friend Joseph Knight Sr. (D&C 12). Here Zion was a set of ideals, a people committed to the ideals of Zion. Matthew Richardson summarizes these chronological parallel events, continuing to the next stage in Joseph's evolving understanding of Zion: "By June 1829 Joseph had completed translating 3 Nephi and had begun working on the small plates of Nephi. It was at this time he learned of 'a city, which shall be called the New Jerusalem' (3 Nephi 21:23)."[121] This Book of Mormon prophecy by Christ in ancient America speaks even more concretely of the meaning of Zion.

> And verily, I say unto you, I give unto you a sign, that ye may know the time when these things shall be about to take place, that I shall gather in from their long dispersion, my people, O house of Israel, and shall establish again among them my Zion . . . and they shall assist my people, the remnant of Jacob . . . that they may build a city, which shall be called the New Jerusalem; and then shall they assist my people that they may be gathered in, which are scattered upon all the face of the land, in unto the New Jerusalem. (See 3 Nephi 21:1, 23–24.)[122]

Richardson continues the conversation, "Then, true to form, Joseph received a revelation admonishing David Whitmer to 'bring forth and establish *my Zion*' (D&C 14:6),"[123] paralleling closely the Book of Mormon text in 3 Nephi 21 where the term *my Zion* was a "city, which shall be called the New Jerusalem." As Smith and Cowdery pushed forward with the Book of Mormon translation, they finally encountered a prophecy by ancient prophet Ether, from approximately 2200 BC. His vision of the last days spoke in detail of this New Jerusalem that eventually would be built in Ether's native land of the ancient Americas:

> [Ether] truly told them of all things . . . that after the waters had receded from off the face of this land [the Americas], it became a choice land above all other lands, a chosen land of the Lord . . . and that it was the place of the New Jerusalem, which should come down out of Heaven, and the Holy Sanctuary of the Lord . . . and that a New Jerusalem should be built up upon this land [the Americas], unto the remnant of the seed of Joseph, for the which things there has been a type . . . and it shall be a land of their inheritance; and they shall build up a holy city unto the Lord, like unto the Jerusalem of old. (See Ether 13:1–8.)[124]

The prophecy spoke of a latter-day people in the chosen land of the Americas as a "remnant of the seed of Joseph," suggesting Jacob's final blessing on his son Joseph, in Genesis.[125] To Smith and Cowdery, translating in 1829, this all pointed to the Book of Mormon project not as an end in itself, but as part of a much broader mission to prepare a people in the land of the Americas to build a city of Zion as a heritage of the biblical Joseph of Israel. This Zion, the New Jerusalem in the Americas, would stand alongside a restored city Jerusalem in the land Israel.

On June 11, 1829, Smith submitted the title page of the Book of Mormon for copyright, and Cowdery delivered the first twenty-four pages to the printer in mid-August 1829. For the next seven months both were occupied in getting the Book of Mormon printed and published; the *Wayne Sentinel* formally announced publication on March 26, 1830. Meanwhile, the topic of Zion remained at the forefront of the Prophet's mind. On the day of the church's formal organization, April 6, 1830, a revelation made clear that throughout the publication process Joseph had been constantly preoccupied with Zion: "Him [Joseph] have I inspired to move the cause of Zion in Mighty power for good & his dilligence I know & his prayers I have heard yea his weeping for Zion I have seen & I will cause that He shall mourn for her no longer for his days of rejoicing are come."[126]

In July 1830, Zion evolved further to include "an inheritance in Zion," in which the Saints would be given their own sacred farmland in Zion.[127] The Prophet received a revelation directed to his wife,"Emma my daughter in Zion,"[128] saying, "If thou art faithful and walk in the paths of virtue before me, I will preserve ~~your~~ <thy> life, and thou shalt receive an inheritance in Zion."[129]

Then in late 1830, Smith became engrossed in Enoch as a prophetic figure for his own ministry, especially in building a Zion people. As he examined the book of Genesis during his biblical retranslation project of the latter half of 1830, he stopped at the mythical Enoch passage: "Enoch walked with God; then he was no more, because God took him" (Genesis 5:24 NRSV).[130] And he made a correction that fused Enoch with Zion in Mormon theology: "And Enoch and all his people walked with God and he dwellt in the midst of Zion and it came to pass

Fig. 18. Doctrine and Covenants 25 was revealed for Emma Hale Smith (1804–1879), wife of Joseph Smith Jr.; Emma assisted as an early transcriber of the Book of Mormon translation.

that Zion was not for God received it up into his own bosom and from thence went forth the saying Zion is fled."[131]

Terryl Givens described Enoch's role in moving toward Zion:

> It is easy to see Joseph Smith as a Moses figure, giving a new law, producing scripture, leading his people out of spiritual bondage

> and into a promised land, speaking with God and angels face to face. But I want to [make] a striking corrective to this parallel that Joseph Smith himself offered. "Moses sought to bring the children of Israel into the presence of God, through the power of the Pri[e]st-hood, but he could not. . . . But Enoch did[,] for himself & those that were with Him." . . . I think [Joseph] believed Enoch offered the model and blueprint for getting all the way to Zion.[132]

In December 1830, Smith recorded an expanded revealed text of Enoch that merged the concepts of Zion, the New Jerusalem of the Book of Mormon, Enoch, and the city of Enoch together in the same prophetic narrative:

> Righteousness and truth will I cause to sweep the earth as with the flood to gether out mine own elect from the four quarters of the earth unto a place which I shall prepare an holy City that my people may gird up their loins and be looking fourth for the time of my coming for there shall be my tabernicle and it shall be called Zion a New Jerusalem and the Lord said unto Enoch then shalt thou and all thy City meet them there and we will receive them into our bosom and they shall us see us and we will fall upon their necks and they shall fall upon our necks and we will kiss each other and there shall be mine abode and it shall be Zion . . . and for the space of a thousand years shall the earth [res]t.[133]

With great anticipation Smith led a party to Jackson County in western Missouri in summer 1831 where advance groups of Latter-day Saints had settled. The appearance of the untamed west was disappointing,[134] but it became a blank canvas for the Prophet's vision of Zion. His revelation of July 20, 1831, became the seminal revelation defining the specific parameters of Zion and the inheritances of the Saints: the location of the city and the temple of Zion; specifics on land acquisition, plot assignment and distribution, and financial transactions; and direction on commerce, printing, publication, and communication (see D&C 57:2–8, 14). The formal city plan, drafted later under the direction of Joseph, created a perfectly square city, similar to John's vision of the heavenly Jerusalem described in Revelation 21:16: "And the city lieth foursquare, and the length is as large as the breadth."[135]

The Book of Mormon also directed Joseph toward the New Jerusalem temple but never provided definitive details. For example, when he was in America, Christ alluded to temple worship in New Jerusalem, saying that "the powers of heaven shall be in the midst of this people; yea, even I will be in the midst of you" (see 3 Nephi 20:22).[136] Ether prophesied that New Jerusalem "should come down out of heaven, and the holy sanctuary of the Lord" (see Ether 13:3),[137] suggesting that the heavenly temple and heavenly city would descend and join the earthly temple and earthly city—together forming the millennial New Jerusalem with its millennial temple. This, of course, was the essence of the revealed Enoch texts of December 1830: "For there shall be my tabernacle, and it shall be called Zion, a New Jerusalem."[138]

This seemed consonant with the apostle John's revelation of the New Jerusalem temple, which cited symbolic elements that would signify worship at this holy temple, such as the name of God that the covenant people would take upon them, the name of the city of God from whence the covenant would originate, and each person's new name associated with personal temple worship. "Him that overcometh will I make a pillar in the temple of my God, and he shall go no more out: and I will write upon him the name of my God, and the name of the city of my God, which is new Jerusalem, which cometh down out of heaven from my God: and I will write upon him my new name" (Revelation 3:12).[139] The large temple planned for the center of New Jerusalem was the first temple Joseph Smith was directed by revelation to build, but his expansive temple vision for Zion in Independence, Missouri, exceeded the time and circumstance of the fledgling Latter-day Saints in rugged far western Missouri. Still, the Book of Mormon provided the underlying genesis for Mormonism's tangible ideal of Zion with the temple at its core. Even today it remains a vision to be fulfilled.

4

Influences on the Temple of the Early Restoration

By all accounts the Latter-day Saint temple-building program of the last two centuries has been extraordinary. Yet its prominence in Mormon consciousness in relation to its actual scale points to a revealing paradox. Today there are over 15 million members of the Church of Jesus Christ of Latter-day Saints, organized into 29,253 local Mormon congregations designed for everyday worship.[1] However, only 144 temples are in operation throughout the entire world.[2] Temple worship for Latter-day Saints is the very pinnacle of spirituality and is considered the highest, most sublime form of sacred worship. Temples are reserved exclusively for select sacred temple rituals such as eternal marriage, the temple endowment, and proxy baptisms and are accessible only to worthy members of the church. Mormon temples contrast in a striking manner to everyday Christian worship in local cathedrals and churches. Adney Komatsu of the LDS First Quorum of the Seventy related this anecdote following the construction of the Tokyo Temple: "The contractor for the Tokyo Temple . . . noted that the Buddhist and Shinto religions in Japan build many shrines and temples, but this was the first time he had heard of a Christian church building a temple. Christian religions are noted for building beautiful chapels and cathedrals, but he had never heard of a Christian temple before. Of the many churches that profess Christianity, The Church of Jesus Christ of Latter-day Saints is the only one that builds temples."[3]

In this chapter we examine the nature of Mormon temple worship, particularly its origins and the ancient temple forms that influenced its emergence. Implicit in the statistics cited above is the obvious fact that Latter-day Saints observe a dual form of worship. They worship both in everyday chapels located in neighborhoods throughout the world and in sacred temples to which they journey from near and far, like a pilgrimage, to do the sacred work of the Lord. What is the precedent for this dual form of worship that seems so totally unique to the world of modern Christianity? As the restoration began to unfold, it became clearer that the temple ideal that Joseph Smith began to construct, and presented to his faithful followers, evoked the heritage of the ancient Israelite temple as if coming from the Hebrew Bible itself. Yet as we see in this chapter, the Mormon temple was also likely influenced by the temple in the Book of Mormon, which itself had its own parallels with Hebrew Bible temple theology. Nevertheless, significant differences in temple plurality, temple space, and temple meaning may delineate a path Joseph Smith might have followed to restore latter-day temple worship. Could it be that the Prophet in fact restored forms of worship found in the temple of ancient Israelite theology but that he accessed many of these forms through the Book of Mormon?

A dual form of worship: Congregational and temple

From the beginning Joseph Smith focused fundamentally on the temple as the center of religious worship. Truman Madsen, a Mormon philosopher, taught that "the earliest documents of the restoration movement are replete with references to consecrated land, to Zion, and to 'the Lord's house' [the temple]. For converts these became an instant and urgent priority. Even before adequate meeting places or chapels were established, temple land was dedicated at Kirtland, Ohio, in 1833 (D&C 94, 95) and at Adam-ondi-Ahman and Far West, Missouri, in 1838 (D&C 115:7–16)."[4] At the same time, of course, the new church held regular congregational Sunday worship services, with sermons, readings, exhortations, and the sacrament. During the early Kirtland period, prior to the completion of the Kirtland Temple, the Saints used private homes or rented spaces for these weekly congregational meetings. In the personal writings of the Prophet we find this entry for Sunday, December 13, 1835:

> At the usual hour, viz. 10. oclock he [Smith] attended meeting at the school-house on the flats. Eldr. Jesse Hitchcock preached a very feeling discourse indeed; in the after noon Eldr. Peter Whitmer [Jr.] related his experiance, after which Pres. F[rederick] G. Williams, related his also; they both spoke of many things connected with the rise and progress of this church of Christ. . . . After these servises closed, the sacrament of the Lord's supper was administered, under the superintendance of Pres. David Whitmer, who presided over the meeting during the day. Pres. Joseph (our author) then made some remarks respecting prayer meetings, and our meeting was brought to a close by invoking heavens blessings upon the audiance.[5]

Beginning in 1836 the Kirtland Temple was used as a gathering place for regular Sunday meetings. A similar pattern continued in Nauvoo, even as the temple there was under construction. Glen Leonard, a Mormon historian, describes where the Saints assembled:

> Until the temple was available for use, Nauvoo had no meetinghouse. The Saints met for a time beginning in October 1842 on a temporary floor on the temple's main level assembly room, and three years later in an enclosed temple. But most large gatherings in Nauvoo assembled during good weather out-of-doors and in bad weather not at all. Preaching took place at designated meeting places in the oak grove on the brow of the hill just west of the temple or, later, at a nearby stand a quarter mile east and a bit north of the unfinished structure.[6]

Along with these congregational Sunday services, Nauvoo temple ordinances were performed in the upper room of Joseph Smith's store in Nauvoo while the members awaited completion of the temple. "Because ordinances of the most sacred nature were to be performed, the room had to be dedicated for the purpose," explained Andrew Ehat. "These ordinances of the priesthood, when performed in enclosed places, were only to be performed in an upper room. Not until Joseph's store was completed in early 1842 was there a place in Nauvoo with a large enough upper room for the various endowment rooms. When everything was complete, the Prophet dedicated the upper story of his brick store before he attended to the ordinances."[7]

This dual form of worship—of both higher temple worship and separate, regular congregational worship—ran counter to the worship patterns of the nineteenth-century Christian world. Why not install only temple worship, or why not adopt simple congregational worship as followed by virtually all other Christian denominations? Where in scripture or practice did Smith get the inspiration to embrace this distinctive, dual form of worship?

A dual pattern of worship is certainly present in the New Testament narrative, especially during the life of Jesus. The Jerusalem temple was the center of his life and ministry, yet he was a master teacher in the life of the synagogue. He purged and reclaimed the temple as his own, "cast[ing] out all them that sold and bought in the temple . . . and said unto them, It is written, My house shall be called the house of prayer" (Matthew 21:12–13).[8] Luke recorded that "his parents went to Jerusalem every year at the Feast of the Passover" (Luke 2:41).[9] At least once during his ministry he made the annual pilgrimage to the Feast of Tabernacles at the Jerusalem temple. The law required all Hebrew males (see John 7:1–14)[10] not to come empty-handed, but to "bring a sheaf of the firstfruits of your harvest unto the priest" for sacrifice (Leviticus 23:10).[11]

Jesus also occupied a commanding presence in the life of the Jewish synagogue and congregational Sabbath worship, where he was often referred to as rabbi: "And Jesus went about all Galilee, teaching in their synagogues, and preaching the gospel of the kingdom, and healing all manner of sickness and all manner of disease among the people" (Matthew 4:23).[12] He "went into Capernaum; and straightway on the sabbath day he entered into the synagogue, and taught. And they were astonished at his doctrine: for he taught them as one that had authority, and not as the scribes" (Mark 1:21–22).[13]

Nonetheless, for Joseph Smith the New Testament narrative was a less attractive model for a modern restoration of dual-form worship.

Herod's temple in the Jerusalem of the first century AD was far removed from the deeper Israelite worship of Solomon's temple of the tenth century BC. Viewed by Christians and even by Jesus as profaned and corrupted, Herod's temple had been built to rival the temples of pagan Rome and Greece, was controlled by the priestly class of Jews who had rejected Christ, and continued traditional animal sacrifice that Christians believed had been abolished with Christ. Similarly, the Jewish synagogue was the center of antipathy and persecution of the early church. According to the New Testament, Stephen, an early deacon, preached to the Jews "of the synagogue, which is called the synagogue of the Libertines, and Cyrenians, and Alexandrians, and of them of Cilicia and of Asia" (Acts 6:9),[14] after which he was summarily executed by stoning for heresy. After the apostle Paul preached in the synagogue in Antioch, "the Jews stirred up the devout and honourable women, and the chief men of the city, and raised persecution against Paul and Barnabas, and expelled them out of their coasts" (Acts 13:50).[15]

The Old Testament should have offered a useful dual-worship model, except that its narratives mention the term *synagogue* only once.[16] The emergence of the synagogue as an institution is mentioned in other sources but barely documented in the Old Testament. This contrasts vividly with the Book of Mormon record in which dual-form worship appears to have been a prominent facet of ancient Nephite religion—the Nephite people worshipped both at the sacred altar of the temple and separately in congregations in their "synagogues, or . . . places of worship" (see 3 Nephi 18:32).[17] Smith's translation of the text added the clarification "or your places of worship," as if to suggest that the term *synagogue* itself was meant to be interpreted more broadly as a place of regular congregational worship, whether Jewish or not.

Though rarely articulated in the narrative, it is nonetheless apparent that these Book of Mormon peoples were not only Hebrew but also Jewish by heritage because founding prophet Lehi and his clan had originated in Jerusalem. During the later First Temple period of the Old Testament in particular, and through the end of the Second Temple period, the ancient Jews of Jerusalem had observed a dual form of worship, with sacred worship at the altar of Solomon's temple, later Zerubbabel's temple, alongside separate congregational worship in the Jewish synagogue. Lehi and his family appear to have imported forms of both these institutions to the New World. We see these forms of worship early in the Book of Mormon timeline, within the sixth century BC. The first appearance of Lehi's altar worship comes after his departure from Jerusalem en route to the promised land: "When he had traveled three days in the wilderness, . . . [Lehi] built an altar of stones, and he made an offering unto the Lord, and gave thanks unto the Lord our God" (see 1 Nephi 2:6–7).[18] During the same period, the first mention of synagogue worship by Nephi comes in his commentary on the writings of Isaiah: "Behold, hath he commanded any that they should depart out of the synagogues, or out of the houses of worship? Behold, I say unto you, nay" (see 2 Nephi 26:26).[19]

In all, the Book of Mormon refers to temples twenty-seven times, altars four times, and sanctuaries ten times—clear evidence of some form of temple worship. At the same time, it references synagogues twenty-five times; as mentioned earlier, the Old Testament mentions the synagogue only once. The prominence of the synagogue in the Book of Mormon is an important marker, suggesting that the synagogue as a religious institution must have been sufficiently established in Jerusalem religious life by the sixth century BC that Lehi's clan chose to import it into the New World.[20] Later, Mormon incorporated firsthand accounts of the synagogue in Book of Mormon history: Alma and Amulek preached "in their synagogues, which was built after the manner of the Jews" (see Alma 16:13).[21] Later, another passage records that after being subjected to congregational discipline, a Zoramite group complained to Alma that they were "despised of all men, because of their poverty; yea, and more especially by our priests; for they have cast us out of our synagogues, which we have labored abundantly to build, with our own hands" (see Alma 32:5).[22] Even after the resurrection, Jesus referred to the synagogue as a center for continued congregational worship in the ancient American church: "Nevertheless ye shall not cast him out of your synagogues, or your places of worship, for unto such shall ye minister . . . and ye shall be the means of bringing salvation unto them" (see 3 Nephi 18:32).[23]

Joseph Smith's earliest impulse during the formative days of the restoration, while the Book of Mormon transcript was at the printer, was to evangelize new converts and establish regular congregational worship. David Whitmer described this early period: "In August, 1829, we began to preach the gospel of Christ. . . . Now, when April 6, 1830, had come [the formal date of the church's founding], we had then established three branches of the 'Church of Christ,' in which three branches were about seventy members: One branch was at Fayette, N.Y.; one at Manchester, N.Y., and one at Colesville, Pa."[24]

Then only five months after the church's formal organization, Oliver Cowdery led a mission to the Lamanites in September 1830, along with companions Peter Whitmer Jr., Parley Pratt, and Ziba Peterson. The objective of this mission, however, was more far-reaching than merely teaching and conversion, for they were to locate a place to build a new city of Zion—and at its center the Prophet had promised a temple. The *Ohio Star* newspaper printed a copy of a covenant Cowdery had penned, dated October 17, 1830:

> I, Oliver, being commanded of the Lord God, to go forth unto the Lamanites, to proclaim glad tidings of great joy unto them, by presenting unto them the fulness of the Gospel, of the only begotten son of God; and also, to *rear up a pillar as a witness where the Temple of God shall be built, in the glorious New-Jerusalem;* and having certain brothers with me, who are called of God to assist me, whose names are Parley, Peter and Ziba, do therefore most solemnly covenant before God, that I will walk humbly before him, and do this business, and this glorious work according as he shall direct me by the Holy Ghost.[25]

Congregational worship continued to flourish in the weekly worship patterns of the Saints even with this emerging temple vision. "During the course of his life," wrote Richard Bushman, "[Joseph Smith] never built a standard meetinghouse, even in Nauvoo, where the Mormon population exceeded 10,000. Although Sunday services were held regularly, the Nauvoo Saints met in houses, public buildings, and an outdoor 'bowery.'"[26] Alongside this congregational worship, the temple remained the church's defining point of reference, spiritually as a center for higher revealed knowledge and physically beginning with the extensive temple complex the Prophet envisioned for the center place of Zion in Independence, Missouri. In so doing it established Mormonism's unique dual form of worship, patterned after the forms of worship in the Book of Mormon.

The formative temple instruction of Moroni

Before examining Book of Mormon temple worship in detail, we must first understand the genesis of Joseph Smith's modern temple views. His history makes clear that in his mind the earliest impulse for the temple came from Moroni, the final Book of Mormon prophet and custodian of the original gold plates. Moroni was more than a visionary encounter in the Prophet's memory; he was a mentor who had a lasting influence. In Smith's *History*, circa summer 1832—his earliest and only history written in his own handwriting—he described the most significant events that marked the beginning of his career as a prophet. The first, according to the *History*'s prospectus, was "'the testamony from on high,' later explained as his first vision of Deity,"[27] when Joseph was fourteen. The second was "'the ministering of Angels,' or the angel Moroni's revelation of the gold plates of the Book of Mormon,"[28] when he was seventeen. In his 1838 history Smith devotes nearly half the narrative of his life before 1827 to detailed descriptions of Moroni's visitations that began September 21, 1823.[29] In the first of these schooling visions, Moroni reportedly told Joseph "that God had a work for [him] to do, and that [his] <name> should be had for good and evil among all nations."[30] Moroni then commenced a teaching pedagogy based on biblical prophecies from the Old and New Testaments.

One detail in Moroni's visitation remained especially vivid to Joseph Smith—Malachi's final prophecy in the Old Testament. In November 1835, now roughly a decade removed from the Moroni visions, the Prophet described his visions of 1820 and 1823 to visitor Robert

Matthews—known colloquially as Prophet Matthias. For Matthews he highlighted only one of Moroni's numerous passages quoted from the Bible—but the one he chose was significant and pointed to the early preeminence of the temple that had remained in Smith's mind. "One I will mention which is ~~this~~ in Malachi 4 behold the day of the Lord cometh &c,"[31] referring to the coming of the Lord to the temple in the latter days.

In fact, taken together, the biblical passages quoted in the Moroni visions (several visions repeated annually that "related the same things")[32] especially focused on three concentric ideas—none of them relating directly to actually translating the Book of Mormon record: a latter-day Zion (referenced in 45 percent of the verses quoted), the gathering of Israel (in 38 percent), and the latter-day temple (in 29 percent).[33] For example, Moroni quoted Isaiah's prophecy of the establishment of the Lord's house (the temple) in the tops of the mountains and that all nations would flow unto it prior to the millennial era (Isaiah 2:2–6). He quoted another Isaiah prophecy of the Lord's latter-day dwelling place (the temple) in Mount Zion; her assemblies would be marked by a cloud and smoke by day, and flaming fire by night, evoking the imagery of the tabernacle of Exodus (Isaiah 4:5–6). He quoted passages concerning temple ritual, the Psalmist's temple hymn of the ritual anointing of Aaron's head and his garments (Psalm 133:1–3), and the Lord's blessing on the (metaphoric temple) mountains of Zion for evermore. He quoted from Joel's expansive prophecy of a future day when the Lord would pour out his spirit upon all flesh and sons and daughters should prophesy, old men should dream dreams, and young men should see visions in Mount Zion (the temple) and Jerusalem (Joel 2:28–30).

However, Moroni's very first prophecy quoted in the vision was accorded the most importance; it was also the last prophecy of the Old Testament, Malachi's well-known prophecy of the coming of the Messiah to the temple and the prophetic return of Elijah the prophet as forerunner: "Behold, I will send my messenger, and he shall prepare the way before me: and the Lord, whom ye seek, *shall suddenly come to his temple,* even the messenger of the covenant, whom ye delight in: behold, he shall come, saith the Lord of hosts" (Malachi 3:1).[34]

Contemporary Christian theologians believed the Malachi prophecy had been fulfilled with Jesus's appearance in the flesh, with John the Baptist as forerunner, before the eventual destruction of the Jewish temple by the Romans in AD 70.[35] But Moroni interpreted this prophecy differently, not as prophecy that had been fulfilled, but as prophecy yet to be fulfilled in advance of the second coming of the Messiah. By choosing this prophecy and placing it first in his instructional vision, Moroni seemed intent on placing the forthcoming Book of Mormon translation project in perspective as part of a broader work of the restoration. This work, Moroni seemed to suggest, would be profoundly centered in the temple.

The Prophet must have paused to consider the meaning of Moroni's quotation of biblical Malachi: "The Lord, whom ye seek, shall suddenly come to his temple." At the time of this 1823 visitation, it had been only three years since Smith's first vision of God and Christ. However, Moroni's recitation of this prophecy occurred *after* the first vision, implying that Malachi's words related to prophecy yet to be fulfilled, of another visitation that God would make to the temple. What temple could the prophecy refer to, and where could it be found? Malachi never identified the temple, but he symbolically described the Lord as the "messenger of the covenant," suggesting that a central purpose in God's coming to the temple would be related to a covenant. Apparently it would be a covenant relating to ancient Israel since Malachi was a prophet in ancient Israel. Malachi's prophecy is rich with Israelite identity and speaks to the "children of Jacob" (Malachi 3:6 NRSV), who possess a deep religious heritage "since the days of your ancestors" but have "turned aside from my statutes [covenants] and have not kept them" (3:7 NRSV).

As though Smith were assembling pieces of a mosaic, the meaning of Moroni's rendition of Malachi's latter-day prophecy of the temple is difficult to miss—it would feature God's covenant with a covenant people of Jacob in a place that the Lord would come to suddenly (the temple), and Smith would somehow have a role in unfolding this prophetic vision. Moroni quoted more of Malachi's prophecy, introducing the prophet figure Elijah, linking him as forerunner in the temple prophecy: "Behold, I will reveal unto you the Priesthood, by the hand of Elijah the prophet, before the coming of the great and dreadful day of the Lord. And he shall plant in the hearts of the children the promises made to the fathers, and the hearts of the children shall turn to their fathers. If it were not so, the whole earth would be utterly wasted at his coming" (Malachi 4:5–6).[36]

For millennia Jews have annually observed Passover with the cup of Elijah the Prophet; an extra place is set at the Passover table in anticipation of Elijah's miraculous return to announce the coming of the Messiah. In Smith's history, Moroni's interpretation of Malachi's prophecy added new meaning by prophetically linking the latter-day temple with Elijah, the forerunner of the coming of the Lord to the temple. These events would precede "the coming of the great and dreadful day of the Lord" (Malachi 4:5) when "all that do wickedly shall burn as stubble" (4:1). In Smith's mind these events were neither symbolic nor allegorical. In 1830 a revelation to Sidney Rigdon made it clear that Elijah had occupied the Prophet's continuing consciousness as a prophetic figure still to make a future appearance: "Behold thou [Sidney] wast sent forth, even as John to prepare the way before me [Christ], & ~~before~~ before Elijah which should come, & thou knew it not."[37]

Six years later the Prophet recorded the fulfillment of the Elijah prophecy in a visionary appearance of Elijah in the Kirtland Temple on April 3, 1836, along with a parallel visitation of Christ:

> After this vision had closed, another great and glorious vision burst upon us, for Elijah, the Prophet, who was taken to heaven without tasting death, stood before us and said behold the time has fully come, which was spoken of by the mouth of Malachi, testifying that he should be sent, before the great and dreadful day of the Lord should come, to turn the hearts of the fathers to the children, and the children to the fathers lest the whole earth be smitten with a curse. Therefore the keys of this dispensation are committed into your hands and by this you may know, that the great and the dreadful day of the Lord is near, even at the doors.[38]

Of the influential role of Elijah on the Prophet's theological development, scholar Gregory Prince related: "From an obscure figure in the early years of the Restoration, Elijah emerged as the dominant figure both in priesthood and in afterlife theology. At the time of Smith's death in 1844, Elijah's importance was second only to that of Jesus Christ."[39] Moreover, by the Nauvoo period not only had Elijah come to the temple in Kirtland, he was at the very center of Mormon temple theology, linked to the doctrine of eternally sealing children to parents and parents to children. Three months prior to his death, the Prophet gave a sermon revealing his final understanding of Elijah's central role in restoration theology:

> Now for Elijah, the spirit power & calling of Elijah is that ye have power to hold the keys of the revelations ordinances, oricles powers & endowments of the fulness of the Melchezedek Priesthood & of the Kingdom of God on the Earth & to receive, obtain & perform all the ordinances belonging to the Kingdom of God even unto the sealing of the hearts of the ~~hearts~~ fathers unto the children & the hearts of the children unto the fathers even those who are in heaven. . . . [W]hat is this office & work of Elijah, it is one of the greatest & most important subjects that God has revealed. . . . [I]f you will receive it this is the spirit of Elijah that we redeam our dead & connect ourselves with our fathers which are in heaven & seal up our dead to come forth in the first resurrection. . . . [T]his is the power of Elijah & the keys of the Kingdom of Jehovah.[40]

In 1876 the church recognized Moroni's Elijah prophecy by making it the first revelation after the introductory revelation in the new edition of the Doctrine and Covenants. Elder Boyd K. Packer of the church's Quorum of the Twelve Apostles commented regarding this placement: "The statement of Malachi concerning Elijah was treated differently from all the others given him [Smith] on that occasion [in September 1823]. It was separated out, considered of unique importance, and registered in a way different from all the rest. . . . There seems to have been guidance in the selection and placement of that quotation as a section in the Doctrine and Covenants. Other references that Moroni quoted, from

Isaiah or Joel or Acts or the 'many other passages of scripture,' were not thus honored."[41]

As the Prophet prepared his 1838 history, he must have appreciated the design of Moroni's mentoring in September 1823, at the dawn of his spiritual preparation for the translation project. Moroni framed the forthcoming translation of the Book of Mormon not as a great literary event—nor as a discovery of a lost ancient record, or a history of the ancient American peoples, or evidence of the calling of a new American prophet. Instead the Book of Mormon would be a part, a significant part to be sure, of a latter-day premillennial work to prepare a covenant people for the coming of the Messiah, the second coming of Christ. Ultimately the Prophet's latter-day work would be centered not in the Book of Mormon itself, but in the broader restoration of the church and the temple and the building of a Zion people.

The temple in the Book of Mormon

From the beginning of the restoration Joseph Smith had a remarkable temple-building focus: he envisioned the Independence, Missouri, temple complex of twenty-four temple buildings on a sixty-three-acre temple lot;[42] a smaller temple at Kirtland, Ohio; two more temples planned for Far West and Adam-ondi-Ahman, Missouri; and then the Nauvoo Temple in Illinois. Had the restoration proceeded as Smith had visualized, there would have been five temples throughout the Midwest region of North America by 1845, all planned or constructed over just a fifteen-year period. Though Smith had intended to restore the temple in fulfillment of biblical prophecy, as reiterated by Moroni, his dynamic vision of temple growth ran counter to the dominant idea of the temple widely embraced for the last twenty-five hundred years by Jews and Christians alike—that of temple worship solely in God's one temple in Jerusalem. This was an obvious paradox. Why would Joseph choose such an ambitious temple vision in contradiction to prevailing nineteenth-century temple understanding? Not surprisingly, it appears that the Prophet's prolific temple vision paralleled Israelite temple worship in

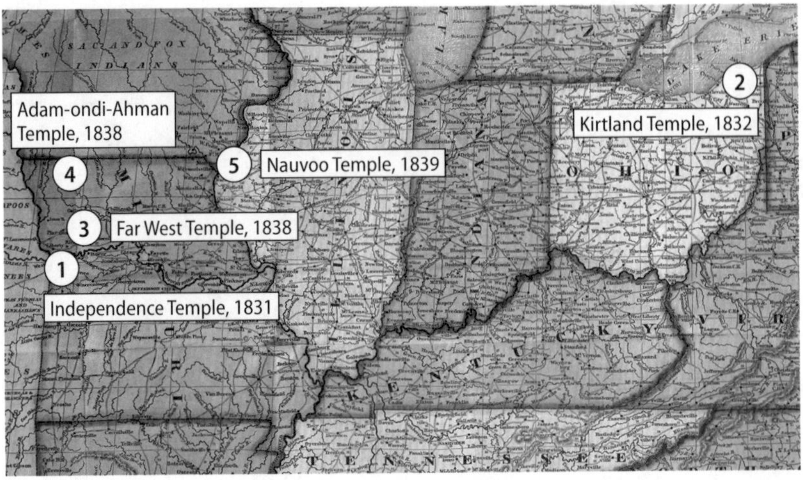

Fig. 19. By the end of Joseph Smith's life in 1844, his ambitious temple vision culminated in what would have been five temples, all conceived in the 1830s.

heritage but adopted the Book of Mormon's broader temple vision in dynamism and practice.[43]

The clearest and only explicit statement of Book of Mormon temple construction tells of the temple of Nephi, built in the sixth century BC in the emerging city of Nephi.

> And I, Nephi, did build a temple; and I did construct it after the manner of the temple of Solomon, save it were not built of so many precious things: for they were not to be found upon the land; wherefore, it could not be built like unto Solomon's temple. But the manner of the construction was like unto the temple of Solomon; and the workmanship thereof was exceeding fine. (See 2 Nephi 5:16.)[44]

Nephi was certainly not alone in building temples in distant lands. A Jewish temple appeared in Elephantine in southern Egypt in 525 BC, only decades after Jewish refugees had fled Israel during the great upheaval following the final destruction of Jerusalem in 586 BC.[45] This coincided with other scripturally documented emigrations from the Jerusalem temple: Ezekiel was taken with the captive Jews to Babylon about 598 BC; Jeremiah was exiled into Egypt with the final Jewish refugees from the destroyed city of Jerusalem about 586 BC; and Lehi fled Jerusalem to the New World shortly after 600 BC. Later, Josephus recorded that Jews in Leontopolis of the Nile Delta region of Egypt in the mid-second century BC "built a temple, and an altar to God, like indeed to that in Jerusalem, but smaller and poorer,"[46] much like Nephi's temple in America that was "not built of so many precious things; for they were not to be found upon the land" (see 2 Nephi 5:16).[47] In response to the Leontopolis temple, the Jewish establishment in Jerusalem, long returned from Babylonian exile, repudiated all distant temple imitations. The temple in Leontopolis was described in the Talmudic literature as idolatrous and illegitimate.[48] Upon learning that another temple might be built by Jewish refugees in Egypt, the Jewish leaders in Jerusalem "enacted a law that the land outside of Judaea be regarded as in a state of defilement. Hence no shrine could be considered sacred if built on ground which is defiled."[49] Despite these restrictions, Book of Mormon temples flourished in a land far away from the establishment Jews of Jerusalem.

According to the Book of Mormon, its first temple, the temple of Nephi, coincided with the coronation of Nephi as king of the people of Nephi. The temple enabled the new Nephite nation to properly vest power in the new king.[50] Then, four hundred years later, the appearance of a second Nephite temple, this one at Zarahemla, emerges in the narrative precisely at the coronation of another king, Mosiah$_2$, by his aging father, Benjamin. Mosiah's coronation was designed to take place not on a random day, but specifically during what seems to have been an observance quite similar to the ancient Israelite temple festival, the Feast of Tabernacles. The Book of Mormon records that

> the people gathered themselves together throughout all the land, that they might *go up to the temple* to hear the words which king Benjamin should speak unto them. . . . And they also took of the firstlings of their flocks, that they might *offer sacrifice and burnt offerings*, according to the law of Moses. . . . And it came to pass that when they came up to the temple, they pitched their tents round

> about, every man according to his family . . . and *they pitched their tents round about the temple,* every man having *his tent with the door thereof towards the temple,* that thereby they might remain in their tents, and hear the words which king Benjamin should speak unto them. (See Mosiah 2:1, 3, 5–6.)[51]

The biblical Feast of Tabernacles (Sukkot) was the final festival of the year in which the entire Israelite population made pilgrimage to the temple and would "dwell in booths seven days; all that are Israelites born shall dwell in booths; that your generations may know that I made the children of Israel to dwell in booths, when I brought them out of the land of Egypt" (Leviticus 23:42–43)[52]—a memorial to the Exodus from Egypt. The Hebrew word *sukkot,* translated "booth" in the King James Bible, also means "tabernacle" or "tent"—hence the Feast of Tabernacles can alternatively be called the Feast of Booths or Feast of Tents. King Benjamin apparently chose his son's coronation to take place when his Nephite nation would be gathering anyway for a great temple festival whose observances paralleled those of the Feast of Tabernacles of ancient Israel. Mormon scholar John Tvedtnes notes that King Solomon had chosen to dedicate the Temple of Solomon during the Feast of Tabernacles, and the coronations of Saul, David, Solomon, Rehoboam, Joash, and other Israelite and Judaic kings may have occurred during the Feast of Tabernacles.[53] This is a curious, yet quite obscure, parallel between the Book of Mormon and the Hebrew Bible, or Old Testament.

Two hundred years later the Book of Mormon narrative introduced a third temple, at Bountiful, the presence of which should be surprising to biblical readers steeped in Jerusalem-only temple theology. After all, the temple of Zarahemla still existed as a center for altar worship for the united peoples of the Nephites and Mulekites (another Israelite group who had emigrated from Jerusalem following the fall of Jerusalem in the sixth century BC). The appearance of the Bountiful temple coincides not with a coronation, but with the appearance of the resurrected Christ in America; however, King Benjamin of Zarahemla had spoken of Christ in his day as "your heavenly King" (see Mosiah 2:19).[54] In other words, in Book of Mormon lore all three major Book of Mormon temples appeared in coronation-like settings, with the third temple at Bountiful the setting for the coming of Christ to the New World. The appearance of these temples in uniquely coronation settings, two historic and the third symbolic, were striking ideas that Smith likely had never noticed before in biblical scripture, suggesting several essential insights.

First, the plurality of three major temples challenged the ancient Deuteronomist assumption of the sole legitimacy of the Jerusalem temple in the Jewish religion of the Old Testament. Despite King Josiah's sweeping edict in 622 BC centralizing all Jewish temple worship at Jerusalem and banning altar worship elsewhere, the Book of Mormon established a clear and tacit precedent of temple building—not just one but multiple temples that would foreshadow in microcosm the temple-building orientation of Smith's early church of the restoration. Second, when Christ appeared in the ancient Americas, the Book of Mormon records that he did so in miraculous splendor and glory—not subtly—at the temple in Bountiful. The people of Bountiful appear to have been uniquely prepared for Christ's temple visitation.[55] Research by John Welch indicates that Bountiful was likely a protected city—located at a strategic narrow neck of land with oceans on two sides, an uninhabitable land of Desolation to the north, and lands on the southern perimeter heavily fortified. "In the first century before Christ," wrote Welch, "the city of Bountiful was a relatively new, small, but important Nephite settlement. . . . The fact that these settlers built, operated, and maintained a temple in this remote and obscure site confirms their devotion to the most orthodox Nephite values and traditional practices."[56] The coming of Christ required the preparation of a temple people in advance of his coming, a key Book of Mormon insight accessible to the Prophet.

Finally, the Bountiful temple narrative in 3 Nephi was the only source in the canon of Judeo-Christian scripture to document temple worship after the death and resurrection of Christ—postresurrection Christian temple worship among an ancient people. When the Prophet first encountered these Book of Mormon passages, temple worship had long been erased from the religious practice of Christians and Jews. While the

Jews awaited the restoration of the prophesied third temple at Jerusalem, early Christians, especially in early Catholicism, had absorbed elements of temple ritual into the church sacrament (the Eucharist service, or Mass).[57] Any notion of separate distinctive temple worship had disappeared, but the Book of Mormon pointed in a different direction: to the restoration of ancient temple worship—not with the Mosaic code, but with Christ at its center, modeled after the postresurrection temple era at Bountiful. The Book of Mormon provided the earliest, indeed only, scriptural source for the meaning of a Christian temple, as if to imply that the Prophet's modern commission might be to reverse the course of Christian history and restore the temple once again to its preeminent place as the holiest place of sacred worship, like the Hebrew Bible's temple, the "House of the Lord."

In addition to these three major temples, the Book of Mormon also described other apparently smaller temple-like "sanctuaries to worship God before the altar" (see Alma 15:17).[58] A body of migrating Nephites "from the land southward, to the land northward" (see Helaman 3:8)[59] strategically cultivated trees and imported timber to "build . . . their temples, and their synagogues, and their sanctuaries" (see Helaman 3:14).[60] During this same period the book of Alma records: "And Alma and Amulek went forth preaching repentance unto the people *in their temples, and in their sanctuaries,* and also in their synagogues, which was built after the manner of the Jews . . . to prepare the minds of the children of men . . . at the time of his coming" (see Alma 16:13, 16).[61] We discussed synagogues earlier in this chapter; their purpose was routine and regular congregational teaching, instruction, and prayer. But what were sanctuaries? These Book of Mormon sanctuaries were clearly described as altar sanctuaries (Alma 15:17), suggesting parallels to the altar sanctuaries only briefly and obscurely mentioned in the Old Testament, for example, in the prophecy of Amos: "And the sanctuaries of Israel shall be laid waste" (Amos 7:9).[62]

Menahem Haran of the Hebrew University of Jerusalem distinguished between temples and altar sanctuaries in the religion of ancient Israel:

> It is essential to make a clear distinction between the temple, as the house of God, and the altar [sanctuary]. A house of God [a temple], to begin with, as even the name implies, was a building, a roofed edifice, while an altar [sanctuary], upon which sacrifices were offered up, . . . was found only in the open. . . . Any temple would be accompanied by an altar placed [outside] in the adjoining court, but not every altar would necessarily be attached to a temple. . . . The solitary altars [sanctuaries] were numerous and scattered throughout the country; there was probably no settlement without its altar, and altars could even be found outside cities, in the countryside.[63]

In summary, we see that Book of Mormon temple worship encompassed multiple forms of expression: temples, probably in various sizes depending on their population centers (for example, Nephi and Zarahemla were likely central and large, and Bountiful was probably regional and smaller, as were possibly others not explicitly named), and numerous altar sanctuaries likely in every community mentioned throughout the book—in both Nephite and Lamanite lands. This Book of Mormon temple model might have seemed at odds with contemporary ideas of ancient biblical temple worship, centered at the great temple of Jerusalem (or earlier at the tabernacle of Moses in the Sinai Peninsula). As recent biblical scholarship has shown, the Book of Mormon model was actually quite consistent with ancient models of diffused expressions of Israelite temple and sanctuary worship; in fact, it was nearly identical. This same impulse seems to have fueled Smith's dynamic temple vision in the nineteenth century, not with open altar sanctuaries that made no sense in a post-Mosaic world, but instead with temples—central temples, regional temples, and community temples, many and varied, large and small.

In 1830 Smith commenced his temple vision with the call for building the great central temple of Zion in Independence, Missouri, with twenty-four temple buildings in the temple complex itself. This was soon followed by the dedication of four more surrounding smaller temples or temple sites in the first fifteen years of his ministry. After Smith's

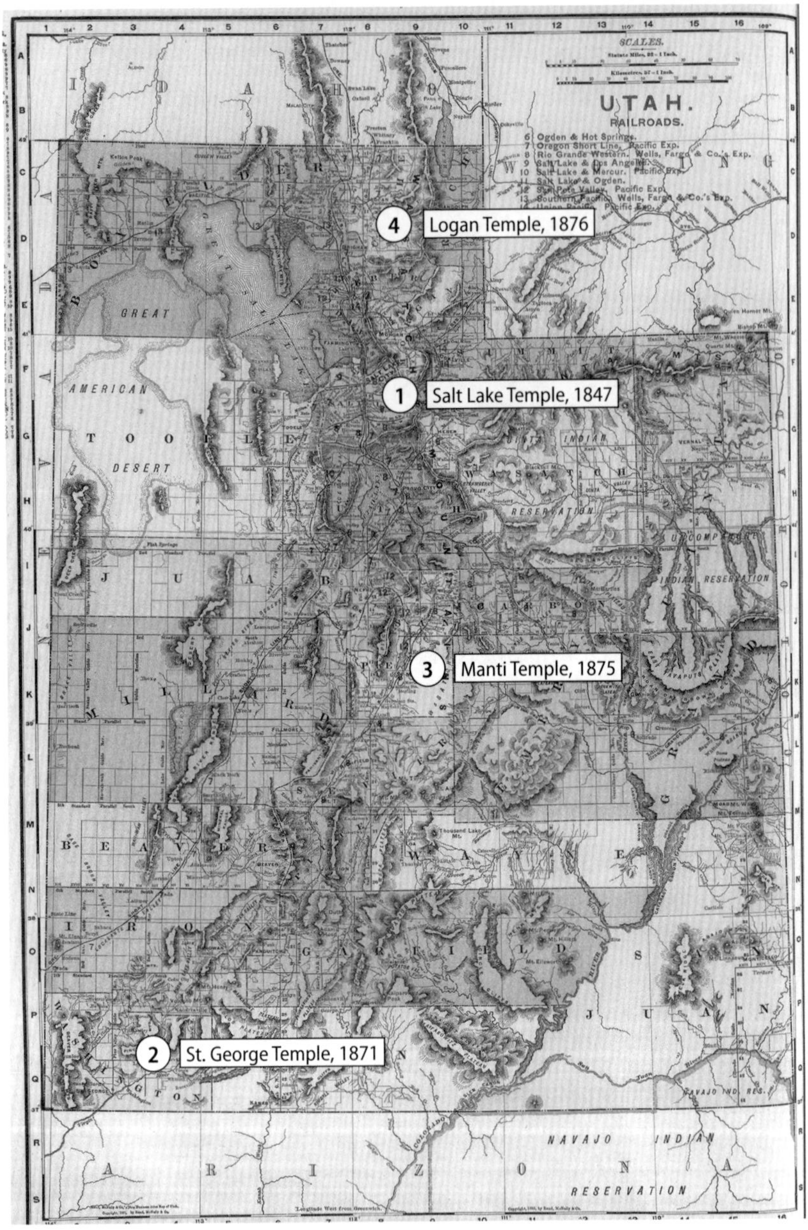

Fig. 20. After the death of Joseph Smith, Brigham Young replicated Smith's temple vision in the western Territory of Utah with an additional four temples, all envisioned during his tenure as leader of the LDS Church. The years given refer to the date of the announcement of the temples.

martyrdom, Brigham Young replicated the Prophet's temple vision with the commencement of constructing the Salt Lake Temple in 1853, a great central temple in the West, surrounded by smaller temples in nearby settlements: the St. George Temple in southern Utah, the Logan Temple in northern Utah, and the Manti Temple in central Utah. During the early construction of the Salt Lake Temple, Young prophesied of his own future vision of Mormon temple building:

> To accomplish this work there will have to be *not only one temple but thousands of them*, and thousands and tens of thousands of men and women will go into those temples and officiate for people who have lived as far back as the Lord shall reveal. If we are faithful enough to *go back and build that great temple which Joseph has written about* [in Independence, Missouri], and should the Lord acknowledge the labor of His servants, then watch, for you will see somebody whom you have seen before, and many of you will see him whom you have not seen before, but you will know him as soon as you see him.[64]

One hundred fifty years after Young's statement, existing latter-day temples vary in size and design: the Salt Lake Temple is 253,000 square feet, the Boston Massachusetts Temple 69,600 square feet, and the Colonia Juárez Chihuahua Mexico Temple 6,800 square feet. Note the parallels between the major temples, apparently smaller sanctuaries, and congregational synagogues of the Book of Mormon and church president Gordon B. Hinckley's 1995 explanation for building small Latter-day Saint temples: "There are many areas of the Church that are remote, where the membership is small and not likely to grow very much in the near future. Are those who live in these places to be denied forever the blessings of the temple ordinances? While visiting such an area a few months ago, we prayerfully pondered this question. The answer, we believe, came bright and clear. We will construct *small temples* in some of these areas, buildings with all of the facilities to administer all of the ordinances. They would be built to *temple standards*, which are much higher than [congregational] *meetinghouse standards*. They would accommodate baptisms for the dead, the endowment service, sealings, and all other ordinances to be had in the Lord's house for both the living and the dead."[65]

In fact, the vast majority of Mormon temples (59 percent) are less than a tenth the size of the Salt Lake Temple, and a significant minority (38 percent) are much smaller—less than a twentieth its size. Mormon temples in the twenty-first century have become ever more local and community-focused. Currently there are 144 operating temples, 14 under construction, and 15 announced. There are 111 temples in North America, 22 in South America, 14 in Europe, 10 in Asia, 4 in the Pacific Islands, 6 in Australia and New Zealand, and 6 in Africa. Reflecting larger LDS populations, Mexico alone has 13 temples, Canada 9 temples, Brazil 8 temples, California 7 temples, Texas 4 temples, and Utah 15 temples. Significantly and symbolically, over three-quarters (79 percent) of the world's Latter-day Saint temples are located in the Americas, the indigenous lands of the ancient peoples of the Book of Mormon.

Defining the meaning of modern temple worship

What was the meaning of temples in a modern Christian world? At the beginning of the restoration in the early 1830s, Smith had virtually no viable temple templates to work with. The Jews of nineteenth-century America had been historical keepers of the Israelite temple tradition, but for centuries their form of worship had centered in the synagogue, not the temple. Bushman commented on other possible temple influences on the early life of the Prophet:

> Joseph's idea of a temple did not come from classical civilization; he omitted Greece and Rome entirely from his many recapitulations of world history. He was familiar with Masons who met in buildings called temples, but Freemasonry was not an attractive model in the aftermath of anti-Masonic political campaigns, and Masonic temples were non-existent in areas where Joseph lived. . . . It is not likely that Joseph ever saw a Masonic temple before he began building [the temple] in Kirtland. Not only did he

> lack models, temples were foreign to the low church Protestants he was familiar with from childhood. . . . Presbyterians and Methodists might casually refer to their meetinghouses as temples but only to add a little dignity to ordinary chapels.[66]

The Old Testament offered a rich trove of temple texts, but its temple worship centered on animal sacrifice, which was clearly not relevant in the postadvent era following the resurrection. Nonetheless, the Prophet had already begun thinking quite early in the restoration about more than the location of the forthcoming temple in Zion. He also envisioned what type of divine worship should someday take place there. As early as January 2, 1831, while the church was still centered in Fayette, New York, and within the first year of the Book of Mormon's publication, the Prophet introduced the idea of "endow," a divine bestowal of "power from on high":

> I gave unto you the commandment, that ye should go to the Ohio: and there I will give unto you my law; and there you shall be endowed with power from on high. . . . And they that have farms that cannot be sold, let them be left, or rented as seemeth them good. See that all things are preserved, and when men are endowed with power from on high, and sent forth, all these things shall be gathered unto the bosom of the church. And if ye seek the riches which it is the will of the Father to give unto you, ye shall be the richest of all people; for ye shall have the riches of eternity.[67]

The revelation's reference to being "endowed with power from on high" suggests that at first the idea of endowment derived from New Testament scripture. After his postresurrection appearance to his New Testament disciples, Christ instructed his disciples to "tarry ye in the city of Jerusalem, until ye be *endued* with power from on high" (Luke 24:49, emphasis added).[68] This promise was believed to have been fulfilled on the Day of Pentecost when the disciples were "all filled with the Holy Ghost, and began to speak with other tongues, as the Spirit gave them utterance" (Acts 2:4)[69]—the day Christians believe the Holy Spirit descended upon the apostles. However, in 1831 the idea of endowment was organic and undeveloped. Its meaning in the Prophet's mind was at once evolving, expanding in meaning and definitional clarity, even as he associated it increasingly (by 1833) with his still-to-be-defined temple worship that had been deeply ingrained into Mormon consciousness with the promise of the temple of Zion in Independence, Missouri.

In fact, the January 1831 endowment revelation revealed Smith's already-broadening understanding of the meaning of endowment in surprising ways. For example, *endow* was an unexpected word in the vocabulary of a twenty-five-year-old unsophisticated young laborer who had never known education, money, or wealth. His parents were poor tenant farmers, moving from rented farm to rented farm. The revelation intimates that Smith was indeed familiar with endowments in the world of education and charity—the revelation spoke of the Saints giving up worldly riches to prepare for an endowment of the riches of eternity. An endowment in common discourse in the 1830s meant a generous financial gift to fund or provide support for a college or sometimes for a member of the clergy, such as a pastor or vicar. The financial gift then enabled the college or teacher to endow its students with learning and knowledge that would provide the recipients with a preparatory foundation for life. Endowment was "that which is given or bestowed on the person or mind by the creator," defined Noah Webster in 1828.[70] This idea of endowment seemed to inspire Joseph: endowment was a gift of spiritual wealth and power given by God to prepare the faithful, not just for life, but for eternal life.

From this early point on, the Prophet became increasingly captivated by a handful of themes related to *endow*—*knowledge*, *intelligence*, *wisdom*, *power*, and *sealing*—that over time progressively developed into the conceptualization of the Mormon endowment. In back-to-back revelations received on December 27, 1832, and January 3, 1833, the church was called on to establish a School of the Prophets.[71] Additionally, the laws of the celestial, terrestrial, and telestial kingdoms were defined with qualifying gradations of spiritual intelligence or light associated with each kingdom: "For intelligence cleaveth unto intelligence; wisdom receiveth wisdom; truth embraceth truth; virtue loveth virtue; light cleaveth unto light; mercy hath compassion on mercy, and claimeth her own; justice continueth its course, and claimeth its own; judgment goeth before the face of him who sitteth upon the throne, and governeth and executeth all things."[72]

The text for the 1833 School of the Prophets, the *Lectures on Faith*, spoke of intelligence and instruction received personally from God; indeed, the content of this 1833 text was quite similar to Lehi's Wisdom-like narrative from the Book of Mormon (2 Nephi 2), itself evoking the ancient Israelite Wisdom tradition of Solomon's temple, discussed in chapter 2: "After man was created . . . God conversed with him face to face. In His presence he was permitted to stand, and from His own mouth he was permitted to receive instruction. He heard His voice, walked before Him and gazed upon His glory, while intelligence burst upon his understanding, and enabled him to give names to the vast assemblage of his Maker's works."[73] Even at this early stage, the school's teachings evoked the imagery of very ancient Israelite knowledge. It is this dimension of Mormon temple understanding that surprised and impressed American literary scholar Harold Bloom:

> What is clear is that Smith and his apostles restated what Moshe Idel, our great living scholar of Kabbalah [the most esoteric Jewish school of thought], persuades me was the archaic or original Jewish religion, a Judaism that preceded even the Yahwist, the author of the earliest stories in what we now call the Five Books of Moses. . . . My observation certainly does find enormous validity in Smith's imaginative recapture of crucial elements in the archaic Jewish religion, elements evaded by normative Judaism and by the Church after it.[74]

Another revelation, received a month after the school's conclusion in April, continued with themes of personal intimacy with God, which was promised to all Saints, not just a select few of the church's leadership: "Verily, thus saith the Lord, it shall come to pass, that every soul who forsaketh their sins, & cometh unto me, & calleth on my name, & obeyeth my voice, & keepeth all my commandments, shall see my face & know that I am. . . . For if you keep my commandments you shall receive of his fulness, and be glorified in me, as I am glorified in the Father. . . . The glory of God is intelligence; or in other words, light, and ~~truth~~ truth."[75] By June 1, 1833, with the anticipation of the recent announcement of the Kirtland Temple, the Prophet was associating the word *endowment* explicitly with the temple: "Yea, verily I say unto you, I gave unto you a commandment, that you should build an House, in the which house I design to endow those whom I have chosen, with power from on high, for this is the promise of the Father unto you, Therefore, I command you to tarry even as mine apostles at Jerusalem."[76] The Book of Mormon had already linked *power* with *sealing*, as in *sealing power*: "I give unto you power, that whatsoever ye shall seal on earth, shall be sealed in heaven; and whatsoever ye shall loose on earth, shall be loosed in heaven; and thus shall ye have power" (see Helaman 10:7),[77] promised God to Nephi. This echoed Christ's similar commission of sealing powers to Peter in the New Testament (see Matthew 16:16–19).

Twenty months later, on February 21, 1835, new apostles Parley P. Pratt, Thomas B. Marsh, and Orson Pratt were ordained to the Quorum of the Twelve Apostles with both ordination blessings and sealing blessings. Cowdery, officiating during the ordinations, then gave an apostolic charge, including a pointed reference to the anticipated endowment:

> Remember you are not to go to other nations, till you receive your endowment. Tarry at Kirtland until you are endowed with power from on high. You need a fountain of wisdom, knowledge, and intelligence such as you never had. Relative to the endowment, I make a remark or two, that there be no mistake. The world cannot receive the things of God. He [God] can endow you without worldly pomp or great parade. He can give you that wisdom, that intelligence in that power which characterized the ancient Saints and now characterizes the inhabitants of the upper world.[78]

Still, if by 1835 the Saints broadly anticipated this temple endowment of divine power, knowledge, and intelligence, the Prophet must have wondered in what way it actually should be revealed or made manifest. The Old Testament offered little precedent; it mentions the word *endue* but not in the context of Israelite temple worship. Though the New Testament spoke of the endowment of power evident on the Day of Pentecost in Acts 2, these miraculous events were never mentioned in connection with the temple.[79]

The Book of Mormon stood alone as the only scriptural source to link this spiritual endowment with the temple. For instance, the apex of Christ's appearance at the Bountiful temple in 3 Nephi, on the second day of his visit, featured a defining spiritual experience culminating in a remarkable outpouring of the Holy Ghost, what Ehat described as a Nephite endowment.[80] The Nephite people had gathered at the temple for the second day of Christ's visit to the Americas:

> [Christ's twelve disciples] did cause that [the people] should be *separated into twelve bodies.* And *the twelve did teach the multitude*; and behold, they did cause that the multitude should kneel down upon the face of the earth, and should *pray unto the Father, in the name of Jesus.* . . . [And the disciples] *ministered those same words which Jesus had spoken—nothing varying* from the words which Jesus had spoken. . . .
>
> [And] when they were all baptized, and had come up out of the water, the Holy Ghost did fall upon them, and they were filled with the Holy Ghost, and with fire . . . and angels did come down out of heaven, and did minister unto them. And . . . behold, Jesus came and stood in the midst, and ministered unto them. . . .
>
> [And] they did not multiply many words, for it was given unto them what they should pray, and they were filled with desire. And it came to pass that Jesus blessed them, as they did pray unto him, and his countenance did smile upon them, and the light of his countenance did shine upon them. (See 3 Nephi 19:5–25.)[81]

The presentation of this experience in 3 Nephi is extraordinary and difficult to overlook, marked by miraculous manifestations of the Holy Ghost, of angels, and of the presence of the resurrected Christ. Could it be that this Nephite experiential endowment, a Pentecostal spiritual experience situated expressly in the temple, may have influenced Smith's expectation for a similar experiential endowment among his Latter-day Saints—at the temple? At the dedication of the Kirtland Temple on March

27, 1836, after the administration of the sacrament toward the conclusion of the all-day service, Smith's history describes a series of miraculous spiritual events: "President F[rederick] G. Williams arose and testified that while Presedent [Sidney] Rigdon was making his first prayer, an angel entered the window, and took his seat between father Smith and himself and remained there during his prayer. President David Whitmer, also saw angels in the house. . . . President Brigham Young gave a short address in tongues, and David W. Patten interpreted, and gave a short exhortation in tongues himself."[82] Later in the evening the Prophet recorded:

> George A. Smith arose and began to prophecy when a voice was heard like the sound of a rushing mighty wind which filled the Temple and all the congregation simultaneously arose being moved upon by an invisible power many began to speak in Tongues and prophecy others saw glorious visions and I beheld the Temple was filled with angels which fact I declared to the <to the congregation> The people in the neighborhood came running together (hearing an unusual sound within and seeing a bright light like a piller of Fire resting upon—the Temple) and [w]ere astonished at what was transpiring The number present on this occasion was 416.[83]

The following Wednesday evening of the dedication week, March 30, 1836, during a solemn assembly at the temple, the Prophet recorded: "The Savior made his appearance to some, while angels ministered unto others, and it was a pentecost and enduement indeed, long long to be remembered, for the sound shall go forth from this place into all the world, and the occurrencies of this day shall be handed down upon the pages of sacred history to all generations; as the day of Pentecost, so shall this day be ~~remembered~~ numbered; and celebrated as a year of Jubilee and time of rejoicing to the saints of the Most High God."[84]

Again, Smith made no mention of the Book of Mormon, instead citing only references to the Day of Pentecost from the New Testament; this was the frame of reference with which most of his Bible-oriented Mormon converts would be familiar.[85] He also never mentioned the Old Testament but introduced a symbolic washing in the Kirtland Temple, similar in form to like rituals in the Exodus account of the tabernacle. This washing was first performed in an upper room of the schooling and printing building adjacent to the Kirtland Temple on January 21, 1836. Later in the same day a symbolic anointing was administered in the west attic room of the temple. Smith records that with these sacred ordinances were sealed upon them "the blessings of Abraham, Isaac and Jacob. . . . The heavens were opened upon us, and I beheld the celestial kingdom of God, and the glory thereof, whether in the body or out I cannot tell. I saw the transcendent beauty of the gate, through which the heirs of that kingdom will enter, which was like unto circling flames of fire. Also the blazing throne of God, wherein was seated the Father and the Son."[86]

A final coda of temple worship in Kirtland again evoked Book of Mormon precedent. In the temple account of 3 Nephi, Jesus had invited each to "feel the prints of the nails in his hands and in his feet" (see 3 Nephi 11:15),[87] at the conclusion of which "they did cry out with one accord, saying: Hosanna! Blessed be the name of the Most High God! And they did fall down at the feet of Jesus, and did worship him" (see 3 Nephi 11:16–17).[88] This culminating Hosanna expression—drawing from both Book of Mormon (Bountiful temple) and New Testament (Jesus's triumphal entry into Jerusalem) narratives—was adopted into the Kirtland Temple dedication by Sidney Rigdon. Called the "Hosanna Shout," this ritual continued as a tradition in Latter-day Saint temple dedications and other congregational ceremonies throughout the restoration.[89] In a separate account Wilford Woodruff described a Kirtland endowment service, which we study in the next section, that concluded with the same Hosanna praise: At the end of the service, Woodruff related, it "was confirmed upon our heads with a shout of all the anointed with uplifted hand to heaven HOSANNA. HOSANNA. HOSANNA. to GOD & the LAMB. Amen. Amen. & Amen."[90]

By 1836, the essential meaning of the temple endowment to the Prophet seemed to be a defining revelatory experience received at the temple, culminating in a miraculous manifestation of the Holy Ghost, including, for those heeding Smith's charge to "solemnize their minds,"[91] the personal ministering of angelic messengers from God and even a ministration by the risen Christ. In developing this understanding, the

Prophet accessed different scriptural ideas from the Old Testament and the New Testament—but also from the Book of Mormon, based on Christ's introduction of sacred worship forms in 3 Nephi and subsequent spiritual manifestations that followed. These took place notably at the temple in the context of a higher form of ritual worship.

Defining and designing temple space

A series of spatial details inconspicuous in the Nephite temple endowment narrative correlate with striking architectural details in the design of the Kirtland Temple, and later of the Nauvoo Temple, suggesting that Smith might have taken notice of these details in the Book of Mormon text and marked them as useful structurally to his emerging temple architecture. First, for instance, the Nephite endowment appeared as a form of liturgical worship that was noticeably set in a postresurrection temple context at the Bountiful temple. Second, the congregation was partitioned into smaller worship groups for temple instruction and prayer. Third, Christ's twelve Nephite disciples officiated in the worship rites at the temple, each of the twelve assigned to a smaller worship group. Fourth, the twelve "ministered" ritual language, repeating word for word "those same words which Jesus had spoken [to the twelve in the temple the day before]—nothing varying from the words which Jesus had spoken" (see 3 Nephi 19:8).[92] Fifth, there was a ritual baptism, likely a rebaptism for those participating if they had previously been baptized into the Nephite church of Christ. Sixth, the twelve formed a solemn prayer group in unified prayer that led to a remarkable spiritual unity and oneness among the congregation: "And they did pray unto Jesus, calling him their Lord and their God. . . . and they did not multiply many words, for it was given unto them what they should pray, and they were filled with desire" (see 3 Nephi 19:18, 24).[93] This group prayer culminated in a final miraculous manifestation—the transfiguration of the prayer group participants in the presence of Christ:

Fig. 21. This historic interior view of the west pulpits in the Kirtland Temple shows the unique system of rolling curtains and veils (including ceiling hooks from which to hang veils around the pulpit areas) that allowed for different worship spaces—congregational assembly, small group instruction and worship, and intimate personal temple worship.

> And it came to pass that Jesus blessed them, as they did pray unto him, and his countenance did smile upon them, and the light of his countenance did shine upon them, and behold they were as white as the countenance, and also the garments of Jesus; and behold the whiteness thereof did exceed all the whiteness, yea, even there could be nothing upon the earth so white as the whiteness thereof . . . ; and he [Jesus] did smile upon the[m] again; and behold they were white, even as Jesus. (See 3 Nephi 19:25, 30.)[94]

These distinct Book of Mormon temple protocols appear to have been carefully accommodated in the architecture of the modern Kirtland Temple, which Smith confirmed was given him in detail by revelation.[95] Eliza R. Snow provided this well-known physical description of the Kirtland Temple's worship spaces—a fundamental worship design that remains evident in temple construction to the present day:

> There was a peculiarity in the arrangement of the inner court [inner hall] which made it more than ordinarily impressive—so much so that a sense of sacred awe seemed to rest upon all who entered; not only the saints, but strangers also manifested a high degree of reverential feeling. Four pulpits stood, one above another, in the centre of the building, from north to south, both on the east and west ends . . . and each of these pulpits was *separated by curtains* of white painted canvas, which were let down and drawn up at pleasure. . . . In addition to the pulpit curtains, were others, intersecting at right angles, which divided the main ground-floor hall into four equal sections—giving to each one-half of one set of pulpits.[96]

Note the temple's architectural organization, with a main hall for congregational solemn assemblies, which was then subdivided by curtains into smaller group worship spaces for temple instruction and prayer. The pulpit areas at opposing ends of the main hall were separated further with curtains and set apart as private areas for personal intimate worship. In the west pulpit area, for example, with the curtains down on April 3, 1836, Smith and Cowdery received a visitation from Christ (associated with the visitation of Elijah the prophet): "We saw the Lord standing upon the breast work of the pulpit. before us, and under his feet was a paved work of pure gold, in color like amber. . . . [H]is voice was as the sound of the rushing of great waters, even the voice of Jehovah, Saying . . . your sins are forgiven you. You are clean before me. . . . For behold I have accepted this house, and my name shall be here; and I will manifest myself to my people, in mercy, in this House, yea I will appear unto my servants, and speak unto them with mine own voice."[97]

Wilford Woodruff's journal offers a rare view into an "endowment" service at the Kirtland Temple, including an unusual mention of the Book of Mormon's use in the temple service. The service began early in the morning, with Woodruff going inside the hung veil of the Aaronic pulpits for personal worship. Beyond this intimate worship space, the larger temple seating space was divided into four smaller group spaces, with a member of the church presidency presiding in each compartment.

> March 23rd. I repaired to the house of the Lord at an early hour in the morning to spend the day in prayer and fasting with the saints in Kirtland, as this was a day [Thursday] set apart for that purpose. Immediately after entering the house in company with several other Elders, I went within the veil and we bowed down before the Lord in the Aronic stand & offerd a morning sacrifice, & the Spirit of God rested upon us with joy to our Souls. I was Called upon, by the Patriarch JOSEPH to read a chapter in the book of Mormon; I then read the third chapter of the Book of Jacob. . . . After I had made some brief remarks upon the subject the congregation took their seats, for the services of the day, in the following order The house being divided into four parts by veils, the females occupied two parts & the males the others. Some of the presidency presided in each appartment.[98]

He next describes a more intimate group worship taking place in each compartment, followed by group prayer with "all as one" praying, which concluded the service. By the end of the service Woodruff's temple service had included personal, small group, and congregational temple worship lasting the entire day:

> The time was taken up during the day in each appartment in singing, exortation, & prayer, some had a tongue, others an interpetation, & all was in order. The power of GOD rested upon the people the gifts were poured out upon us some had the administering of angels & the image of GOD sat upon the countenances of the Sants. at 4 oclock PM. the Veils were all rolled up together which brough the whole congregation in full view of each other and while the presence of the LORD filled the house the congregation of the Saints fell upon their knees & all as one man, vocally poured forth rejoicing. supplication & Prayer, before the God of Israel which closed the services of the day, after contributing for the support of the poor.[99]

Fig. 22. The Community of Christ Temple in Independence, Missouri, features a large sanctuary designed for congregational worship.

The patterns of worship at the Kirtland Temple—the various smaller worship spaces, the progressive worship flow, the divinely intimate forms of ceremonial worship, the sublime revelatory experiences recorded—are similar to the Nephite endowment recorded in 3 Nephi. Obviously missing was temple baptism, which had been a central part of the Nephite endowment.

Visitors to modern LDS temple open houses are sometimes surprised at the inner architecture of the temple. Expecting a large sanctuary with intricate décor reminiscent of a grand cathedral, instead they encounter a sequence of smaller rooms connected to each other by ornate staircases and inner hallways. Each room is tastefully decorated and labeled with a unique purpose: sealing rooms for marriages; endowment rooms for instruction; the baptistry with a font resting on the backs of twelve oxen; and a celestial room, architecturally designed to reflect the very presence of God. The smaller architectural worship spaces alone provide evidence of the Book of Mormon's influence on the early temple endowment and its temple spaces.

By contrast, the Community of Christ (formerly the Reorganized Church of Jesus Christ of Latter Day Saints) dedicated its first temple, the Independence Temple, in 1994, near Kansas City, Missouri. The Community of Christ identifies its origins with Joseph Smith, but its early leaders did not adopt the newer forms of temple worship that Smith had taught in Nauvoo. Its first prophet-president, Joseph Smith III and son of Joseph Smith, was a child during the Kirtland Temple years and had been only ten years old when complete temple ordinances were formally introduced by Smith in Nauvoo in the early 1840s. The striking architectural design of the Community of Christ's Independence Temple by Gyo Obata features a great basilica-style sanctuary evoking the spiral shell of the nautilus with a stainless steel spire rising 300 feet.[100] The sanctuary itself seats 1,600 and has a large pipe organ with 60 stops, 102 ranks, and 5,685 pipes. The central room is surrounded by various public spaces: a museum, bookstore, theaters, lecture hall, and meditation chapel.[101] The entire temple is reminiscent of a large Christian cathedral rather than an early Mormon temple like Kirtland; missing is the personal intimate and ritual worship portrayed in the postresurrection Bountiful temple narrative of the Book of Mormon.

In 1842, Joseph Smith introduced the more complete Nauvoo temple endowment, considered a new and great revelatory vista. The architectural design of the Nauvoo Temple's various worship spaces, together with the progressive patterns of its worship, reflected the distinctive early features of the Kirtland Temple endowment service—personal intimate ritual worship with the Lord, small-group instructional worship, and a sublime group prayer culminating in the presence of the Lord. Finally, in Nauvoo, even baptism was incorporated into the temple. Prior to the Nauvoo Temple the Prophet had introduced the doctrine of baptism for the dead: "On 10 August 1840, Seymour Brunson, member of the Nauvoo High Council, died in Nauvoo. The Prophet took the occasion of his funeral, on 15 August 1840, to deliver the first discourse on the doctrine of baptism for the dead," recounted Andrew Ehat and Lyndon Cook.[102]

Within weeks these proxy baptisms were being performed in the Mississippi River. Several months later, Smith's thinking evolved as he clarified by revelation that these proxy baptisms were to be treated with more reverence than a routine baptism performed in any body of water. After the completion of the temple, these proxy baptisms were to be observed only in the temple. A revelation recorded on January 19, 1841, disclosed:

> I grant unto you a sufficient time to build a house unto me, and during this time your baptisms shall be acceptable unto me. But, behold, at the end of this appointment, your baptisms for your dead shall not be acceptable unto me. . . . For, verily I say unto you, that after you have had sufficient time to build a house to me, wherein the ordinance of baptizing for the dead belongeth, and for which the same was instituted from before the foundation of the world, your baptisms for your dead cannot be acceptable unto me.[103]

This revelation marked a culmination for the Prophet of the complete expression of a symbolic spiritual journey as taught in the temple, for these proxy baptisms were to be performed among the most sacred ordinances of the forthcoming Nauvoo Temple:

> Therefore, verily I say unto you, that your anointings and your washings, and your baptisms for the dead, and your solemn assemblies <January 19> and your memorials for your sacrifices, by the sons of Levi, and for your oracles in your most holy places, wherein you receive conversations and your statutes and judgments, for the beginning of the revelations and foundation of Zion, and for the glory, honor, and endowment of all her municipals, are ordained by the ordinance of my holy house which my people are always commanded to build unto my holy name . . . that I may reveal mine ordinances therein, unto my people.[104]

At last, with the incorporation of proxy baptism into the temple, the modern temple would include virtually all the hallmarks of the Book of Mormon temple as expressed originally in the Nephite endowment.

5

Priesthood Restorations, Origins, and Influences

PRIESTHOOD IS A DEFINING PRIORITY for new religion. Judaism began with the Levitical Priesthood when God told Moses in the visions of Sinai to "anoint Aaron and his sons, and consecrate them, that they may minister unto me in the priest's office" (Exodus 30:30).[1] In the formative days of his early ministry, Jesus of Nazareth established priesthood as foundational to his early church: "He ordained twelve, that they should be with him, and that he might send them forth to preach" (Mark 3:14–15).[2] Early Catholicism asserted the primacy of hierarchical priesthood, with archbishops, bishops, priests, and deacons. Conversely, Protestant Reformers such as Martin Luther in Germany, Zwingli in Zurich, and Calvin in Geneva rejected Catholic authority, arguing that the Bible as the Word of God stood alone as the supreme source of authority, "the supremacy of Holy Scripture."[3] True authority was vested in believers via access to the Bible. "We are all priests, as many of us as are Christians,"[4] proclaimed Luther, hence introducing the idea of a priesthood of all believers.

Three hundred years later in 1829 in the burned-over district of Protestant upstate New York, Joseph Smith's new American religion developed its own unique priesthood traditions. First, like Catholics, Smith asserted that priestly authority was indeed requisite for the valid administration of the ordinances of salvation. An April 1830 revelation taught that "although a man shouldest be baptized an hundred times [without the new church's authority] it availeth him nothing . . . wherefore enter ye in at the ~~at~~ gate as I have commanded."[5] Nor could one merely assume this authority on his own; even Joseph Smith and

Oliver Cowdery authenticated their own priesthood ordinations, recording being ordained initially in a divine visitation from John the Baptist.[6] Yet the requirements for Mormon ordination were remarkably egalitarian. According to a December 1830 revelation, "As many as shall come before my servants, Sidney Rigdon and Joseph Smith Jr, embracing this calling and commandment, shall be ordained and sent forth to preach the everlasting gospel among all nations."[7] This was the beginning of a lay priesthood that Mormons are known for to this day, in which priesthood ordination was available to all worthy men, even to the uneducated classless frontiersmen of North America.[8] This proletarian "practice even the most republican of Presbyterians and Methodists rejected," remarked David Holland, professor of history at Harvard Divinity School.[9]

Joseph Smith instituted a hierarchical priesthood, including Mormonism's system of apostolic succession. In contrast to Catholicism's claim to lineal apostolic succession from the apostle Peter through a long line of Roman bishops over the centuries, Smith claimed a revealed apostolic succession from Peter, James, and John, who visited Smith and Cowdery in May/June 1829.[10] The earliest Mormon priesthood hierarchy included apostle, elder, priest, and teacher, nearly identical to the Book of Mormon priesthood offices of 3 Nephi. The obvious model for hierarchical priesthood would have been Catholicism, but Joseph Smith had little exposure to formal Catholicism in Protestant upstate New York—he never mentions it in his early history. Many Irish Catholics had immigrated to America to help build the Erie Canal beginning in 1817, but there were no Catholic congregations in all of western New York during Smith's early life.[11] Richard Bushman discussed concepts of the priesthood:

> Priesthood was associated with Roman Catholicism and the old regimes of Europe. The radical [Protestant] religious tradition from which many Mormon converts came denounced priesthood as popish, emphasizing preaching rather than sacraments administered by priests. Universalists like Joseph Smith's grandfather linked priesthood with priestcraft and preaching the gospel

> for hire. In most New England churches, ministers were ordained as pastors of specific congregations and were not admitted to a priesthood at all. The idea of priesthood descending in a line of authority was Roman, not Puritan.[12]

Where did Mormonism's priesthood innovations come from? Several scholars have argued that the Book of Mormon provided Joseph Smith with the blueprint for priesthood.[13] Book of Mormon priesthood practices influenced the early restoration, especially in three notable areas that clearly distinguished early Latter-day Saint priesthood from surrounding Catholic and Protestant priesthood ideas: (1) the surprising emergence of priesthood orders as a defining dimension of Mormon priesthood meaning and governance, (2) the unique hierarchy of Mormon priesthood offices that was markedly priestly in a nonpriestly Protestant world, and (3) the model of priests and teachers in Mormon congregational worship as a reflection of apparently Israelite priesthood forms.

The emergence of priesthood orders and Book of Mormon influence

Early in the restoration Joseph Smith introduced the idea of priesthood orders, which would have been foreign to the mostly Protestant world that Mormonism was surrounded by. In the nineteenth century religious orders were the domain of Catholicism, whose various orders, today numbering in the hundreds, found their origins over a thousand years earlier—for example, the Order of Saint Benedict (Benedictines) founded in the sixth century AD, the Order of the Holy Cross in AD 1131, and the Society of Jesus (Jesuits) in 1540. Early in the Mormon restoration Smith probably knew little of these orders, given the intense discrimination against Catholicism in North America, especially in nineteenth-century New York State.[14] In Protestantism religious orders appeared only later—for example, Anglican orders for women in the 1840s and men in 1866, Methodist (Wesleyan) orders of Deaconesses in 1890, and Lutheran orders beginning in 1927.[15]

Smith developed priesthood orders using a different historical lens reminiscent of the heritage of priestly orders of antiquity—the ancient Aaronic Priesthood order from the Old Testament and the ancient Melchizedek order that evoked the legacy of Abraham in biblical scripture, the latter receiving decided influence from the Book of Mormon in its form and expression. He especially seemed intent on restoring the lost Melchizedek Priesthood order of antiquity, as if to say that modern Mormon priesthood was more than a restoration of various priesthood offices such as apostle, elder, priest, and teacher—significant in itself—but was also a restoration of the ancient priesthood itself. In his view the priesthood of the modern age must be the same as the authentic original priesthood of antiquity. In 1842 Smith remarked "that the spirits of men are eternal, that they are governed by the same priesthood that Abraham, Melchisdedek, and the Apostles were; that they are organized according to that priesthood which is everlasting, 'without beginning of days or end of years.'"[16] This contrasted with mainstream Christian views that priesthood was new with Christ, while Old Testament priesthoods had long ago been done away.

The appearance of priesthood orders in the early restoration

The historical record of June 3, 1831, documents the earliest impression of what would become the Melchizedek order in the restoration; however, the earliest historical reference to what would become the Aaronic order actually appeared in revelation fifteen months later, in September 1832.[17] This order of appearance is important because the Book of Mormon never mentions an order relating to Aaron, only one relating to Melchizedek, which is referred to as the "high priesthood being after the order of his [God's] Son [and] Melchizedek . . . was also a High Priest after this same order" (see Alma 13:7, 14).[18] Thus by June 1831 Smith's emerging priesthood theology had recognized elements of the Melchizedek order as salient. Its meaning and significance is documented in Alma's discourses in the Book of Mormon, but the Aaronic order, a purely biblical order, had yet to become a part of his priesthood teachings.

Thus, at the fourth church conference in Kirtland, Ohio, newly called church historian John Whitmer recorded: "June 3, 1831, A general conference was called, and a blessing promised, if the elders were faithful, and humble before him. . . . After the business of the church was attended to according to the Covenants. The Lord made manifest to Joseph that it was necessary that such of the elders as were considered worthy, should be ordained to the high priesthood."[19] The minutes of the 1831 conference reported that "Brs. Lyman Wight John Murdock Reynolds Cahoon Harvey Whitlock & Hyrum Smith were ordained to the high Priesthood under the hand <of> br. Joseph Smith jr."[20] Ezra Booth, who was also ordained to the high priesthood but soon thereafter left the church, wrote in the fall of 1831: "Many of [the Mormonite preachers] have been ordained to the High Priesthood, or the order of Melchisedec; and profess to be endowed with the same power as the ancient apostles were."[21]

Still, at this very early period of the restoration the idea of a modern "order of Melchisedec" for Latter-day Saints was not understood as it is today. Instead, it appears that worthy men were selectively chosen and ordained to the high priesthood, which effectively meant ordination to the office of high priest. Citing an early November 1831 priesthood revelation,[22] William V. Smith, a Mormon scholar, noted: "The word 'priesthood' in the[se] early revelations was not the designator of a class of individuals or offices. It named an office."[23] Matthew C. Godfrey further described the priesthood: "Apparently [even] in 1832, the concept of priesthood, especially what the high priesthood was, was still nebulous among Church members, even though both the Bible and the Book of Mormon contained teachings about it."[24] Even so, Booth's 1831 comment points to an early connection between the high priesthood and the order of Melchizedek, suggesting that for Smith it seems to have been an early priority to cite the heritage of this ancient priestly order, whether or not the order itself was fully constituted as a class or group of modern priesthood holders. In 1831 this was not the case, but by 1835 it was.

Either way, at this early point in the restoration, the Book of Mormon's apparent influence on Smith's 1831 introduction of the high priesthood seems unmistakable; in all of scripture the term *high priesthood* is found only in the Book of Mormon. William Smith concluded, "Early Mormons saw the Book of Mormon version of high priesthood as the June 1831 'Joseph Smith' high priesthood."[25] In 1832 the high priesthood became more definitively associated with Melchizedek and with the order of Melchizedek. In March 1832 the Vision revelation (D&C 76) "emphasized that the high priesthood carried the name of Melchizedek," clarified Godfrey. "Those who inherited the celestial kingdom, the vision declared, were 'priests of the Most High, after the order of Melchizedek, which was after the order of Enoch, which was after the order of the Only Begotten Son'" (D&C 76:57).[26]

The second order, the Aaronic, appeared for the first time in a revelation dated September 22–23, 1832—as the "priesthood [of] Aaron and his seed" (D&C 84:18).[27] The September priesthood revelation marked a new plateau of understanding, though still an intermediate step in the Prophet's full understanding of the priesthood. According to Godfrey, it "traced the lineages of the two priesthoods, noting that the greater priesthood was held by Moses, who received it from a line of individuals (including Melchizedek) who ultimately had received it from God. Aaron, meanwhile, held the lesser priesthood, which passed to his descendants until it reached John the Baptist. As Joseph's translation of the Bible emphasized, both priesthoods were of an eternal nature (see D&C 84:6–27)."[28] The September revelation defined the Melchizedek as the "greater priesthood" and the Aaronic as the "lesser priesthood." By 1835 the Prophet would teach that the Aaronic was "an appendage to the greater, or the Melchisedek priesthood."[29]

Priesthood authority, offices, and orders

The ordinations to the high priesthood on June 3, 1831, are sometimes confused with what modern Latter-day Saints consider the restoration dates of the Aaronic Priesthood that took place on May 15, 1829, and the Melchizedek Priesthood in May/June 1829; these dates are well known in LDS missionary and teaching pedagogy. Of the Aaronic Priesthood, Smith recorded in his 1838 history:

> A Messenger from heaven, descended in a cloud of light, and having laid his hands upon us, he ordained us, saying unto us; "Upon you my fellow servants in the name of Messiah I confer the priesthood of Aaron. . . . The messenger who visited us on this occasion and conferred this priesthood upon us said that his name was John, the same that is called John the Baptist in the new Testament. . . . It was on the fifteenth day of May, Eighteen hundred and twenty nine.[30]

This Aaronic Priesthood account seems clear enough, but it is retrospective and recorded nine years after the event itself, reflecting a later, more evolved understanding of priesthood orders. Of the Melchizedek Priesthood, Smith recorded in his 1838 history: "The messenger who visited us on this occasion [May 15, 1829] and conferred this priesthood upon us [John the Baptist] said . . . that he acted under the direction <of> [apostles] Peter, James, and John, who held the keys of the priesthood of Melchisedeck, whi[c]h priesthood he said should in due time be conferred on us."[31] Historians later dated the apostolic visit of Peter, James, and John to be "late May or early June 1829—soon after the visit of John the Baptist."[32] What seems clear in retrospect, but may not have been completely clear to Smith or Cowdery at the time, is that the two seminal ordination events of May/June 1829 and then June 3, 1831, separated by about twenty-four months, addressed different yet distinctly important dimensions of the Melchizedek Priesthood.

In fact, the historical timeline of events suggests the restoration of three important priesthood dimensions in sequential order, each with its own distinct meaning: (1) priesthood *authority* to officiate in the rituals and ordinances of God—at first to baptize, and then separately to confer the Holy Ghost, restored by revelation in May and June 1829; (2) priesthood *offices* for those called to specific priesthood roles and responsibilities, restored by August 1829 and again in June 1831 with the high priesthood;[33] and (3) priesthood *orders* with specific authorities to officiate in different domains of the work of the Lord, outlines of which were beginning to emerge in September 1832.

Smith himself fused these three dimensions together in his later accounts of the priesthood restoration, leading in practice to various short forms or partial expressions of ordination that obfuscated the several essential meanings of ordination.[34] For example, William F. Cahoon recorded in his autobiography: "I was ordained a priest under the hands of Oliver Cowdery at a conference of elders held at the town of Orange, Ohio on the 25th October 1831."[35] William E. McLellin's confirmation of ordination to elder was even shorter: "And on the 24th [August 1831] I was ordained an Elder in The Church of Christ."[36] Both men were ordained very early in the restoration when the idea of priesthood orders was not well understood and was still missing from Mormon discourse. A later convert, Charles Henry Hales, gave a more complete statement: "I was ordained a priest in the Aaronic priesthood at conference held in Scarborough Township in December 1837."[37] Similarly, Lorenzo Brown recorded: "January 17, 1839. Brother Obed Crosby was ordained to the office of priest and myself as teacher, both offices pertaining to the lesser or Aaronic Priesthood."[38]

Much is to be gained by actually considering the historical meaning of each of the three dimensions separately. Merging any two of these dimensions leads to a loss of meaning and identity—for example, how is the meaning of priesthood orders uniquely different from the meaning of priesthood offices, or from priesthood *authority*? Very early in the restoration priesthood authority simply meant divine authorization to act in the name of God, without reference to priesthood based on Book of Mormon protocol and angelic visitations. Authority was then distributed or delegated via ordination to specific priesthood *offices* (for example, elder, priest, or teacher) without mention of priesthood order—but that began to change in the mid-1830s.

Religious *orders* usually refer to a fellowship, a brotherhood (or sisterhood in Catholic and Protestant orders), or a community of persons who are set apart from the world and devoted to common principles of religious service and devotion. Among early Mormons, members were set apart by ordination, but with a unique focus on authorities and rights to minister in different salvific rites and priesthood service responsibilities—referred to in the revelations as keys, which were dependent on the order to which one was ordained. The early September 1832 priesthood revelation with its deliberate identification of two priesthood orders also specified their different keys. "This greater priesthood [Melchizedek] administereth the gospel and holdeth the keys of the mysteries of the kingdom even the key of the knowledge of God therefore in the ordinances thereof the power of Godliness is manifest . . . for without this no man can see the face of God even the father and live."[39] This implied keys for officiating in the more transcendent forms of priesthood service such as temple worship (which was anticipated with the temples planned for Independence, Missouri, and then Kirtland, Ohio) and church governance (already a centerpiece of the November 11, 1831, revelation on the high priesthood). Of the Aaronic order the revelation explained: "which [Aaronic] priesthood holdeth the keys of the ministring of Angels and the preparatory gospel which gospel is the gospel of repentance and baptisam and the remission of sins."[40] These keys related to officiating in salvific rites and more visible expressions of religious devotion—baptism, the sacrament, faith, and repentance.

Nearly a century later, in 1919, LDS Church president Joseph F. Smith decided that the best model for priesthood ordination was the Prophet's original ordination to the Aaronic order, recorded in his history of 1838, involving a clear conferral of select authorities belonging to that priesthood order:

> Having laid his hands upon us, he [John the Baptist] ordained us, saying unto us; "Upon you my fellow servants in the name of Messiah *I confer the priesthood of Aaron,* which holds the keys of the ministring of angels and of the gospel of repentance, and of baptism by immersion for the remission of sins." . . . He said this Aaronic priesthood *had not the power of laying on of hands, for the gift of the Holy Ghost*, but that this should be conferred on <us> hereafter and he commanded us to go and be baptized, and gave us directions that I should baptize Oliver Cowdery, and afterward that he should baptize me.[41]

Note the distinctive separation of authorities by priesthood order. Even today, an LDS priesthood ordination includes all three formal and discrete elements: authority, priesthood order, and priesthood office. For example, a recent edition of the *Church Handbook of Instructions* prescribed the protocol for a typical priesthood ordination:

> The priesthood holder who performs the ordination:
>
> 1. Calls the person by his full name.
> 2. *States the authority* by which the ordination is performed (Aaronic or Melchizedek Priesthood).
> 3. *Confers the* [*order of the*] *Aaronic or Melchizedek Priesthood,* unless it has [previously] been conferred.
> 4. *Ordains the person to an office* in the Aaronic or Melchizedek Priesthood and bestows the *rights, powers, and authority* of that office. (Priesthood keys are not bestowed in conferring the priesthood or ordaining to one of these offices.)
> 5. Gives a priesthood blessing as the Spirit directs.
> 6. Closes in the name of Jesus Christ.[42]

What was the source for Smith's priesthood orders? We noted earlier William Smith's conclusion that the June 1831 "'Joseph Smith' high priesthood" was the same as that presented in the Book of Mormon, which itself was linked to Melchizedek.[43] Nonetheless there remained a fascination with Melchizedek and biblical orders in some marginal niches of eighteenth- and nineteenth-century Protestantism, and we see pockets of evidence of this in different places. For example, the eighteenth-century leader of the Seventh Day Baptists of Ephrata, Pennsylvania, was said to be "pre-ordained to be a priest after the order of Melchizedek."[44] And during the anti-Masonic activism of the 1820s in New York, ministers in Livonia (thirty-five miles from Palmyra) drafted a resolution in 1828 against "the order of Melchisedick [of Freemasonry], when Christ is the only priest after that order."[45]

The book of Hebrews in the New Testament likely inspired some of these modern Christian views of Melchizedek: "If therefore perfection were by the Levitical priesthood, (for under it the people received the law,) what further need was there that another priest should rise after the order of Melchisedec, and not be called after the order of Aaron?" (Hebrews 7:11).[46] Most Christians interpreted the new Melchizedek priest to be Christ. Melchizedek himself was originally mentioned in Genesis 14 as a biblical high priest and king of Salem, presiding over an order of priests ordained to the service of the Lord.[47] Adam Clarke, renowned Methodist theologian in the early 1800s, described the role of Melchizedek in the priesthood:

> Melchisedec had a priesthood more than four hundred years (422) before the law [of Moses] was given; and David prophesied, Psa. 110:4, that another priest should arise after the order of Melchisedec, nearly five hundred years (476) after the law was given. The law [of Moses], therefore, did not contain the original priesthood; this existed typically in Melchisedec, and really in Jesus Christ. . . . The order of Aaron being now abrogated, to make way for that which had preceded it, the order of Melchisedec.[48]

Nonetheless, for most nineteenth-century Christians, Melchizedek or Aaronic Priesthood referred only to historical constructs that had long since been done away with the advent of Christ and his apostolic priesthood. Historian Mark Staker maintained that Alexander Crawford, a Canadian Restorationist minister, expounded the idea in 1827 that historically there had been "three priesthoods: 'the patriarchal,' 'the Aaronical,' and a priesthood of Jesus Christ. Sometimes Crawford referred to these priesthoods in his writing as the 'order of Melchizedec,' the 'order of Aaron,' and the 'office as priest' of Jesus Christ."[49] Campbell articulated the same view with three different dispensations of religions—the Patriarchal, Jewish, and Christian ages of the world—a notable clarification of Crawford's view. According to Staker, "Campbell, influenced by Crawford, had little use for Judaism, early Israel, or anything connected to pre-Christian priesthood. Christian priesthood was a 'new priesthood' that grew out of Christ's ministry and had no relationship with the past."[50]

The influence of the Book of Mormon's Melchizedek order

Joseph Smith would have been aware of these ideas concerning Melchizedek that were circulating so close to home. Nonetheless, the evidence suggests that his formative thinking about priesthood in the early restoration gained impetus and clarity after the translation of the Book of Mormon in 1829. The clearest description of the Melchizedek order in the Book of Mormon comes from Alma's discourse to the people of Ammonihah, a sophisticated community of defecting Nephites that evidently had once included a high priesthood of an ancient American Melchizedek order.[51] Alma's careful exposition of what he calls priesthood ordination—which encompassed authority, office, office (calling), and order (high priesthood)—provided a conceptual blueprint for the Prophet's development of priesthood orders among the Latter-day Saints:

> This High Priesthood [was] after the order of [God's] Son, which order was from the foundation of the world. . . . Now they were ordained after this manner: Being called with a holy *calling*, and *ordained* with a holy ordinance, and taking upon them the High Priesthood of the *holy order*, which calling, and ordinance, and High Priesthood, is without beginning or end; thus they become High Priests forever, after the order of the Son of the only begotten of the Father. . . . Now as I said concerning the holy order of this High Priesthood: There were many which were ordained and became High Priests of God. . . . Yea, humble yourselves even as the people in the days of Melchizedek, who was also a High Priest after this same order which I have spoken, who also took upon him the High Priesthood forever. (See Alma 13:7–10, 14.)[52]

What is striking in this Book of Mormon passage is this original description of the Melchizedek Priesthood as the "high priesthood *after the order of the Son* [*Christ*]," and *not* the order of Melchizedek, as described in the book of Hebrews. In other words, Melchizedek entered into the priesthood order of the Son of God: "a high priest after this same order [of the Son] which I have spoken, who [Melchizedek] also took upon him the high priesthood forever." By contrast, biblical passages articulate precisely the opposite interpretation: that Christ became a member of the order of Melchizedek. For example, the well-known messianic Psalm 110 of David declared: “The Lord hath sworn, and will not repent, Thou [Messiah] art a priest for ever after the order of Melchizedek” (Psalm 110:4).[53] And the Epistle to the Hebrews in the New Testament articulated the same view: “So also Christ glorified not himself to be made an high priest; but he that said unto him, Thou art my Son, to day have I begotten thee. . . . Thou art a priest forever after the order of Melchisedec” (Hebrews 5:5–6).[54] Once again, the Book of Mormon thrust Christ into the center of theology, in this case priesthood theology.

So which version—biblical or Book of Mormon—seems to have influenced Smith’s early understanding of this Melchizedek Priesthood order? Not surprisingly, it appears to be the Book of Mormon variation, “priesthood after the order of the Son.” For example, when Smith began his retranslation of the Bible in June 1830 he inserted new textual material, including Genesis 14:27–28, which suggested that not only Melchizedek but also ancient prophet Enoch had been ordained to this holy order of the Son of God: “And thus having been approved of God he [Melchizedek] was ordained <~~a~~> a high Preist after the order of the covenent which God made with Enoch it being after the order of the Son of God. . . . And now Melchizedeck was a Priest of this order.”[55] Similarly, Smith’s early retranslation of Hebrews 7:3 read: “For this Melchizedek was ordained a priest after the order of the Son of God. . . . And all those who are ordained unto this priesthood are made like unto the Son of God.”[56]

Finally, in 1835 Smith’s revelation on priesthood showed his definitive understanding of priesthood orders, their author, and their origin:

> There are, in the church, two Priesthoods, namely: the Melchisedek, and the Aaronic, including the Levitical Priesthood. Why the first is called the Melchisedek priesthood, is because Melchisedek was such a great high priest: before his day it was called the holy priesthood, after the order of the son of God; but out of respect or reverence to the name of the Supreme Being, to avoid the too frequent repetition of his name, they, the church, in ancient days, called that priesthood after Melchisedek, or the Melchisedek priesthood.[57]

In sum, priesthood was organized and manifest fundamentally in priesthood orders and was centered in Christ as its eternal author, with Melchizedek as its great exemplar.

The influence of the Book of Mormon's high priest

Yet still another important indication of the Book of Mormon's influence was the office of high priest itself. In June 1831 Smith's introduction of the high priesthood restored the ancient office of high priest. High priests had long been part of Old Testament history. The presiding priest of the ancient Jerusalem temple was a high priest, and great Old Testament patriarchs were high priests: Melchizedek was "the great high priest and leader of the sons of heaven,"[58] according to Margaret Barker, and "Adam as the original high priest was a widely based and widely known temple tradition."[59] The New Testament affirmed that Christ himself was a high priest "after the order of Melchisedec" (Hebrews 5:6).[60] Nevertheless, what seems to have truly inspired Smith was the idea that in the restored priesthood there would be numerous high priests, an idea not visible in the biblical narrative.[61] In Smith's early restoration all worthy priesthood bearers could be ordained high priests like the great high priests of old—"it was the privilege of every Elder present to be ordained to the High priesthood [i.e., high priests],"[62] the Prophet proclaimed at a conference in October 1831. They would "be endowed with the same power as the ancient apostles,"[63] stated Booth. Bushman made this important observation, amended to more accurately reflect my thesis:

> Bible commentators generally concluded that only two men [were high priests of the order of Melchizedek]: Melchizedek and Christ. It was a messianic priesthood. . . . In [Smith's] expansion, Enoch received the [High] Priesthood [i.e., the office of high priest] along with Melchizedek and Christ. Moreover, the revision said, the high priesthood was to be bestowed on "as many as believed on his name." Far from being a messianic priesthood, all believers were to be ordained high priests, a presumptuous act from the viewpoint of Protestant scholarship. . . . They were all to become Enochs and

> Melchizedeks. . . . Joseph was trying to install them in the order of the Son of God, "to stand in the presence of God; to do all things according to his will."[64]

These teachings reflected a deep biblical heritage pointing back to the earliest periods of Israelite priesthood history, but parallels with high priests in the Book of Mormon are just as clear and uniquely influential. In Alma's church of Christ "there were *many* which were ordained and became High Priests of God" (see Alma 13:10);[65] they became "High Priests forever, after the order of the Son of the only begotten of the Father" (see Alma 13:9).[66] Melchizedek "was also a High Priest after this same order which I have spoken, who also took upon him the High Priesthood forever" (see Alma 13:14).[67] Alma's passage described the calling, ordination, mission, and qualifications of high priests; Melchizedek was the exemplar among high priests, but most of all he was a representative member of the order—the priesthood order of the Son of God.

The seminal Book of Mormon insights of the order of Melchizedek led Smith to dramatically reconstitute the leadership structure of the new church, to be defined in terms of priesthood orders rather than simply priesthood offices—for example, elders, apostles, and bishops. The governing leadership of the church became the presidency of "the Melchisedek priesthood, [with] three presiding high priests [the First Presidency]."[68] The leadership of geographic locales, such as stakes (similar to dioceses) in Kirtland, Ohio; Far West or Adam-ondi-Ahman, Missouri; or Nauvoo, Illinois, were stake presidencies with presiding high priests—quite similar to high priests Ammon and Giddonah that presided over Alma's regional churches in Jershon and Giddonah in the Book of Mormon narrative. This model of governance through priesthood orders contrasted with Catholic governance through priesthood offices, that is, bishops and archbishops, and with Protestant democratic governance through the pastoral priesthood of all believers.

The local Mormon bishopric, also consisting of three high priests,[69] were not merely pastoral officers in a congregation but were "the presidency of [the Aaronic] priesthood and [held] the keys, or authority of the same"[70] in the service of their congregation. An unspoken meaning underlying these concepts was the principle that, because priesthood orders were timeless, church governance through priesthood orders was timeless as well. The restoration of priesthood orders in the modern day was merely a restoration of the ancient and venerable archetypes used in governing God's people in the past, "governed by the same priesthood that Abraham, Melchisdedek, and the Apostles were,"[71] explained the Prophet.

Mormonism's early priesthood offices and hierarchy

In 1829 Smith and Cowdery instituted a priesthood hierarchy with four priesthood offices (disciple, elder, priest, and teacher) that became a foundation for the restoration of the church (shortly thereafter the office of disciple was changed to apostle). This initial selection of priesthood offices was virtually identical to that instituted by Christ in the ancient Americas as recorded in 3 Nephi of the Book of Mormon: disciple, elder, priest, and teacher. Like some Christian pastors of the nineteenth century, Smith and Cowdery sought a restoration of the ancient gospel of Christ and attracted many converts desiring the purest restoration of the apostolic church. Walter Scott of the Protestant restoration movement articulated: "The professors of our holy religion having unhappily strayed from the scriptures and true Christianity, there seemed to be no remedy in anything but a return to original ground . . . resembling, more or less, the churches planted by the Apostles, or the church of Jerusalem instituted by the Lord Jesus himself."[72]

The restoration among the Latter-day Saints, however, was different. Rather than look entirely to forms of the ancient New Testament church, Smith sought to find lost elements of the ancient church wherever they could be found in all ages of the world. In 1842, Smith recorded a revelation describing his inspiration as follows:

> For it is necessary in the ushering in of the dispensation of the fulness of times; which dispensation is now beginning to usher in, that a whole, and complete and perfect union, and welding together of dispensations and keys, and powers and glories should

> take place, and be reveal'd, from the days of Adam even to the present time; and not only this, but those things that never have been reveal'd from the foundation of the world; but have been kept hid from the wise and prudent; shall be revealed unto babes and sucklings, in this, the dispensation of the fulness of times.[73]

Thus, with the Book of Mormon translation before him, one accessible source was the church of Christ of the ancient Americas. In fact, the pattern of the restoration of priesthood offices suggests that the Book of Mormon was the Prophet's *earliest* source for priesthood restoration, and only later did he follow with priesthood restorations from the New Testament. The distinctions are subtle here, but meaningful.

For example, in 1829 Smith and Cowdery deferred a restoration of the priesthood offices of the New Testament church and instead chose first to restore the arrangement of ancient priesthood offices of the Nephite church of the Book of Mormon—disciple, elder, priest, and teacher—that had existed for centuries prior to the coming of Christ in ancient America. The New Testament, by contrast, variously mentions offices such as apostle, prophet, pastor, teacher, evangelist, elder, bishop, and deacon. "Alexander Campbell [Protestant restorationist leader] argued strongly that there were only two legitimate offices in the ancient church, bishop and deacon," noted Gregory Prince, "and that only these two offices should be present in the modern church."[74] Nonetheless, in Mormonism the offices of bishop and deacon of the New Testament church were added two years *after* the original Nephite priesthood offices, in 1831.[75]

Book of Mormon influences on priesthood offices

This ordering of events signaled essential distinctions in the Mormon interpretation of Christ's priesthood purposes at his coming in the meridian of time—and countered traditional assumptions about Christian priesthood. As illustrated earlier in this chapter with Campbell's views on the priesthood, for centuries Catholic and Protestant clergy had assumed that Christ brought a *new* gospel, with *new* ordinances and *new* priesthood. Paul seemed to intimate as much in writing to the Corinthians: "When that which is perfect is come, then that which is in part shall be done away" (1 Corinthians 13:10).[76] Pope Leo I (AD 440–461) made a similar argument: "Now a new and indestructible Temple has been erected [in Rome] . . . ordained in honor of Christ, the prophet after the order of Melchizedek, . . . not after the order of Aaron whose priesthood . . . ceased with the Law of the Old Testament."[77]

The Book of Mormon narrative, however, framed the priesthood events of the advent of Christ quite differently. For centuries prior to the appearance of the resurrected Christ, the ancient priesthood offices of elder, priest, and teacher had consistently met the needs of the Nephites. Then with Christ's coming to the ancient Americas, these venerable offices were not done away. They continued uninterrupted, though they were changed to reflect the reality of the church after the resurrection, for example, in the means of administering the sacrament, or Eucharist. The Book of Mormon thus defined the meaning of Christ's priesthood purposes at the meridian of time in a different light, as a restoration of ancient and noble priestly institutions whose rites had for centuries, even millennia, pointed to the centrality of Christ as the Messiah of sacred theology. Finally their priestly purposes would be fulfilled. Barker's central thesis, explained Dean Collinwood and James McConkie, was that "Jesus [was] a restorer of a religion that had been lost rather than . . . an inventor of something new."[78] Said Barker herself, "The gospel as it was first preached by Jesus, and as it was developed and lived by the early church, concerned the restoration of the true temple. This explains how Christian doctrine was able to develop so quickly; it was the expression of a long established set of beliefs in the light of the life and work of Jesus."[79] This, of course, is the thesis of this book: The early Mormon restoration developed quickly and definitively precisely because it was a restoration of ancient and familiar ways originating first in the Book of Mormon, but then inevitably evoking the early observances of biblical Israelite religion since the Book of Mormon peoples emigrated from historic Jerusalem in the sixth century BC.

One obvious difference appeared confusing very early in the restoration: the governing leadership of the church in 3 Nephi was twelve *disciples*, while Mormon converts were taught—during most of the nineteenth century and today—that the New Testament church had been led by twelve *apostles*. If both branches of Christ's church—one in Jerusalem and the other in the Americas—were inaugurated by Christ, then why the difference in leadership titles? Modern scholars suggest that in the earliest New Testament church in Jerusalem the term used to describe Christ's chosen twelve was more akin to *disciples*. Though appearing in the earliest New Testament writings of Paul as a missionary calling, the term *apostles* as a description of Christ's chosen twelve was likely a later development in the canonized New Testament Gospels. According to research by Taylor Petrey, "Neither Mark nor John calls the twelve as a group or any individual member of that group 'apostles' or 'apostle,' suggesting that the early independent traditions of John and Mark did not originally designate this group with a special title. Mark just calls these disciples the twelve"[80]—for example, "And he [Jesus] ordained twelve, that they should be with him, and that he might send them forth to preach" (Mark 3:14).[81]

The Book of Mormon's reference to the twelve disciples of the Nephite church thus appears to parallel the recent scholarly view of the early New Testament church, and in 1829 Smith and Cowdery appeared to have adopted the disciple model with reference to the highest leadership roles in the new church. But it is clear that over time they came to believe that the roles of disciple (from the Book of Mormon) and apostle (from the New Testament) were interchangeable, and they changed the designation to apostle.[82] Thus, in the early restoration, ordinations were made to teacher, priest, or elder, and some elders also received the office of apostle until the number of these elders/apostles reached twelve.[83] For example, John Whitmer's preaching license verified that "he is an Apostle of Jesus Christ, an Elder of this Church of Christ."[84] Prince continued: "Initially the term 'disciple' referred to those possessing this authority, but in late 1829 the term switched to 'apostle.' . . . Since the Book of Mormon spoke of twelve 'disciple/elders,' it appears that the total number of apostle/elders was initially limited to twelve. As growth required more administrative officers, additional elders were called [except] without the title of apostle."[85]

David Whitmer, nearly sixty years after witnessing and having been involved in the earliest priesthood ordinations,[86] lamented the church's departure from purely Book of Mormon priesthood offices, including the shift from *disciples* to *apostles*:

> As you know, the teachings of Christ are the same in the New Testament and in the Book of Mormon . . . but the teachings of Christ in the Book of Mormon are pure, plain, simple and full. Christ chose "twelve" [in the Book of Mormon] and called them disciples or elders, not apostles, and the "twelve" ordained elders, priests, and teachers. These are all the spiritual offices [necessary] in the Church of Christ, and their duties are plainly given.[87]

Nonetheless, a number of parallels seem apparent between roles of the New Testament twelve and the Book of Mormon twelve. For example, Jesus ordained the twelve in the Jerusalem church and imbued them with governing stewardship of church doctrines, ordinances, and priesthood. He did the same with the twelve disciples in the ancient Nephite church in the Americas. Of the lengthy instruction Christ gave the Nephites at the temple in Bountiful during his seminal visitation, nearly half (46 percent)[88] was directed formally and exclusively to the twelve as leaders of his new church.

Among the rights and roles given by Christ to the ancient American twelve disciples, at least seven appeared to be influential in priesthood governance patterns in the early restoration, including the twelve's duties as (1) presiding officers over priesthood authority—the two separate authorities relating to baptism and conferring the Holy Ghost; this likely included the right to delegate dissemination of priesthood authority to others (see Moroni 3:1); (2) stewards of sacred ritual and protocols, such as baptism, ordination, and sacrament; (3) interpreters and keepers of doctrinal integrity, for example, as Christ differentiated between what "is not my doctrine" (see 3 Nephi 11:30)[89] and what "is my doctrine. . . .

And whoso shall declare more or less than this, and establish it for my doctrine, the same cometh of evil" (see 3 Nephi 11:30, 40);[90] (4) official recorders of the scriptural canon (see 3 Nephi 23:7–14; 24:1), for example, "I command you that ye shall write these sayings after I am gone . . . that these sayings which ye shall write shall be kept and shall be manifested unto the Gentiles" (see 3 Nephi 16:4);[91] (5) eyewitnesses of the resurrected Christ: "Ye shall testify that ye have seen me, and that ye know that I am" (see 3 Nephi 12:2);[92] (6) keepers of sacred temple rituals, such as the Nephite endowment-like ritual, and custodians of the word-perfect preservation (see 3 Nephi 19:8) and replication of Christ's ritualized experiential instruction, prayer, and spiritual communion given during his visit at the Bountiful temple in the ancient Americas (3 Nephi 19); and (7) chief guardians of church identity charged with naming and defining the essence of the identity of Christ's church in ancient America, for example, "if it be called in the name of a man, then it be the church of a man; but if it be called in my [Christ's] name, then it is my church, if it so be that they are built upon my Gospel" (see 3 Nephi 27:8).[93]

This understanding of the Nephite twelve, along with the New Testament's apostleship, formed an essential scriptural foundation for priesthood governance in the restoration; this became increasingly apparent the same month the Book of Mormon translation was completed. A June 1829 revelation informed Cowdery and Whitmer that "I speak unto you, even as unto Paul mine apostle, for you are called even with that same calling with which he was called."[94] Later in 1829, while writing the "Articles of the Church of Christ," Cowdery confirmed, "Behold I am Oliver I am an Apostle of Jesus Christ by the will of God the Father & the Lord Jesus Christ."[95] In April 1830, one week before the church's formal organization, David Marks, a local preacher, wrote after visiting the Whitmers, "They further stated, that twelve apostles were to be appointed, who would soon confirm their mission by miracles."[96]

Then in a revelation marking the official organization of the new church, dated April 10, 1830, Joseph Smith "was called of God, and ordained an apostle of Jesus Christ, an elder of the church . . . also to Oliver Cowdery . . . who was also called of God, an apostle of Jesus

Christ, an elder of the church, and ordained under his hand."[97] Finally, on March 28, 1835, revelation confirmed the formal calling of "twelve travelling counsellors [who] are called to be the twelve Apostles, or special witnesses of the name of Christ, in all the world."[98] To this day members of the Quorum of the Twelve Apostles of the Church of Jesus Christ of Latter-day Saints are referred to by the title *Elder,* consistent with Book of Mormon practice in which the Nephite twelve "were called the elders of the church" (see Moroni 3:1),[99] but also reflecting New Testament protocol of referring to the New Testament twelve as "the apostles and elders" in Jerusalem (see Acts 15:2–6, 22–23; 16:4).

Priests and teachers in the Book of Mormon: Reflections of ancient Israel

Of all the priesthood offices of the early restoration, the two offices of priest and teacher held symbolic significance—almost as the DNA of early Mormon priesthood. Not only did these modern offices seem to be patterned after the Book of Mormon priesthood offices of the same name, but the book's history enables us to trace a pathway back in time to what appears to be a priesthood heritage quite similar to the ancient Israelite priesthood. Priests and teachers first appear in the Book of Mormon narrative at a key moment in history: the creation of the new Nephite nation in the early sixth century BC, the coronation of Nephi as first king, the founding of a new city of Nephi, and the construction of the first Nephite temple in the New World. Coinciding with these events, Nephi announced, "I, Nephi, did consecrate Jacob and Joseph, that they should be priests and teachers over the land of my people" (see 2 Nephi 5:26).[100]

What is the religious significance of these twin priesthood offices—priest and teacher—to the modern restoration, and why did they persist for a thousand years of Nephite history? The first clue to answering this question relates to their essential status as priesthood servants in community worship, as we see in the timing of the appearance of Nephite priesthood. The founding of priests and teachers in the ancient Americas appeared to be centered in the founding of the Nephite temple in the recently established Nephite nation, perhaps several decades after Lehi's people journeyed to and settled in the New World. Nephi described the new temple: "And I, Nephi, did build a temple; and I did construct it after the manner of the temple of Solomon, save it were not built of so many precious things: for they were not to be found upon the land; wherefore, it could not be built like unto Solomon's temple. But the manner of the construction was like unto the temple of Solomon; and the workmanship thereof was exceeding fine" (see 2 Nephi 5:16).[101]

If Nephi intended to replicate the Temple of Solomon in the New World of the Americas, then he also would have imported the same forms of worship as used in the Temple of Solomon. At the very center of Solomon's temple worship was Hebrew, or Israelite, priesthood; and the twin core offices of this priesthood were priests and Levites. In Jerusalem, priests officiated at the temple, interpreted the law, and governed congregations. Levites were charged with ministering with the priests in a supporting role in their service to the lay people of the congregation.

Could it be that Nephi restored replicas of these two Israelite priesthood offices in the ancient Americas with the Nephite offices of priest and teacher and then accessed a legacy of these Israelite offices essentially through the Book of Mormon? Let us look more closely at how these two core priesthood offices would have functioned in the community of the Nephites. I compare this to priesthood service in Jerusalem and at Solomon's temple to round out our understanding of what these priesthood offices might have borrowed from the Old World; Nephi remained as perhaps the lone Nephite survivor able to document Jerusalem priesthood culture in and around the Temple of Solomon. I then examine how Joseph Smith restored these priesthood offices and how their development evoked the models first of Book of Mormon priesthood service, which inevitably evoked a legacy of apparent ancient Israelite priesthood service. I begin first with the ancient models of priests.

Essential roles of priests under Nephi

In Nephite culture priests and teachers must have worked closely together as companion priesthood offices; evidently, though, the priests were the higher office. Nephi's brother Jacob wrote: "I, Jacob, and my brother Joseph, had been consecrated priests, and teachers of this people, by the hand of Nephi. And we did magnify our office unto the Lord, taking upon us the responsibility, answering the sins of the people upon our own heads" (see Jacob 1:18–19).[102] In Smith's translation of the Book of Mormon text, the priesthood title *teacher* is used, rather than the biblical title *Levite.* In ancient Jersualem only members of the tribe of Levi (which included both priests and Levites) were set apart by God for priesthood service. The Nephite people had no persons of Levite lineage among their founding colonists—Lehi was from the Israelite tribe of Manasseh (see Alma 10:3). Nevertheless, Nephi never explains his actions—whether the ordination to these offices was Levitical or not (clearly it was not); he acted in his new role as prophet-king to establish the ordained offices of priest and teacher to officiate among the people of Nephi and at the new temple of Nephi.[103]

As editor, Mormon never details the differences in commissioned responsibilities of priests versus teachers. Prince assumed that "responsibilities were common to the two offices,"[104] but I propose a different explanation. Instead, those acting in the two offices appear to have officiated alongside each other—similar to Levites ministering with priests in ancient Jerusalem. Indeed, a careful reading of the Book of Mormon text indicates that Jacob must have been ordained to the higher office of priest and Joseph to teacher.[105] We see this in the opening words of Jacob's temple speech in 2 Nephi 6–10, probably delivered at or near the time of Nephi's coronation,[106] thereby linking Jacob's priestly office with Nephi's kingship: "I, Jacob, having been called of God, and ordained after the manner of his holy order, and having been consecrated by my brother, Nephi, unto whom ye look as a king or a protector" (see 2 Nephi 6:2).[107]

John Welch researched the royal connection between priests and kings: "An essential part of the temple ascension of new potentates in the ancient world was to install temple priests and administrators who would rule under the new king. This consecration usually occurred at the temple."[108] Thus, in Jerusalem King David installed Abiathar as his chief priest. At David's death, King Solomon deposed Abiathar and installed Zadok as his chief priest of the Jerusalem temple (see 1 Kings 2:26–35). Similarly, just as in Jerusalem, one of King Nephi's earliest official acts was to install his brother Jacob as first priest, and therefore chief priest, in the city of Nephi and in the new temple of Nephi. As temple priest, Jacob likely would have officiated during Nephite ceremonial holy days; for example, Jacob's narrative on sin and atonement (Jacob 2–4) may have been part of Nephite observances of a form of the Israelite Day of Atonement, with Jacob officiating (see especially Jacob 2:2–3; 4:5, 11–12). King Nephi further charged Jacob with the priestly responsibility of being chief religious scribe and keeper of sacred texts and revelations: "Nephi gave me, Jacob, a commandment concerning the small plates, upon which these things are engraven. And he gave me, Jacob, a commandment that I should write upon these plates, a few of the things which I considered to be most precious . . . and that I should preserve these plates, and hand them down unto my [priestly] seed, from generation to generation" (see Jacob 1:1–3).[109]

Jacob not only was first chief priest among the Nephites, but his descendants continued the sacred priestly office by lineage. Over several centuries Jacob's descendants dutifully continued to write upon these small plates even as the Nephite nation slid into spiritual decline, always keeping the sacred trust of preserving and transmitting the priestly small plates record—before us today as the books of Jacob, Enos, Jarom, and Omni in the Book of Mormon.

Duties Nephite priests might have imported from the Temple of Solomon

So what priestly forms could the Nephite priests have imported from Jerusalem and from Solomon's temple of the Old Testament? Jerusalem priests in the First Temple (Solomon's temple) period were governed by the responsibilities set forth in the Blessing of Moses on the tribe of

Levi, recorded in the Deuteronomy 33:10: "They shall teach Jacob thy judgments, and Israel thy law: they shall put incense before thee, and whole burnt sacrifice upon thine altar" (Deuteronomy 33:10).[110] Beginning with the latter role, the priest's essential role related to rituals and ordinances, especially at the altar. "The priest's role began when . . . the blood [of an offering] had to be brought into immediate contact with the altar," noted Roland de Vaux, a historian of ancient Israel. "Similarly, it was always a priest who presented and who placed upon the altar that part of the sacrifice which belonged to God. . . . The priest was, then, in a very real sense, the 'minister of the altar.'"[111]

In addition to their service at the temple altar, priests also held the divine right to preside over teaching and over administrative judicial matters in the community or congregation, as specified in the Blessing of Moses. Moses Buttenwieser elaborated: "Throughout pre-exilic times the expounding of the Torah and the administration of justice remained the specific functions of the priests. [The Blessing of Moses] declares that the priests are the guardians of God's teachings and Law, and that it is their mission to teach God's judgments and Torah to Israel (Deut. xxxiii. 9, 10), while the Deuteronomic code decrees that all difficult criminal as well as civil cases be referred to the priests."[112]

Note the parallels of these ancient biblical priests with the Nephite priests—patterns hidden beneath layers of textual narrative but nonetheless present—for Nephite priests apparently had quite similar vital roles in teaching and preserving doctrinal integrity, administering ordinances, and judicial administration. For example, when King Benjamin of the second century BC "consecrated his son Mosiah to be a ruler and a king over his people . . . [he] appointed priests to teach the people, that thereby they might hear and know the commandments of God, and to stir them up in remembrance of the oath which they had made" (see Mosiah 6:3).[113] Later, "Alma, having authority from God, ordained priests; even one priest to every fifty of their number," and charged them to be stewards of doctrinal integrity: "And he commanded them that they should teach nothing save it were the things which he had taught, and which had been spoken by the mouth of the holy prophets" (see Mosiah 18:18–19).[114]

Priests handled judicial disputes for the king: "And Alma laid the case before their king, Mosiah. And Mosiah consulted with his priests" (see Mosiah 27:1).[115] Priests administered judicial discipline in the religious community, as when Zoramite members complained that "our priests . . . have cast us out of our synagogues, which we have labored abundantly to build, with our own hands" (see Alma 32:5).[116] And Book of Mormon priests officiated in ancient baptismal rites in Zarahemla (Alma 6:1–2), in Sidom (Alma 15:13), and after Christ's coming in Bountiful (3 Nephi 11:21–27). In summary, Book of Mormon priests had broad-ranging priesthood leadership roles among the community, resembling all three dimensions outlined in the Blessing of Moses: teaching, judicial, and sacred rituals. These long-held roles of priests provided a basic model for the essential defining characteristics of priests in the early restoration.

Essential roles of teachers under Nephi and Levites under Solomon

The same type of essential model for teachers in the Book of Mormon priesthood may also be present, for they too will become exemplars for the modern priesthood restoration. The role of teachers in the Book of Mormon likely parallels that of Levites in the Old Testament. The official priesthood actions of Nephi's brother Joseph as the first ordained teacher are never documented nor even mentioned. Instead, throughout Book of Mormon history the teachers seem to officiate in a support capacity, ministering in a subordinate role to the priests. In Alma's church in the second century BC, teachers first acted as protector or guardian against sin, under the direction of the priests: "Those who committed sin that was in the church . . . were brought before the priests, and delivered up unto the priests by the teachers; and the priests brought them before Alma, who was the high priest" (see Mosiah 26:6–7).[117] Second, they preached the word of God, but again in a support role to the priests who presided over doctrinal integrity: "Every Church [had] their priests and their teachers, and every priest preach[ed] the word according as it was delivered to him by the mouth of Alma" (see Mosiah 25:21).[118]

This passage implies that as teachers were involved in teaching and preaching, self-evident given their title, they did so under the auspices of the priests. During King Benjamin's reign teachers were also associated with the temple service, offering "sacrifice and burnt offerings, according to the law of Moses . . . and had appointed just men to be their teachers . . . who had taught them to keep the commandments of God" (see Mosiah 2:3–4).[119]

There was another role that the Nephite teachers probably imported from the Levites of Jerusalem and Solomon's temple that involved administration in the temple—this may not seem relevant to the development of Smith's early priesthood views, but in fact the pattern of teachers working alongside priests in the service of the congregation was a subtle but salient protocol that appears in the early restoration, which we will see in the next section. For example, in the Jerusalem temple the Levites served closely with, but in a supportive, subordinate role to the priests.[120] We see this when King David organized the priesthood for service in Solomon's temple before his death; he "gathered together all the princes of Israel, with the priests and the Levites . . . to set [forth] the work of the house of the Lord." His address to the Levites reveals their specific priesthood responsibilities:

> For by the last words of David the Levites were numbered. . . . Because *their office was to wait on the sons of Aaron [the priests]* for the service of the house of the Lord, in the courts, and in the chambers, and in the purifying of all holy things, and the work of the service of the house of God; both for the shewbread, and for the fine flour for meat offering, and for the unleavened cakes, and for that which is baked in the pan, and for that which is fried, and for all manner of measure and size; and to stand every morning to thank and praise the Lord, and likewise at even; and to offer all burnt sacrifices unto the Lord in the sabbaths, in the new moons, and on the set feasts, by number, according to the order commanded unto them, continually before the Lord: and that they should keep the charge of the tabernacle of the congregation, and the charge of the holy place, and the charge of the sons of Aaron their brethren, in the service of the house of the Lord. (1 Chronicles 23:27–32, emphasis added)[121]

If Nephi restored a replica of the priesthood service of Solomon's temple, along with the temple architecture discussed earlier, then the Nephite teachers probably performed temple duties similar to those performed by the Levites in their temple service: purifying, preparing, baking, frying, cleansing, and cleaning.[122] Most important, they would have provided these services in support of the priests of the temple.

Second, the Jerusalem Levites were fundamentally charged with teaching and preaching in the temple, in the synagogue, and in the community—again similar to the roles of the Nephite office of teacher. G. Ernest Wright of Harvard Divinity School described the foundational role of Levites as teachers:

> We have the persistent tradition in the O.T. that one of the chief functions of the Levites was the work of teaching and exposition. References to this function are to be found in Deut. xxxiii 10; 2 Chron. xvii 7–9; xxxv 3 and Neh. viii 7–9. Indeed, the legal work of the tribe of Levi was probably its most extensive and important function, especially when we note the breadth of meaning given to the word torah. Von Rad has recently called attention to this aspect of Levitical duty, and has made out an excellent case for the view that both Deuteronomy and the Holiness Code are examples of the expository teaching and preaching carried on by the Levites. Neither of these works is primarily a juridical document; it is instead a type of exposition which points to a history behind it and to a certain kind of personnel responsible for it.[123]

Wright, however, wondered why this Levite teaching role is given so little attention in the Old Testament; similarly, the Book of Mormon gives little attention to the role of teachers. Wright further suggested that since the religious record was kept by priests, it therefore centered mostly on priestly functions: "One may well wonder why it is that we do not hear more about such teachers. The answer would probably be that the O.T. literature concerned with Levites was, with the exception of Deuteronomy, mostly written by the Jerusalem priesthood [of temple priests], or by a Levite who was connected with the Jerusalem Temple in which Levites were assistants of the altar-clergy, guards, judges and musicians."[124] In the same way we may know little about Nephite teachers precisely because the Book of Mormon record was kept by priests and the kings and prophets they served under.

Yet the duties of the Levites were broader still than simply their central commission to teach and interpret the law. For example, according to the Old Testament, they were porters at the temple gates (1 Chronicles 26:13–19), stewards over the treasures of the house of God and the treasures of the dedicated things (1 Chronicles 26:20–28), officers and judges in all the business of the Lord and in the service of the king (1 Chronicles 26:29–30), as well as singers and musicians who should prophesy with harps, with psalteries, and with cymbals and the horn (1 Chronicles 9:33; 25:1, 5). The picture that emerges here is of Levites as respected teachers and sacred servants in the community and at the temple. It makes sense that we would see the same kind of status with regard to teachers in Nephite society.

Priests and teachers in the restoration

So how did Smith, Cowdery, and other early Mormon leaders utilize priests and teachers in the early restoration, and how did their roles compare to ancient Book of Mormon priesthood models, which themselves were likely derived from hidden ancient biblical models? In the early restoration the very first priesthood offices to be revealed to the Prophet were priests and teachers, specified in revelation in June 1829. The revelation was addressed to Cowdery and Whitmer, suggesting they were called to search out and find twelve disciples, who would then find and ordain priests and teachers—reflecting closely Book of Mormon protocol: "And behold you are they which are ordained of me to ordain priests and teachers to declare my gospel, according to the power of the Holy Ghost which is in you, and according to the callings and gifts of God unto men."[125]

The September 1832 revelation on priesthood orders (D&C 84), discussed earlier in this chapter, clarified the priest as the higher office in the lesser Aaronic Priesthood order: "<the> office of teachers and deacons are necessary appendages belonging to the lesser priesthood which priesthood [priest] was confirmed upon Aaron and his Sons."[126] Elders were also among the first priesthood offices to serve in the early restoration, so that the full complement of revealed priesthood offices—disciples, elders, priests, and teachers—matched precisely the priesthood offices of the Nephite church of Christ.

Elders served in a missionary outreach capacity to find new converts and build local church congregations or branches. Their revelatory commission of missionary outreach was defined in the 1829 "Articles of the Church of Christ," but note that this wording closely matched Christ's concluding missionary charge to the Nephite twelve before his final ascension (3 Nephi 27:20)—and later, Mormon underscored the importance of Christ's charge by quoting from it again at the end of the Book of Mormon record (Moroni 7:34). The missionary charge given to the elders of the early restoration—"& now I speak unto [the] Elders of the Church again Behold thus shall ye say repent all ye ends of the Earth & come unto me & be baptized in my name which is Jesus Christ & endure to the end & ye shall be saved"[127]—compares closely to the passages in 3 Nephi and Moroni.

While elders were traveling and finding new converts, priests and teachers were commissioned to stay behind and serve the congregation in the community. Priests were leaders of the congregation, and teachers ministered in a supporting role. Even the modern duties of the priests and teachers were patterned after the roles of the Book of Mormon priesthood—priests as ordained priesthood leaders were to govern the congregation, administer church ordinances, and oversee the priesthood; and teachers were to act as ordained priesthood emissaries, with a special commission to be protectors of the congregation. Their divine commissions were contained in the 1830 "Articles and Covenants of the Church of Christ" (see D&C 20), the successor document to Cowdery's 1829 Articles:

> The Priests' duty is to preach, teach, expound, exhort and baptize, and administer the Sacrament, and visit the house of each member, and exhort them to pray vocally and in secret, and also to attend to all family duties; and ordain other Priests, Teachers, and Deacons, and take the lead in meetings. . . .

> The Teachers' duty is to watch over the Church always, and be with them, and strengthen them, and see that there is no iniquity in the Church, neither hardness with each other, neither lying nor back-biting nor evil speaking; and see that the Church meet together often, and also see that all the members do their duty.[128]

In David Whitmer's mind, with the restoration of these essential Book of Mormon offices in 1829, the restoration of the church of Christ from its original presentation in 3 Nephi had been fulfilled; the restored church was now complete and had commenced its latter-day mission:

> In August, 1829 . . . [t]he following six Elders had then been ordained: Joseph Smith, Oliver Cowdery, Peter Whitmer, Samuel H. Smith, Hyrum Smith, and myself. The Book of Mormon was still in the hands of the printer, but my brother, Christian Whitmer, had copied from the manuscript the teachings and doctrine of Christ, being the things which we were commanded to preach. We preached, baptized and confirmed members into the Church of Christ, from August, 1829, until April 6th, 1830, being eight months in which time we had proceeded rightly; the offices in the church being Elders, Priests and Teachers. . . . There were six elders and about seventy members before April 6th, and the same number of elders and members after that day.[129]

As the church began forming congregations, or branches, it turned its attention to ordaining priests and teachers to provide basic priesthood service—often with priests presiding (in some branches an elder might preside, or later even a high priest). In essence, however, priests and teachers were the bulwark priesthood servant-leaders to the congregation in the community. The broader pattern observed here is indistinguishable from Alma's Book of Mormon model in which traveling elders "went forth from city to city, and from one house of worship to another, establishing churches, and consecrating priests and teachers throughout the land" (see Alma 23:4).[130]

We see this pattern with one of the church's earliest branches in New York, the Colesville Branch, when its first stalwart leaders were

Fig. 23. Hyrum Smith, Joseph's older brother, was ordained an elder in 1829, a priest in 1830, and a high priest in 1831.

specifically ordained priests. Hyrum Smith—loyal brother to the Prophet, one of eight witnesses testifying to have handled the Book of Mormon plates, and one of the original six members of the church at its founding April 6, 1830—was ordained to the office of priest on June 9, 1830[131] (he previously had been ordained an elder in 1829 prior to the church's official inauguration on April 6, 1830). As a priest Hyrum was then called to preside over the Colesville Branch with approximately nineteen members.[132] In September 1830, Newel Knight, a long-time friend of the Prophet and the first person baptized in Colesville (in May 1830), was ordained a priest and sometime thereafter also called to preside over the Colesville Branch, alongside Hyrum for a time and then alone.[133] At the same time Newel's uncle Hezekiah Peck likely served as an ordained teacher in the branch.[134]

We see a similar pattern in the Manchester Branch in New York. Martin Harris—one of three witnesses to testify of a personal manifestation of Moroni displaying the Book of Mormon plates, scribe during the early translation, and financier of the Book of Mormon's publication—was ordained a priest, also on June 9, 1830, and appears to have been a priesthood leader in the Manchester Branch. He was called to lead the exodus of the Manchester congregation to Kirtland in May 1831.[135] The Prophet's father, Joseph Smith Sr., was also an ordained priest in the Manchester Branch.[136] William Smith, brother of the Prophet, was an ordained teacher in Manchester.[137]

We see another example of this priest-teacher congregational stewardship model again in the minutes of a "general conference held on Damond's creek, Calloway County, Kentucky, Sept. 2,1836," in which Apostle Thomas B. Marsh presided with several apostles present. Since Marsh and his fellow apostles were "about to leave this region of country," Marsh delivered his departing instructions to the priests and teachers, mostly addressing their administrative and judicial duties:

> A short address was delivered from the chair [Marsh], showing the necessity of there being kept by the Tennessee conference, a church record of all names belonging to the several branches of said conference, and also a record of all the proceedings of all courts and çonferences held within the bounds of said conference. And that a clerk should be chosen, or appointed, by this conference, to keep the records, and be a standing clerk while the church should remain in this region. And also, that the priests and teachers bring from their several branches, the names of such as had been added since the last conference &c. agreable [agreeable] to the articles and covenants."[138]

In fact, this priest-teacher model of congregational priesthood service was used widely throughout the church during the early years of the restoration. In England, Heber C. Kimball recorded in fall 1837 that priests and teachers were ordained to officiate side by side in local supervision of newly organized church branches in Preston, England: "We divided the Church into several branches and ordained priests and teachers to preside over them. Thursday evening was appointed for prayer meetings to be held in different parts, and on Sundays for the whole church [all church branches] to assemble in the Cock Pit [a rented hall in Preston], when the Sacrament was administered, and such instructions given, as were thought necessary, for their spiritual prosperity and advantage."[139]

We even see statistical evidence of the priest-teacher model in the church's European mission program—especially calling more priests to provide backbone congregational priesthood service, assisted by teachers and then deacons. This was notably evident in England, where only a decade after the church's organization British membership growth was greater than in America. On July 6, 1840, Brigham Young recorded: "I attended a general conference of the Church in Britain, in the Carpenter's Hall . . . Elder P. P. Pratt, President; William Clayton, Clerk. There were represented 41 branches, comprising 2,513 members, 56 elders, 126 priests, 61 teachers and 13 deacons. Increase the last three months, 842 members, 22 elders, 74 priests, 23 teachers and 5 deacons."[140] On average, according to Young's census, there were 61 members per branch, serviced by 3 priests and 1 teacher per branch, and 1 deacon in every 3 branches.

Less than a year later, Parley P. Pratt recorded in his autobiography a similar emphasis on the number of priests utilized for British priesthood service: "On the 6th of April, 1841, the Council of the Twelve assembled at Manchester [England], in the Carpenter's Hall, for the first time to transact business as a quorum, in the presence of the Church in a foreign land. . . . The representations of the Churches and conferences throughout the kingdom were then called for. The total numbers of which were as follows: 5,814 members; 136 elders; 303 priests; 169 teachers; and 68 deacons, besides about 800 souls who had emigrated to America during the year, who were not included in this representation."[141]

The commission to priests and teachers in the early restoration

Given the priests' scriptural mandate for sacrament service in the early restoration, we should expect to see many historical accounts documenting priests administering the sacrament. Surprisingly, this is not the case, which may seem curious to modern observers given the visible practice in the modern LDS Church of young priests officiating in the sacrament. What appears more common in the historical record are accounts of sacramental administration by various prominent church officials, and frequently elders. For example, at a priesthood leadership meeting on March 30, 1836, just after the dedication of the Kirtland Temple, the First Presidency personally administered the sacrament. What is relevant to our thesis of Book of Mormon influence is to note that they followed exactly the protocol of Christ's first sacrament administration at the Bountiful temple as recorded in 3 Nephi. Christ first gave the sacramental emblems to the twelve disciples, who then distributed the emblems to the congregation.

> The [First] presidency, the 12 [apostles], the seventies, the high ~~co<u>ncils~~ councils, the Bishops and their entire [Aaronic Priesthood] quorums, the Elders, and all the official members in this [Kirtland] stake of Zion amounting to about 300 met in the [Kirtland] temple of the Lord. . . . [M]essengers were dispatched for bread and wine. . . . [T]he bread <& wine> was then brought in, and I [Joseph Smith] observed that we had fasted all the day, and lest we faint; as the Saviour did [with the Nephites at Bountiful] so shall we do on this occasion, we [the First Presidency] shall bless the bread and give it to the 12 [apostles] and they to the multitude, after which we shall bless the wine and do likewise.[142]

According to the Prophet's personal writings, several days later, on Sunday, April 3, 1836, "T. B. Marsh [Thomas B. Marsh] & D. W. Patten [David W. Patten] spoke in the A.M. to an attentive audience of about 1000 persons. In the P. M. he [Joseph Smith] assisted the other Presidents in distributing the elements of the Lords Supper to the church, receiving them from the ~~Hands~~ 'Twelve' [apostles] whose privilige it was to officiate in the sacred desk this day."[143]

This does not mean that priests and teachers were not involved at all in the sacrament, but rather that their sacramental involvement in various small branches throughout the world probably went unnoticed in most official church records. The sacrament was a rite observed so frequently, and particularly in Mormonism so simply, as to be otherwise unremarkable in the episodic diaries of church leaders. For example, Brigham Young recorded in his diary that on Sunday March 17, 1839, "I held a meeting with the brethren of the Twelve and the members of the Church in Quincy, Illinois. . . . We broke bread and partook of the sacrament."[144] On Sunday, June 30, 1839, he noted: "I met with the church in Montrose, and we partook of the Sacrament."[145] In eleven references to the sacrament in Young's diary, he never mentioned *who* administered the sacrament, only that it occurred. Also, those whose records, journals, and diaries were preserved in church repositories were mostly prominent church officials who recorded their noteworthy achievements and faith-promoting experiences as they traveled from land to land, state to state, and conference to conference. We see much less of local church affairs in small branches such as Colesville or Manchester, New York, or, say, Warrensville, Ohio.

However, modern revelation gave priests and teachers another specific mandate in the modern church that evoked the Book of Mormon's commission to priests and teachers (similar to the biblical charge to priests and Levites) to be spiritual guardians and protectors of the congregation in the community. According to the 1830 "Articles and Covenants of the Church of Christ" (D&C 20), the priests' duty is to "preach, teach, expound, exhort . . . and visit the house of each member. . . . The Teachers' duty is to watch over the Church always, and be with them, and strengthen them, and see that there is no iniquity in the Church, neither hardness with each other, neither lying nor back-biting nor evil speaking."[146]

This charge was followed quite diligently. For example, the church periodical *Millennial Star*, published in the nineteenth-century, offered this imperative to priests and teachers:

> But the system to which we refer as established in the Church of Christ to preserve the Saints from evil, is that of sending Priests and Teachers to visit the houses of members and converse with them and find out their spiritual condition. If Priest and Teachers were to discharge the duties of their office, according to the revelations which have been given upon this subject, Latter-day Saints would almost be a perfect people. . . . Every Priest or Teacher who visits the houses of the Saints, according to the command of the Lord, should endeavor to get the spirit of his office and to talk to those whom he visits under its influence. He should endeavor to find out everything connected with the lives of the family by the searching power of the Spirit of God, and to give them instructions according to those things which are brought to light.[147]

From the earliest days of the restoration there appears to have been a particular emphasis on this spiritual guardian role of priests and teachers. In a well-known LDS account, William F. Cahoon, an eighteen-year-old priest, tells of visiting Joseph Smith's home as an ordained teacher in late 1831:

> Being young, only about seventeen [eighteen] years of age . . . I went to his [the Prophet's] door and knocked, and in a minute the Prophet came to the door. I stood there trembling, and said to him, "Brother Joseph, I have come to visit you in the capacity of a teacher, if it is convenient for you." He said, "Brother William, come right in, I am glad to see you; sit down at that chair there and I will go and call my family in." They soon came in and took seats. He then said, "Brother William, I submit myself and family into your hands," and then took his seat. . . .
>
> [At the conclusion of the visit the Prophet] said, "God bless you, Brother William; and if you are humble and faithful, you shall have power to settle all difficulties that may come before you in the capacity of a teacher." I then left my parting blessing upon him and his family, as a teacher, and took my departure.[148]

Just before Brigham Young's death in 1877, his last conversation with his counselor in the First Presidency, George Q. Cannon, focused on this congregational guardian role: "His great anxiety seemed to rest on the necessity of a more thorough Visitation of every member of the Church by the Priests and Teachers."[149]

The revelatory mandate of teachers as protectors against iniquity was especially vivid. William Hartley discussed their role:

> In 1834 and 1835, the Missouri teachers quorum tackled a variety of tasks that required adult abilities: two labored with a brother having a tobacco problem, one worked with a couple having domestic difficulties, two tried to settle a dispute about steers, one labored with a person "for lying and extortion," and one took a deacon along to "settle a quarrel" among three "housewives." . . . A contemporary analogy said elders "quarried the stone" and sent it to Zion, where Aaronic Priesthood bearers "polished" it. In February 1838 the Missouri high council recommended that each neighborhood "choose for themselves a teacher, who is skilled in the work of God, faithful in his ministry, full of the Holy Ghost, and a friend to Joseph Smith . . . to take the watch-care over them and preside . . . who shall be assisted by the other teachers and deacons in the branch."[150]

The evolution of priests and teachers in the restoration

Over time the priest-teacher congregational stewardship model of the early restoration became increasingly strained. Adult men had always comprised the Aaronic Priesthood quorums of priests, teachers, and deacons (which were added in 1831), but the advent of the Nauvoo temple endowment in the 1840s required that men be ordained elders in the Melchizedek Priesthood for temple worship. As the Aaronic Priesthood quorums diminished in size the church called Melchizedek Priesthood men to be acting priests, teachers, and deacons. In 1849 Brigham Young "formally requested that leading brethren, including 'the best high priests, the most substantial men,' act in the lesser priesthood."[151]

Meanwhile, beginning in Nauvoo in the 1840s, bishops increasingly assumed more complete congregational leadership responsibility over local wards, including directing the work of priests, teachers, and deacons per their scriptural mandate of 1835 to preside over the

Aaronic Priesthood. After the Mormon settlement of the West, "the bishops, who often served for life, were temporal and spiritual leaders. They filled roles resembling those of pastor, constable, judge, arbitrator, foreman, and mayor. For assistants they had [bishopric] counselors and local Aaronic Priesthood bearers."[152] Surprisingly, during this period the prominence of teachers increased because of their congregational guardian and protector mandate:

> The basic ward officers for the pioneer Utah period were the bishopric and the teachers' quorum, then called block teachers or ward teachers. Under direction of the bishop, teachers visited members in their homes, settled disputes, and helped the needy. Teachers and bishoprics heard charges of wrongdoing and decided guilt or innocence. Bishops, as Church judges, conducted inquiries regarding sin and held bishops' courts, if necessary, to excommunicate, disfellowship, or exonerate. During the reformation (LDS) of 1856–1857, bishops and teachers saw to the catechizations interviews, and rebaptism of members.[153]

Priests, meanwhile, "were the primary visiting watchmen, assisted by the teachers. But in practice priests operated as regular teachers and usually met with [the] teachers quorum."[154] As it became increasingly difficult to find older men to act as teachers to serve in the ward, some bishops turned to calling young men and boys "ranging in age from ten to their twenties."[155] Because this involved the problem of "asking boys to do men's work,"[156] other bishops resisted. Nonetheless, the First Presidency in 1877 established an apprentice policy that "the experienced priest or teacher should have as a companion a young man, so that the latter may have the opportunity of learning the duties of his calling."[157] Finally, in 1908, responding to President Joseph F. Smith's call to give boys "something to do that will make them interested in the work of the Lord," the church adopted fixed age groups for Aaronic Priesthood ordinations: age twelve for deacons, fifteen for teachers, eighteen for priests, and twenty-one for elders.[158]

In 1916 the church formally proposed a master list of Aaronic Priesthood duties. The priests' duties were essential in the Mormon community: "Administer the sacrament, including taking it to the infirm who are not able to attend meeting; assist in ward teaching, act as Sunday school officers and teachers, act as Mutual officers and teachers, perform the ordinance of baptism, . . . act as messengers for bishopric, hold cottage meetings, assist the elders, do missionary work in the ward, . . . supervise the collection of fast offerings, help bishop to take care of tithes."[159] The teachers' duties were more complementary and supportive: "Assist in ward teaching; assist with the sacrament, and seeing that the [sacrament] service is in order; become instructors for boy scouts; collect ward funds; take charge of meetings now and again and furnish speakers, singing, etc., . . . act as officers in Sunday school; help clerk of branch; serve as choir members; serve as ushers in gatherings, and as order monitors."[160]

Indeed, viewing these 1916 Aaronic Priesthood protocols and looking back in time, we can see that, though in a modern context, the essence of Book of Mormon priesthood service is present. Because of its apparent legacy from ancient Jerusalem through Lehi and Nephi, this service was reminiscent of the Old Testament priesthood service models of priests and Levites as given in the original Blessing of Moses on Levi—of teaching, administration and judging, and administering the ordinances of God. Certainly, it appears that Joseph Smith and his early restoration leaders attempted to replicate the Book of Mormon models of priesthood in 1829 with fair fidelity. The restoration of New Testament offices in the church in 1831—that of deacon, but particularly that of bishop with its innovative calling as presiding officer of the (Old Testament's) Aaronic Priesthood—affected the congregational leadership mandate of priests and teachers, but their priesthood service responsibilities remained unaffected. What did change over the remainder of the century was not so much the roles or responsibilities of the Aaronic Priesthood but the continued concern over staffing—finding qualified, worthy priests, teachers, and deacons to serve the priesthood needs of the growing church.

Once again, this brings us back to familiar themes with the Book of Mormon and its influence on Joseph Smith's priesthood innovations. The protocols behind Smith's innovations often were inspired by Book of Mormon models and meanings, but because of the Book of Mormon's own origin in the Judeo-Israelite religious milieu of Jerusalem, his innovations often reflected early biblical narratives. As if to stress that religion is rarely new, but instead is marked by periods of renewal and restoration, Smith restored the ancient Melchizedek and Aaronic Priesthood orders in 1831–1832, the Book of Mormon and New Testament priesthood offices from the ancient church of Christ in 1829–1831, and the enduring legacy of the priesthood service of priests and Levites of Moses. For these last offices he drew not from the Old Testament but from the priests and teachers of the Book of Mormon, replicating even the titles of these official Book of Mormon priesthood offices. As we have seen, Book of Mormon priesthood models were not adopted as an exact template but rather as a foundational platform from which to build useful and relevant priesthood roles of service in the modern restoration.

6

The Meaning of the Book of Mormon in the Early Restoration

WE CONCLUDE OUR EXPLORATION into one of the defining paradoxes of the Mormon restoration of the nineteenth century—that between Joseph Smith and the Book of Mormon. My research suggests that this relationship between modern prophet and the ancient scripture he recovered is in fact complex and intricate, often imperceptible on the surface of official church history or prophetic discourse. Though often portrayed as being derivative from Joseph Smith, the Book of Mormon appears to have had a profound formative impact on his doctrinal and institutional development during the nascent days of the Mormon restoration. This finding alone frames the Book of Mormon in a different light and recommends new avenues of exploration and scholarship—both within Mormonism and without. "[The Book of Mormon] contributes little to LDS ritual (aside from the wording of sacramental prayers)," averred Grant Hardy, "even though its narratives are central to the religious experience of adherents."[1] Yet the findings of this book suggest deeper correlations between Book of Mormon ritual expression and meaning and modern Mormon ritual expression, especially with regard to baptism, the sacrament, and the meaning of temple worship in the postresurrection era that are distinct from purely biblical interpretations.

For others, Smith's relationship with the book—indeed, his vital reliance upon Book of Mormon forms and observances for religious development—recommends a more nuanced consideration of the book itself, not merely as a religious text but as a repository of ancient religious conventions such as institutions, theologies, rites, ordinances, and rituals. Similar to Hardy's landmark study of the Book of Mormon "as literature—a genre that encompasses history, fiction, and scripture"[2]—my work here explores the Book of Mormon in a novel way: It identifies the ideas and institutions of the Book of Mormon text that Smith himself judged to be distinctive, valuable, and beneficial to his work in the early restoration. It then places a spotlight focus on the constitution of those ancient religious forms, their presentation, history, provenance, and correlations with other known scripturally documented forms and then connects them to their parallel expression in the restoration in the modern church.

In fact, Joseph Smith did use the Book of Mormon even in some of his most significant sermons and appearances, but in so doing he sensed that he walked a tightrope between acceptance and derision. His purpose implicitly seems to have been to establish in the minds of his listeners that the Book of Mormon was scripture, quietly asserting comparable equivalence to the Bible. He, and indeed many of his listeners, referred to the Book of Mormon loosely in biblical terms, as the *Mormon Bible* or the *Golden Bible.* The account of his speaking before a group of Washington dignitaries in February 1840 is revealing:

> Joseph Smith ("Jo Smith" as known to fame) has held one or two meetings here [Washington, DC]. . . . The Prophet, or inspired penman, (whichever title he prefers, for he averred to the meeting that he was inspired to write the golden Bible, or the "Book of Mormon," a copy of which he held in his hand,) is a stout, square-built man of about thirty or thirty-five years of age, of prepossessing manner, and look, and shrewd mind. . . . He quotes from the New Testament readily in his addresses. He took good care, as there was an intelligent congregation, including several members of congress, present, to say but little about the "Book of Mormon." He averred, however that nobody wrote it but him, and that it contained nothing contrary to the Bible, or its virtue.[3]

Smith prudently avoided saying very much at all about the Book of Mormon on this occasion and certainly did not quote from its contents—a provocation he likely sensed would have risked contention, scorn, ridicule, and his very reputation among those governing elite he had traveled nearly a thousand miles to meet. Instead he quoted from the New Testament; the writer of the Washington account underscored the wisdom of Smith's approach, for he was speaking to "an intelligent congregation, including several members of congress." Of course Smith knew, as any intelligent person knew, that the Bible, whose stories and narratives provided the truest metaphors for virtuous living, was the most broadly embraced book of scripture in the Western world, the foundation of Western religion, and the divine inspiration of modern democracy. The Book of Mormon might aspire to a similar standing, but any reasoned observer among Smith's nineteenth-century audiences—Mormon or not—would have known that such a comparison would be viewed by most as incredible, implausible, and unbelievable. Even his actions during his Washington speech reflect the reality of this tacit tension between new and old: He held the new book of scripture, the Book of Mormon, in his hand, but he never opened it, taking "good care . . . to say but little about [it]." The old book of scripture, the Bible, he never held—but quoted it verbatim from memory. Nonetheless, both books were conspicuously present in the same public forum—as scripture.

Still, if the biblical religious milieu of the nineteenth century affected Smith's public use of the Book of Mormon, the book's manifest identity as ancient scripture seems to have influenced how he approached its content. To Smith the Book of Mormon was historical—concrete, tangible, grounded, and existential—and from this historical narrative emerged the revelatory, visionary, and theological impulses that defined its identity as a sacred text. "Most recent sacred texts consist of doctrinal expositions, ritual instructions, moral codes, scriptural commentary, or devotional poetry," declared Hardy. "The Book of Mormon, by contrast, is narrative—a much rarer genre of religious writing—and for examples of canonized sacred history one would have to look to previous millennia and writings such as the Christian Gospels, the historical portions of the Hebrew Bible, Buddhist Jataka stories, or Hindu Puranas and epics such as the Mahabharata and the Ramayana."[4]

Learning from the Prophet's schooling

We have documented carefully Joseph Smith's relationship with the book of scripture that commenced his legacy as a nineteenth-century leader of American religion. Scholars have studied the impact of the Book of Mormon as a sign of Smith's prophethood—the miraculous account of ancient gold plates recovered from the ground by divine assistance from an angel. We now fill in an important space on an incomplete canvas that has been missing for nearly two centuries. To conclude that the Book of Mormon did indeed influence the Prophet is a beneficial contribution, but this would be an understatement. The Book of Mormon—with its depth and breadth—influenced the theological DNA for the church's first formal statement of doctrine (the "Mormon Creed") articulated in the "Articles and Covenants of the Church of Christ" in 1830. It provided a tangible vision and theology of Zion with an American New Jerusalem and a scriptural heritage anchored in the New World. It defined the meaning of Christ-centered temple worship in a postresurrection world where altar sacrifice was replaced with endowed instruction and communion with Christ as seen in the Nephite endowment.

Especially valuable to Smith's doctrinal development was the portrayal in the Book of Mormon of two contrasting periods of the church of Christ in the New World, perfectly straddling the meridian of time. Alma's church of Christ of 150 BC offered a portrait of Christian religion *before* the birth of Christ. Then Nephi's church of Christ, inaugurated at the coming of Christ to the New World, revealed a transformed Christian religion *after* the resurrection of Christ. Alma's church was a forerunner to the coming of Christ to the New World anciently; it thus offered to Smith a prophetic metaphor that his latter-day church might similarly become a forerunner for the apocalyptic coming of Christ at the end of days. The before/after historical contrast also suggested other insights—for example, that baptism was not merely a New Testament innovation instituted by Christ, which was broadly assumed by most of Christianity, but was a timeless ritual that had disappeared into the scribal shadows of Old Testament history. Christ therefore was a restorer of baptism during his ministry in Jerusalem.

Notice too that the Book of Mormon became a seminal resource to the Prophet on different levels. At a clearly visible level, it provided a noticeable repository of New World prophecies, doctrines, and liturgical rites that were instantly accessible, tangible, and concrete, yet were novel with distinctive facets and nuanced meanings. We saw this, for example, in the unique resurrection emphasis of Christ's introduction of the sacrament in the Book of Mormon, with its distinctive covenantal sacramental language in 3 Nephi: "And this shall ye do in remembrance of my holy body, which I have shewn unto you" (see 3 Nephi 18:7),[5] compared to the New Testament: "This is my body which is given for you: this do in remembrance of me" (Luke 22:19).[6]

On a more subtle level, the Book of Mormon opened a trove of theological insights that carried the Prophet deep into religious history. Many Book of Mormon prophecies, rituals, and doctrines were not exclusive to ancient American religion; they appeared connected to the traditions and heritage of ancient Israelite religion going back millennia into Israelite history. This relationship was evident in the Book of Mormon's presentation of the Melchizedek Priesthood order with its brotherhood of many high priests or in the ascension theology of Adam and the Garden of Eden narratives that evoked the ancient Wisdom traditions, which have been documented by scholars as appearing during the period of the ancient Temple of Solomon or even earlier. These connections are remarkable in and of themselves, but they provided new and deep avenues of prophetic meaning and direction to the Prophet.

These examples, and others cited in our exploration, suggest the notion of provenance in the Book of Mormon—its uninterrupted religious lineage that traces back in time to early prophetic narratives and worship forms captured anciently by original scribes, editors, and redactors. Rituals, theologies, and doctrines of the early restoration seem to stem directly from Book of Mormon worship forms, which in turn seem to have clear correlations with ancient Old Testament rites, rituals, forms, and meanings. The problem of a nineteenth-century explanation of the Book of Mormon text in which Smith wrote the Book of Mormon as his own repository of religious ideas, innovations, and writings—like John Wesley's Articles of Religion and their codification into the Methodist *Book of Discipline*—is that it ignores the work's historic origins. A similar problem arises if an art historian were to admire the image but ignore the religious origins and sacred meanings behind Michelangelo's *Creation of Adam* painted on the ceiling of the Sistine Chapel. Provenance is evidence of historic origin, authenticity, and timeless value in a work.

A frequently recurring pattern in Smith's newly emerging church is the fairly rapid introduction of religious forms—such as the offices of elders, priests, and teachers or the protocols for baptism and the sacrament. The establishment of these forms appeared in June 1829—the same month the Book of Mormon translation was completed. This was but one year after Smith's first formal revelation in July 1828, yet nearly a year before the church's formal inauguration in April 1830.

Remarkably, these innovations appeared not only quickly, but distinctively—that is, their forms and their presentations were uniquely different from the current, competing Christian orthodoxies. In some cases their presentation remained surprisingly constant over time, even to the present day—for example, with baptism or the sacrament of the Lord's Supper. This suggests that these early innovations were not entirely new. They were not simply the product of new and spontaneous revelation, nor did they appear as an amalgamation of neighboring Christian protocols. Instead, as we have seen, they appear to have been sourced, derived, and adapted from earlier forms that Smith and his associates had so recently discovered in the Book of Mormon narrative. With the completion of the translation in June 1829, and then the careful preparation of the printer's manuscript later the same year, these Book of Mormon protocols were accessible and freshly imprinted upon the minds of Joseph Smith and Oliver Cowdery in advance of their emerging roles as builders of the early restoration.

However, other liturgies and doctrines matured over longer periods of time, showing a progression that often started with exposure to a Book of Mormon text early in the Prophet's development, in 1828 and 1829. We saw this in the development of Latter-day Saint priesthood, from the restoration of two separate Book of Mormon forms of authority in May/June 1829 to the restoration of Book of Mormon priesthood offices (disciple/elder, priest, and teacher) in summer 1829, followed by New Testament priesthood offices (bishop and deacon) in early 1831. Then came the Book of Mormon restoration of the Melchizedek Priesthood order in June 1831 with ordinations to the high priesthood (office of high priest), followed by the Aaronic Priesthood order recorded for the first time in September 1832, and finally the culminating revelation on priesthood in 1835 when the Quorum of the Twelve Apostles was formally established based on both New Testament and Book of Mormon precedent.

We saw the same type of steady progression in temple theology, beginning with the restoration of the Book of Mormon's expansive temple vision centered around the temple of Zion in 1830, the New Testament idea of spiritual endowment in 1831, then the Book of Mormon precedent of connecting endowment with the temple in 1833 (the forthcoming Kirtland Temple), leading to the experiential Kirtland Temple endowment in 1836 patterned after the Nephite endowment, and continuing finally to the full expression of endowment theology in the Nauvoo Temple in 1842. These longer patterns of development, for both priesthood and temple, suggest that the Prophet must have carefully studied, pondered, cross-referenced, and compared Book of Mormon temple and priesthood texts with similar Old Testament and New Testament texts through the decade of the 1830s. Rather than translating the Book of Mormon and then walking away from it, leaving it as a mere symbol of his prophethood, the Prophet returned to it again and again. Original Book of Mormon innovations pointed to Old Testament observances or New Testament doctrines, which in turn led to more careful examination and comparison among these scriptural records. This careful study inspired new revelations, each with a provenance tracing back to Book of Mormon theology—the Constitution of the Church of 1830 (D&C 20), the Vision revelation of 1832 (D&C 76), and the priesthood revelations of 1831 (D&C 68), 1832 (D&C 84), and 1835 (D&C 107)—each marking plateaus of definitive understanding.

Another insight emerges from our exploration relating to assumptions about *how* the restoration took place—that is, how God revealed scripture and divine protocol during the early days of Mormonism. Like many devout Christians believing the Bible to be the infallible and inerrant word of God,[7] many Latter-day Saints also assumed that the Book of Mormon and the revelations that followed were given by God with inerrancy—divinely and perfectly, without human fault. In fact, however, during the early restoration we see the production of modern scripture as challenging, evolving, and improving even as Smith and the leaders of the restoration matured and learned to continuously translate, transcribe, record, and properly codify scripture for publication. To be sure, an 1831 revelation told several ordained elders that "whatsoever they shall speak when moved upon by the Holy Ghost shall be Scripture shall be the will of the Lord shall be the mind of the Lord shall be the voice of the Lord & shall be the power of God unto Salvation."[8]

Nevertheless, the process of composing the restoration's scriptural canon was an active, living work of speaking, recording, revising, redacting, and constantly perfecting the revealed word of God. After the book's publication in 1830, the Prophet began "extensive updating of the grammar" in 1837,[9] adding to the 1840 (third edition) the words: "Carefully Revised by the Translator."[10] Frequent revisions also occurred with the revelations as restoration theology matured and evolved. For example, Smith's earliest revelations of July 1828 (D&C 3) and February 1829 (D&C 4) speak of God in the second person, but those recorded in April 1829 or later are written in the first-person voice of Jesus Christ with proclamations such as "I am Jesus Christ" (coinciding closely with Smith and Cowdery's recent translation of the visitation of Christ to the Americas). In 1835 Smith added new revelatory material to an existing early revelation of August 1830, addressing the use of wine in the sacrament (D&C 27),[11] doubling the length of the original revelation. This kind of revisionary revelation is pronounced throughout the early revelations of the restoration. In their introduction to the facsimile edition of Smith's early revelations, Robin Jensen, Robert Woodford, and Steven Harper wrote in the Joseph Smith Papers:

> Joseph Smith and his followers considered his revelations to be true in the sense that they communicated the mind and will of God, not infallible in an idealized sense of literary flawlessness. "The revelations were not God's diction, dialect, or native language," historian Richard Bushman has written. "They were couched in language suitable to Joseph's time." Smith and others appointed by revelation (including Oliver Cowdery, Sidney Rigdon, John Whitmer, and William W. Phelps) edited the revelations based on the same assumption that informed their original receipt: namely, that although Smith represented the voice of God condescending to speak to him, he was limited by a "crooked broken scattered and imperfect language." The November 1831 conference resolved that he should "correct those errors or mistakes which he may discover by the holy spirit."[12]

The foundational influence of the Book of Mormon

It is useful to examine the meaning of the Book of Mormon as a resource to early Mormonism's development by considering not only its presence during the early restoration but also the possibility of its absence: What would the restoration have been without the Book of Mormon—not merely as a sign of Smith's prophethood, but as a trusted fount of ancient religion? Rodney Stark observed that "the Book of Mormon, first published in 1830, may not have added enough doctrinal novelty to the Christian tradition to have made Mormonism more than a Protestant sect."[13] And Harold Bloom concluded that "with the Book of Mormon, we arrive at the center of Joseph Smith's prophetic mission, but hardly at any center of Mormonism, because of Smith's extraordinary capacity for speculative development in the fourteen years that remained to him after its publication."[14]

Smith, however, offered a contrasting view in 1834: "Take away the Book of Mormon, and the revelations, and where is our religion? We have none; for without a Zion, and a place of deliverance, we must fall; . . . and if we are not sanctified and gathered to the places where God has appointed, <with all> our former professions and our great love for the bible, we must fall, we cannot stand, we cannot be saved; for God will gather out his saints from the gentiles."[15] The seminal touchstones that remained at the top of Smith's consciousness—Zion, God's sanctified appointed places [temples], the gathering of God's people from the Gentiles—all were foundational Book of Mormon themes. Indeed they were the three dominant themes of Moroni's early schooling visions of 1823 to 1827.

Without the Book of Mormon, Joseph Smith would have had access only to biblical tradition—the Old and New Testaments—and of course to his growing body of divine revelations recorded in the voice of God. The restoration then would have developed as a religion of essentially biblically inspired origins. It might have struggled for survival alongside innumerable other Protestant offshoots seeking new and inspired insights into countless biblical texts and interpretations. Is it conceivable that without the Book of Mormon, Mormonism might have slipped into history as one of many nineteenth-century restorationist movements that attempted to return to Christ's pure and original religion of the New Testament, like the Campbellites, the Millerites, or the Christadelphians? These early movements ultimately struggled unsuccessfully to establish religious differentiation; despite their early popularity, they never achieved sustained and compelling clarity and demarcation amid myriad competing claims of salvation in the crowded milieu of nineteenth-century Christianity.

In the end, some will come away from this exploration saying that this evidence makes a case for Joseph Smith's divine calling as a modern-day prophet. How could this boy-prophet in his early twenties have produced a nearly six-hundred-page historical scriptural text in two months' time, simultaneously presenting in concrete form complex rites, rituals, theologies, and doctrines that evoke a deep provenance from ancient religious traditions at a profound level of understanding?

This kind of reasoning falls just short of the mark; it inevitably leads to the kind of heuristic thinking identified early in this book that the Book of Mormon was merely a derivative document from the Prophet. The evidence in the remaining pages of this book points to the Book of Mormon as its own historical source document. To the Prophet its narratives were rich and compelling; its revelations became models for his own revelations. Its rites and rituals captured deep and nuanced meanings of a covenant people of God that were at once familiar because of its biblical provenance yet were unique and distinctly different from other Christian interpretations because the book's religious traditions had developed completely independently in the New World setting of the ancient Americas. The book appeared in 1829 as ancient scriptural history, quite unlike other modern-day religious commentaries accessible to the Prophet from theologians like Wesley, Swedenborg, Campbell, or Scott. Its narrative presentation was uneven, difficult to read, and sometimes difficult to follow, with biases and contradictions reflecting the writings and views of hundreds of historical priests, prophets, scribes, and redactors over the span of a thousand years of antiquity.

For Smith and his companions, the historical value of the Book of Mormon was innate and never in doubt. "To the very end of the Joseph Smith era, the Book of Mormon was read, followed, and even clung to by the leaders and members of the early Church," said Welch. "On the way to Carthage Jail, Hyrum Smith knew right where to go to find Ether 12:37–38, which he read aloud as his final source of solace and strength before he was murdered: 'Thou has been faithful; wherefore . . . thou shalt be made strong. . . . Farewell . . . until we shall meet before the judgment-seat of Christ, where all men shall know that my garments are not spotted with your blood.'"[16]

On June 26, 1844, the night before their martyrdom, brothers Joseph and Hyrum Smith spent their final hours while imprisoned in Carthage Jail reading and listening to Book of Mormon historical narratives of persons experiencing divine rescue. "During the evening," wrote friend and eyewitness Dan Jones, "the Patriarch [Hyrum] read and commented upon copious extracts from the Book of Mormon, the imprisonments and deliverance of the servants of God for the Gospels sake; Joseph bore a powerful testimony to the guards of the divine authenticity of the Book of Mormon—the restoration of the Gospel, the administration of angels, and that the Kingdom of God was again upon the Earth, for the sake of which he was at that time incarcerated in that prison, and not because he had violated any law of God or of man."[17]

There seems little doubt that the Book of Mormon had a deep influence on the life and mission of Joseph Smith and on the meaning and identity of the modern church that he founded in nineteenth-century North America.

Notes

Preface

1. Joseph Smith Jr., History, circa Summer 1832, *The Joseph Smith Papers*, http://josephsmithpapers.org/paperSummary/history-circa-summer-1832?p=1.

Introduction

1. Terryl L. Givens, *By the Hand of Mormon: The American Scripture That Launched a New World Religion* (New York: Oxford University Press, 2002), 85.

2. David J. Whittaker, "The Book of Daniel in Early Mormon Thought," in *By Study and Also by Faith: Essays in Honor of Hugh W. Nibley*, ed. John D. Lundquist and Stephen D. Ricks (Salt Lake City: Deseret Book and FARMS, 1990), 1:159.

3. Joseph Smith, Junior, author and proprietor, *The Book of Mormon: An Account Written by the Hand of Mormon, upon Plates Taken from the Plates of Nephi* (Palmyra [NY]: Grandin, 1830), title page. *The Joseph Smith Papers*, http://josephsmithpapers.org/paperSummary/book-of-mormon-1830?p=7.

4. Joseph Smith, Junior, trans., *The Book of Mormon: An Account Written by the Hand of Mormon, upon Plates Taken from the Plates of Nephi* (Kirtland, OH: P. P. Pratt and J. Goodson; printed by O. Cowdery & Co., 1837). *The Joseph Smith Papers*, http://josephsmithpapers.org/paperSummary/book-of-mormon-1837?p=7.

5. Book of Mormon (1830 ed.), iii.

6. Book of Mormon (1830 ed.), title page.

7. Book of Mormon (1830 ed.), iii.

8. Book of Mormon (1830 ed.), title page.

9. Revelation, 9 December 1830 [D&C 36], 39th. Commandment Decm. 9th. AD 1830, *The Joseph Smith Papers*, http://josephsmithpapers.org/paperSummary/revelation-book-1?p=33. See Doctrine and Covenants (hereafter D&C) 36:8.

10. Revelation, 20 July 1831 [D&C 57], *The Joseph Smith Papers*, http://josephsmithpapers.org/paperSummary/revelation-20-july-1831-dc-57?p=1. See D&C 57:1–3, emphasis added.

11. Revelation, 26 April 1838 [D&C 115], *The Joseph Smith Papers*, http://josephsmithpapers.org/paperSummary/revelation-26-april-1838-dc-115?p=2. See D&C 115:7–8.

12. Orson F. Whitney, *Life of Heber C. Kimball* (Salt Lake City: Deseret Book, 1888), 208–9.

13. The state of Missouri issued an extermination order in 1838 to remove Mormons from its borders, which was legally in effect until the formal rescinding by Governor Christopher Bond in 1976. The intense persecution in frontier Missouri precluded the completion of the three Missouri temples, though Mormons believe eventually they will be constructed.

14. James E. Talmage, *House of the Lord* (Salt Lake City: Deseret Book, 1912), 105–6.

15. The Church of Jesus Christ of Latter-day Saints, "Temples," http://www.lds.org/church/temples/find-a-temple.

16. W. A. Morris, *The Writings of Alexander Campbell: Selections Chiefly from the Millennial Harbinger* (Austin, TX: Eugene Von Boeckmann, 1896), 399–400.

17. See, for example, Zechariah 6:11–15 or Ezekiel 40–48.

18. The constitution of the Hamburg Temple, the first Reform congregation, established in 1817, called for "a dignified and well-ordered ritual according to which the worship service shall be conducted on the Sabbath and holy days and on other solemn occasions, and which shall be observed in their own temple, to be erected especially for this purpose. Specifically, there shall be introduced at such services a German sermon, and choral singing to the accompaniment of an organ." "Constitution of the Hamburg Temple (December 11, 1817)," Heritage: Civilization and the Jews: Public Broadcasting Service, http://www.pbs.org/wnet/heritage/episode6/documents/documents_3.html. See also Michael Meyer, *Response to Modernity: A History of the Reform Movement in Judaism* (Detroit, MI: Wayne State University Press, 1995); also Jehuda Reinharz and Walter Schatzberg, eds., *The Jewish Response to German Culture: From the Enlightenment to the Second World War* (Lebanon, NH: University Press of New England, 1985); Paul R. Mendes-Flohr and Jehuda Reinharz, eds., *The Jew in the Modern World: A Documentary History* (New York: Oxford University Press, 1995); and "The Origins of Reform Judaism," Jewish Virtual Library, American-Israeli Cooperative Enterprise, http://www.jewishvirtuallibrary.org/jsource/Judaism/The_Origins_of_Reform_Judaism.html.

19. William Whiston, trans., *The Works of Flavius Josephus: The Learned and Authentic Jewish Historian and Celebrated Warrior* (Baltimore: Armstrong and Plaskitt, 1835), 603.

20. Book of Mormon (1830 ed.), 268, emphasis added.

21. Menahem Haran, *Temples and Temple Service in Ancient Israel* (Winona Lake, IN: Eisenbrauns, 1995), 16.

22. Terryl L. Givens, "The Prophecy of Enoch as Restoration Blueprint" (paper presented at the Leonard J. Arrington Mormon History Lecture, Utah State University, Logan, Utah, September 16, 2012), 9.

23. Vision, 16 February 1832 [D&C 76], *The Joseph Smith Papers*, http://josephsmithpapers.org/paperSummary/vision-16-february-1832-dc-76?p=5.

24. Grant Underwood, "Book of Mormon Usage in Early LDS Theology," *Dialogue: A Journal of Mormon Thought* 17/3 (1984): 52–53.

1. The Formative Influence of the Book of Mormon

1. *The Uniform System for Teaching Families* (Salt Lake City: The Church of Jesus Christ of Latter-day Saints, 1973).

2. John-Charles Duffy, "The New Missionary Discussions and the Future of Correlation," *Sunstone*, September 2005, 28–46; and Richard O. Cowan, "Richard Lloyd Anderson and Worldwide Church Growth," in *The Disciple as Witness: Essays on Latter-day Saint History and Doctrine in Honor of Richard Lloyd Anderson*, ed. Stephen D. Ricks, Donald W. Parry, and Andrew H. Hedges (Provo, UT: FARMS, 2000), 105–15.

3. Parley P. Pratt, *A Voice of Warning, and Instruction to All People or, an Introduction to the Faith and Doctrine of the Church of Jesus Christ of Latter-Day Saints*, 8th ed. (Liverpool: Richards, 1846).

4. See Peter Crawley, "Parley P. Pratt: Father of Mormon Pamphleteering," *Dialogue: A Journal of Mormon Thought* 15/3 (1982): 13–26; see n. 8.

5. "Time of universal restoration that God announced long ago through his holy prophets" (Acts 3:21 NRSV).

6. Charles H. Bliss, *Is Baptism Essential to Salvation?* (1890), LDS Pamphlet Library, http://ldspamphlets.org/Is_Baptism_Essential.htm.

7. John Morgan, *Plan of Salvation* (1881), LDS Pamphlet Library, http://ldspamphlets.org/Plan_of_Salvation.htm.

8. Jana Riess and Phyllis Tickle noted: "Early Mormons rarely quoted from the [Book of Mormon] in their speeches and writings; in one nineteenth-century LDS periodical, *Elders' Journal*, the Bible was cited forty times more often than the Book of Mormon. Although early Mormons believed that the book was an authentically ancient record and that its miraculous appearance signaled that they were living in the 'latter days,' they didn't strongly emphasize its teachings. . . . It wasn't until 1961 that a year-long course in the Book of Mormon became required for freshman students at Brigham Young University, and it was the 1980s before the Book of Mormon was cited regularly in General Conference talks by Church leaders." Jana Riess and Phyllis Tickle, *The Book of Mormon: Selections Annotated & Explained* (Woodstock, VT: Skylight Paths Publishing, 2005), xiii. See Noel B. Reynolds, "The Coming Forth of the Book of Mormon in the Twentieth Century," *BYU Studies* 38/2 (1999): 8.

9. Richard L. Bushman, *Joseph Smith: Rough Stone Rolling* (New York: Knopf, 2005), 85, second emphasis added.

10. Alexander Campbell, "The Mormonites," *Millennial Harbinger* 1/2 (1831): 91.

11. Andrew F. Ehat and Lyndon W. Cook, comps. and eds., *The Words of Joseph Smith: The Contemporary Accounts of the Nauvoo Discourses of the Prophet Joseph* (Provo, UT: Religious Studies Center, Brigham Young University, 1980), 33–34.

12. Ehat and Cook, *Words of Joseph Smith*, 35.

13. *Journal of Discourses*, 16:73.

14. *Journal of Discourses*, 13:335.

15. Grant Underwood, "Book of Mormon Usage in Early LDS Theology," *Dialogue: A Journal of Mormon Thought* 17/3 (1984): 58–59.

16. Reynolds, "Coming Forth of the Book of Mormon," 8.

17. John W. Welch, "The Book of Mormon as the Keystone of Church Administration," in *A Firm Foundation: Church Organization and Administration*, ed. David J. Whittaker and Arnold K. Garr (Provo, UT: Religious Studies Center, Brigham Young University, 2011), 26.

18. Alexander Campbell, "Delusions," *Millennial Harbinger* 1/2 (1831): 95.

19. Revelation, 22–23 September 1832 [D&C 84], *The Joseph Smith Papers*, http://josephsmithpapers.org/paperSummary/revelation-22-23-september-1832-dc-84?p=2. See D&C 84:54–57.

20. "In the same way, every good tree bears good fruit, but the bad tree bears bad fruit. . . . Thus you will know them by their fruits" (Matthew 7:17, 20 NRSV).

21. Fawn Brodie, *No Man Knows My History: The Life of Joseph Smith*, 2nd ed. (New York: Knopf, 1971).

22. Harold Bloom, *The American Religion: The Emergence of the Post-Christian Nation* (New York: Simon & Schuster, 1992).

23. See Lucy Mack Smith, Scott Facer Proctor, and Maurine Jensen Proctor, *The Revised and Enhanced History of Joseph Smith by His Mother* (Salt Lake City: Bookcraft, 1996).

24. Bushman, *Rough Stone Rolling*, 31–32.

25. History, 1838–1856, volume A-1 [23 December 1805–30 August 1834], *The Joseph Smith Papers*, http://josephsmithpapers.org/paperSummary/history-1838-1856-volume-a-1-23-december-1805-30-august-1834?p=4.

26. Letterbook 1, History, circa Summer 1832, *The Joseph Smith Papers*, http://josephsmithpapers.org/paperSummary/letterbook-1?p=7.

27. John A. Widtsoe, *Joseph Smith as Scientist* (Salt Lake City: Deseret Book, 1908), 134.

28. Lucy Mack Smith and Preston Nibley, *History of the Mormon Joseph Smith by His Mother and Devoted Member of the Church of Jesus Christ of Latter Day Saints* (Whitefish, MT: Kessinger, 2004), 82.

29. Smith and Nibley, *History of the Mormon Joseph Smith*, 90.

30. Pomeroy Tucker, *Origin, Rise, and Progress of Mormonism: Biography of Its Founders and History of Its Church* (New York: Appleton, 1867), 17.

31. *Journal of Discourses*, 19:105.

32. History, 1838–1856, volume A-1 [23 December 1805–30 August 1834], *The Joseph Smith Papers*, http://josephsmithpapers.org/paperSummary/history-1838-1856-volume-a-1-23-december-1805-30-august-1834?p=5. The original first sentence read: "and that his name was Nephi.<* Moroni> <*Evidently a clerical error; see Book Doc & Cov., Sec 50, par 2; Sec 106, par 20; also Elder's Journal Vol. 1, page 43. Should read Moroni.>" (ibid.).

33. Some of the sixty-nine verses quoted by Moroni deal with multiple themes. For example, twenty scriptural verses refer to temple themes, thirteen to the second coming, thirty-one to latter-day Israel, fourteen to the destructions of the last days, two to Elijah the prophet, thirty-one to latter-day and millennial Zion, twenty-six to the gathering of Israel, and four to latter-day prophets. My research is based on accounts in Joseph Smith's 1838 History (History, 1838–1856) and Oliver Cowdery, "Letter VI, to W.W. PHELPS, Esq," *Messenger and Advocate* 1/7 (April 1835): 109–12.

34. Cowdery, "Letter VI, to W.W. Phelps," 112.

35. Evidence of Joseph's growing realization of a broader mission as prophet is first documented in a revelation the Prophet received in March 1829, recorded in the 1833 Book of Commandments and modified in the 1835 edition of the Doctrine and Covenants: "& I will establish my Church yea even the church which was taught by my Desiples." Revelation, March 1829 [D&C 5], *The Joseph Smith Papers*, http://josephsmithpapers.org/paperSummary/revelation-march-1829-dc-5?p=1. See also 1833 Book of Commandments 4:5.

36. H. Donl Peterson documents the following visits by Moroni based on accounts from Joseph, his mother, David Whitmer, and Oliver Cowdery: During the night of September 21, 1823 (three visits); the morning of September 22, 1823, at the fence surrounding the fields of the family farm (one visit); at the Hill Cumorah on or soon after September 22, 1823, as Joseph visually saw the plates in a stone box (one visit); consecutive annual night visits on September 21 of 1824, 1825, and 1826 (three visits); early in the year 1827 while returning from a trip to Manchester (one visit); the night of September 21 and predawn hours of September 22, 1827, when Moroni gave Joseph physical custody of the plates (one visit)—for a total of ten visits. Another twelve visits occurred between June 1828, beginning with the lost-manuscript-of-Lehi incident, and June 1829, when Joseph finished the translation and Moroni takes back the original records. See H. Donl Peterson, *Moroni: Ancient Prophet, Modern Messenger* (Springville, UT: Cedar Fort, 2008), 121–24.

37. Lucy Mack Smith, *Biographical Sketches of Joseph Smith the Prophet and His Progenitors for Many Generations* (Liverpool: Richards, 1853), 85.

38. Russell Goodman, "Ralph Waldo Emerson," in *Stanford Encyclopedia of Philosophy*, http://plato.stanford.edu/entries/emerson.

39. Richard Lyman Bushman and Dean C. Jessee, "Joseph Smith and His Papers: An Introduction," *The Joseph Smith Papers*, http://josephsmithpapers.org/intro/joseph-smith-and-his-papers-an-introduction?p=3.

40. Terryl L. Givens, "Joseph Smith's American Bible: Radicalizing the Familiar," *Journal of the Book of Mormon and Other Restoration Scripture* 18/2 (2009): 17.

41. Book of Mormon (1830 ed.), 586.

42. See Michael Broyles, *Beethoven: The Emergence and Evolution of Beethoven's Heroic Style* (New York: Excelsior Music, 1987).

43. Melvyn Bragg, *The Book of Books: The Radical Impact of the King James Bible 1611–2011* (Berkeley, CA: Counterpoint Press, 2011), 6.

44. Grant Hardy, *Understanding the Book of Mormon: A Reader's Guide* (New York: Oxford University Press, 2010), 352–54.

45. Richard Van Wagoner and Steve Walker, "Joseph Smith: 'The Gift of Seeing,'" *Dialogue: A Journal of Mormon Thought* 15/2 (1982): 51.

46. Quoted in Francis W. Kirkham, "The Manner of Translating The Book of Mormon," *Improvement Era*, October 1939, 596–97.

47. Stephen D. Ricks, "Joseph Smith's Translation of the Book of Mormon," Neal A. Maxwell Institute for Religious Scholarship, http://publications.maxwellinstitute.byu.edu/fullscreen/?pub=934.

48. Royal Skousen, "How Joseph Smith Translated the Book of Mormon: Evidence from the Original Manuscript," *Journal of Book of Mormon Studies* 7/1 (1998): 24.

49. Stanford Carmack, "The Implications of Past-Tense Syntax in the Book of Mormon," *Interpreter: A Journal of Mormon Scripture* 14 (2015): 119. Carmack continued: "This means that the large doses of *did* [as in Moroni "*did arrive* with his army"] found in the [Book of Mormon] text apparently did not arise *ex nihilo*, that there was an historical, though obscure, basis for their systematic patterns of use. All the evidence presents a picture of the BofM as an EModE [Early Modern English] text that is difficult to refute. The data indicate that the BofM is similar to texts from the middle of the 16th century." Carmack, "Implications of Past-Tense," 120. Mormon scholar Daniel Peterson explained: "The 'Elizabethan era,' which Carmack says 'appears to be the epicenter' of English Book of Mormon syntax and which is often viewed as a 'golden age' in English history and literature—for the most part, it's also the age of Shakespeare—covers the reign of Queen Elizabeth I, from 1558 to 1603." Peterson, "Defending the Faith: The Very Surprising Language of the Book of Mormon," *Deseret News*, August 21, 2014. See also Stanford Carmack, "A Look at Some 'Nonstandard' Book of Mormon Grammar," *Interpreter: A Journal of Mormon Scripture* 11 (2014): 209–62; and Stanford Carmack, "What Command Syntax Tells Us about Book of Mormon Authorship," *Interpreter: A Journal of Mormon Scripture* 13 (2015): 175–217.

50. Skousen, "How Joseph Smith Translated the Book of Mormon," 25, 27, 29.

51. Skousen, "How Joseph Smith Translated the Book of Mormon," 31.

52. Blake T. Ostler, "The Book of Mormon as a Modern Expansion of an Ancient Source," *Dialogue: A Journal of Mormon Thought* 20/1 (1987): 104.

53. Brant A. Gardner, *The Gift and Power: Translating the Book of Mormon* (Salt Lake City: Greg Kofford Books, 2011), 156.

54. Gardner, *Gift and Power*, 236.

55. Gardner, *Gift and Power*, 242–43.

56. Kirkham, "Manner of Translating," 630–31. The form of the original quotation is question and answer between Joseph Smith III, the Prophet's son, and his mother, Emma Smith; the quotation here removes the questions and reports only Emma's responses in continuous form.

57. "History of the Book of Mormon," *Contributor* 5/10 (July 1884): 362–63.

58. History, 1838–1856, volume A-1 [23 December 1805–30 August 1834], *The Joseph Smith Papers*, http://josephsmithpapers.org/paperSummary/history-1838-1856-volume-a-1-23-december-1805-30-august-1834?p=11.

59. See Book of Mormon (1830 ed.), iii; also Ricks, "Joseph Smith's Translation of the Book of Mormon."

60. Quoted in Ehat and Cook, *Words of Joseph Smith*, 34, emphasis in the original.

61. Remarks delivered on October 25, 1831, Sirenes Burnet home, Orange, Cuyahoga County, Ohio. Source: Oliver Cowdery record copied into the Far West Record, Book of Abraham Project, http://www.boap.org/LDS/Parallel/1830-33/25Oct31.html. See also Minutes, 25–26 October 1831, *The Joseph Smith Papers*, http://josephsmithpapers.org/paperSummary/minutes-25-26-october-1831?p=4

62. Revelation, March 1829 [D&C 5], *The Joseph Smith Papers*, http://josephsmithpapers.org/paperSummary/revelation-march-1829-dc-5?p=1. See D&C 5:4.

63. Robin Scott Jensen, Robert J. Woodford, and Steven C. Harper, eds., *Manuscript Revelation Books*, facsimile edition, first volume of the Revelations and Translations series of *The Joseph Smith Papers*, edited by Dean C. Jessee, Ronald K. Esplin, and Richard Lyman Bushman (Salt Lake City: Church Historian's Press, 2009), 19. See D&C 9:7–9.

64. See Gerald E. Smith, "Evidence of Extemporaneous Change and Correction in the Book of Mormon Translations," unpublished working paper, 2015.

65. Book of Mormon (1830 ed.), 270–71, emphasis added.

66. Book of Mormon (1830 ed.), 23, emphasis added.

67. Thanks to an anonymous reviewer for this helpful insight.

68. Grant Hardy, introduction to *Book of Mormon: The Earliest Text*, ed. Royal Skousen (New Haven: Yale University Press, 2009), xix.

69. *The Book of Mormon: The Earliest Text*, ed. Royal Skousen (New Haven: Yale University Press, 2009), 745–89.

70. Hardy, introduction to *Book of Mormon: The Earliest Text*, xix.

71. Roger Terry, "What Shall We Do with Thou? Modern Mormonism's Unruly Usage of Archaic English Pronouns," part 2, *Dialogue: A Journal of Mormon Thought*, forthcoming.

72. John W. Welch and Larry E. Morris, *Oliver Cowdery: Scribe, Elder, Witness* (Provo, UT: Neal A. Maxwell Institute for Religious Scholarship, 2006), 17.

73. Larry E. Morris, "The Private Character of the Man Who Bore That Testimony: Oliver Cowdery and His Critics," *FARMS Review* 15/1 (2003): 317, 338.

74. History, 1838–1856, volume A-1 [23 December 1805–30 August 1834], *The Joseph Smith Papers*, http://josephsmithpapers.org/paperSummary/history-1838-1856-volume-a-1-23-december-1805-30-august-1834?p=21.

75. *Messenger and Advocate* 1/1 (October 1834): 15.

76. History, 1838–1856, volume A-1 [23 December 1805–30 August 1834], *The Joseph Smith Papers*, http://josephsmithpapers.org/paperSummary/history-1838-1856-volume-a-1-23-december-1805-30-august-1834?p=23.

2. Influences on Doctrine and Theology

1. Terryl L. Givens, *Wrestling the Angel: The Foundations of Mormon Thought: Cosmos, God, Humanity* (New York: Oxford, 2015), 184–85.

2. David Whitmer, *An Address to All Believers in Christ: By a Witness to the Divine Authenticity of the Book of Mormon* (Richmond, MO, 1887), 73.

3. Revelation, 26 April 1838 [D&C 115], *The Joseph Smith Papers*, http://josephsmithpapers.org/paperSummary/revelation-26-april-1838-dc-115?p=2. See D&C 115:4.

4. History, circa 1841, fair copy, *The Joseph Smith Papers*, http://josephsmithpapers.org/paperSummary/history-circa-1841-fair-copy?p=3. See also Dean C. Jessee, "The Early Accounts of Joseph Smith's First Vision," *BYU Studies* 9/3 (1969): 9; and John W. Welch, ed., *Opening the Heavens: Accounts of Divine Manifestations, 1820–1844* (Provo, UT: Brigham Young University Press, 2005).

5. History, circa Summer 1832, *The Joseph Smith Papers*, http://josephsmithpapers.org/paperSummary/history-circa-summer-1832?p=3.

6. *The Doctrines and Discipline of the Methodist Episcopal Church*, 14th ed. (New York: John Wilson and Daniel Mitt for the Methodist Connection, 1808), 6.

7. Revelation Book 1, Articles and Covenants, circa April 1830 [D&C 20], *The Joseph Smith Papers*, http://josephsmithpapers.org/paperSummary/revelation-book-1?p=37. See D&C 20:5.

8. Thanks to Terryl, Givens for this insight.

9. History, 1838–1856, volume A-1 [23 December 1805–30 August 1834], *The Joseph Smith Papers*, http://josephsmithpapers.org/paperSummary/history-1838-1856-volume-a-1-23-december-1805-30-august-1834?p=3. See Joseph Smith—History 1:21–25.

10. History, 1838–1856, volume A-1 [23 December 1805–30 August 1834], *The Joseph Smith Papers*, http://josephsmithpapers.org/paperSummary/history-1838-1856-volume-a-1-23-december-1805-30-august-1834?p=4. See Joseph Smith—History 1:21–25.

11. History, 1838–1856, volume A-1 [23 December 1805–30 August 1834], *The Joseph Smith Papers*, http://josephsmithpapers.org/paperSummary/history-1838-1856-volume-a-1-23-december-1805-30-august-1834?p=4.

12. History, circa Summer 1832, *The Joseph Smith Papers*, http://josephsmithpapers.org/paperSummary/history-circa-summer-1832?p=3.

13. James B. Allen and John W. Welch, "The Appearance of the Father and the Son to Joseph Smith in 1820," in Welch, *Opening the Heavens*, 39.

14. History, 1838–1856, volume A-1 [23 December 1805–30 August 1834], *The Joseph Smith Papers*, http://josephsmithpapers.org/paperSummary/history-1838-1856-volume-a-1-23-december-1805-30-august-1834?p=2. See Joseph Smith—History 1:8.

15. According to Turner, "Joseph had a little ambition; and some very laudable aspirations; the mother's intellect occasionally shone out in him feebly, especially when he used to help us solve some portentous question of moral or political ethics, in our juvenile debating club, which we moved down to the old red school house on Durfee

street, to get rid of the annoyance of critics that used to drop in upon us in the village; and subsequently, after catching a spark of Methodism in the camp meeting; away down in the woods, on the Vienna road, he was a very passable exhorter in evening meetings." O. Turner, *History of the Pioneer Settlement of Phelps & Gorham's Purchase, and Morris' Reserve* (Rochester: Alling, 1852), 214. The reference to *exhorter* is ambiguous here and, considered in full context, seems to imply that Turner was referring to Smith's evening activities with the debating club where he could be described as an effective "exhorter." Another interpretation: Methodists could become licensed exhorters if they were members in full standing, which Smith was not; it may have been possible, though, that he attended evening camp meetings and informally gave scriptural exhortations in the period before summer 1822, the time frame of Turner's association with Smith.

16. Pomeroy Tucker, *Origin, Rise, and Progress of Mormonism: Biography of Its Founders and History of Its Church* (New York: Appleton, 1867), 18.

17. John Matzko, "The Encounter of the Young Joseph Smith with Presbyterianism," *Dialogue: A Journal of Mormon Thought* 40/3 (2007): 70.

18. Richard Lyman Bushman, *Joseph Smith and the Beginnings of Mormonism*, reprint ed. (Chicago: University of Illinois Press, 1987), 53.

19. Matzko, "Encounter of the Young Joseph Smith with Presbyterianism," 70–71.

20. Lucy Mack Smith, History, 1844–1845, *The Joseph Smith Papers*, http://josephsmithpapers.org/paperSummary/lucy-mack-smith-history-1844-1845?p=49. The entire passage is marked by three large X's, which JSP editors interpreted to mean strike-out.

21. Lucy Mack Smith, History, 1845, *The Joseph Smith Papers*, http://josephsmithpapers.org/paperSummary/lucy-mack-smith-history-1845?p=100.

22. Linda King Newell and Valeen Tippetts Avery, *Mormon Enigma: Emma Hale Smith*, 2nd ed. (Champaign: University of Illinois Press, 1994), 27.

23. Bushman, *Joseph Smith and the Beginnings of Mormonism*, 94.

24. Matzko, "Encounter of the Young Joseph Smith with Presbyterianism," 68.

25. The Prophet's official historical account compiled in 1839 records: "Mr Harris having returned from this tour ['to the city of New York . . . to Professor Charles Anthon'] he left me and went home to Palmyra, arranged his affairs, and returned again to my house about the twelfth of April Eighteen hundred and twenty eight, And commenced writing for me while I translated from the plates, which we Continued untill the fourteenth of June following, by which time he had written one hundred and sixteen <pages> of manuscript on foolscap paper." History, 1838–1856, volume A-1 [23 December 1805–30 August 1834], *The Joseph Smith Papers*, http://josephsmithpapers.org/paperSummary/history-1838-1856-volume-a-1-23-december-1805-30-august-1834?p=11.

26. Robin Scott Jensen, Robert J. Woodford, and Steven C. Harper, eds., *Revelations and Translations, Volume 1: Manuscript Revelation Books*, vol. 1 of the Revelations and Translations series of *The Joseph Smith Papers*, edited by Dean C. Jessee, Ronald K. Esplin, and Richard Lyman Bushman (Salt Lake City: Church Historian's Press, 2011), 9, 11. See also D&C 3:16–18.

27. Bushman, *Rough Stone Rolling*, 69.

28. Matzko, "Encounter of the Young Joseph Smith with Presbyterianism," 72.

29. Revelation, Fayette Township, Seneca Co., NY, to Oliver Cowdery, David Whitmer, and the future twelve disciples, June 1829. Featured version, titled "Chapter XV," typeset [ca. early 1833] for Book of Commandments, 34–35. *The Joseph Smith Papers*, http://josephsmithpapers.org/paperSummary/revelation-june-1829-b-dc-18?p=1.

30. John W. Welch, "The Book of Mormon as the Keystone of Church Administration," in *A Firm Foundation: Church Organization and Administration*, ed. David J. Whittaker and Arnold K. Garr (Provo, UT: Religious Studies Center, Brigham Young University, 2011), 22.

31. Scott H. Faulring, "The Book of Mormon: A Blueprint for Organizing the Church," *Journal of Book of Mormon Studies* 7/1 (1998): 63.

32. Robert J. Woodford, "The Articles and Covenants of the Church of Christ and the Book of Mormon," in *Sperry Symposium Classics: The Doctrine and Covenants*, ed. Craig K. Manscill (Provo, UT: Religious Studies Center, Brigham Young University, 2004), 103–16.

33. Revelation Book 1, Articles and Covenants, circa April 1830 [D&C 20], *The Joseph Smith Papers*, http://josephsmithpapers.org/paperSummary/revelation-book-1?p=38. See also *Evening and the Morning Star* 1/1 (June 1832): 1.

34. Book of Mormon (1830 ed.), 579.

35. Book of Mormon (1830 ed.), 582.

36. My analysis of thirty-nine phrases suggests that 18 percent matched Book of Mormon phrases exactly; 49 percent matched within a few words; 21 percent matched Book of Mormon, Old Testament, or New Testament phrases roughly equally; and 13 percent matched phrases from the Old or New Testaments.

37. "Of God, and of the Holy Trinity," *The Westminster Confession of Faith and Catechisms* (Lawrenceville, GA: Orthodox Presbyterian Church, Christian Education & Publications, 2007), 8 (chapter 2:1).

38. Confessio Augustana, The Augsburg Confession, AD 1530, *Creeds of the Evangelical Protestant Churches*. Christian Classics Ethereal Library, http://www.ccel.org/ccel/schaff/creeds3.iii.ii.html.

39. Book of Mormon (1830 ed.), 544.

40. Book of Mormon (1830 ed.), 476.

41. Book of Mormon (1830 ed.), 476–77.

42. Book of Mormon (1830 ed.), 477.

43. Book of Mormon (1830 ed.), 544.

44. "that they may be one, as we are one" (John 17:22 NRSV).

45. Andrew F. Ehat and Lyndon W. Cook, comps. and eds., *The Words of Joseph Smith: The Contemporary Accounts of the Nauvoo Discourses of the Prophet Joseph* (Provo, UT: Religious Studies Center, Brigham Young University, 1980), 60.

46. David Paulsen, "The Doctrine of Divine Embodiment: Restoration, Judeo-Christian, and Philosophical Perspectives," *BYU Studies* 35/4 (1995): 13–14.

47. Paulsen, "Doctrine of Divine Embodiment," 21.

48. Givens, *Wrestling the Angel*, 94.

49. Book of Mormon (1830 ed.), 257, emphasis added.

50. *Messenger and Advocate* 1/6 (March 1835): 96, emphasis added.

51. Adam Clarke, "Commentary Romans 3, note 2," in *The Adam Clarke Commentary*, http://www.studylight.org/com/acc/view.cgi?bk=44&ch=3.

52. Charles Partee, *The Theology of John Calvin* (Louisville, KY: Westminster John Knox Press, 2008), 249.

53. Thomas H. Olbricht, "Walter Scott as Biblical Interpreter," in *Walter Scott: A Nineteenth-Century Evangelical*, ed. Mark G. Toulouse (St. Louis, MO: Chalice, 1999), 90, emphasis added. "During his term as an evangelist of the Mahoning Baptist Association (1827–30) in Ohio," wrote Christian author Peter M. Morgan, "Scott developed the Five Finger Exercise as a summary of the plan of salvation used for preaching and teaching purposes. Typically Scott would ride into a village and find a group of children. He would have them hold up their left hands and, beginning with the thumb, point to each finger and repeat the words 'faith, repentance, baptism, remission of sins, gift of the Holy Spirit.' He often paired 'and eternal life' with the Holy Spirit, on the little finger. The children would repeat the game until they had mastered the 'faith in their fingers.' He would then send them to their homes to tell their parents that a man would preach that same gospel that night at the schoolhouse. They were not to forget to tell their parents the faith of their hands." Peter M. Morgan, "Five Finger Exercise," in *The Encyclopedia of the Stone-Campbell Movement* (Grand Rapids, MI: Eerdmans, 2004), 338–39.

54. Terryl Givens and Fiona Givens, *The God Who Weeps: How Mormonism Makes Sense of Life* (Salt Lake City: Ensign Peak, 2012), 94.

55. Book of Mormon (1830 ed.), 254, emphasis added.

56. Book of Mormon (1830 ed.), 253.

57. Samuel Morris Brown, *In Heaven as It Is on Earth: Joseph Smith and the Early Mormon Conquest of Death* (New York: Oxford University Press, 2012), 23.

58. Brown, *In Heaven as It Is on Earth*, 19.

59. Brown, *In Heaven as It Is on Earth*, 23.

60. Brown, *In Heaven as It Is on Earth*, 35.

61. Remarks by Joseph Smith, recorded by Wilford Woodruff in "Sermon Delivered at Yelrome, Hancock County, Ill. on Sunday May 14, 1843," Book of Abraham Project, http://www.boap.org/LDS/Parallel/1843/14May43.html.

62. Book of Mormon (1830 ed.), 80.

63. History, 1838–1856, volume A-1 [23 December 1805–30 August 1834], *The Joseph Smith Papers*, http://josephsmithpapers.org/paperSummary/history-1838-1856-volume-a-1-23-december-1805-30-august-1834?p=41.

64. Revelation Book 1, Vision, 16 February 1832 [D&C 76], *The Joseph Smith Papers*, http://josephsmithpapers.org/paperSummary/revelation-book-1?p=123. See D&C 76:37–39, 42–43.

65. Revelation, 27–28 December 1832 [D&C 88:1–126], *The Joseph Smith Papers*, http://josephsmithpapers.org/paperSummary/revelation-27-28-december-1832-dc-881-126?p=3. See D&C 88:21–22; reordering of the text is mine.

66. Bushman, *Rough Stone Rolling*, 199.

67. History, 1838–1856, volume A-1 [23 December 1805–30 August 1834], *The Joseph Smith Papers*, http://josephsmithpapers.org/paperSummary/history-1838-1856-volume-a-1-23-december-1805-30-august-1834?p=198.

68. *Journal of Discourses*, 16:42.

69. Bushman, *Rough Stone Rolling*, 17.

70. Book of Mormon (1830 ed.), 222.

71. Bushman, *Rough Stone Rolling*, 200–202.

72. Brown, *In Heaven as It Is on Earth*, 16.

73. Book of Mormon (1830 ed.), 435.

74. The Mosiah$_2$ coronation is recorded in the first four chapters of the book of Mosiah, in the 1830 edition (of thirteen chapters total in Mosiah), and is 6,861 words in length. By comparison, the book of Moroni is 5,838 words, and Mormon's personal writings preserved in the internal book of Mormon (excluding Moroni's writings recorded in the internal Book of Mormon) were 6,150 words.

75. Matthew L. Bowen, "Becoming Sons and Daughters at God's Right Hand: King Benjamin's Rhetorical Wordplay on His Own Name," *Journal of the Book of Mormon and Other Restoration Scripture* 21/2 (2012): 7.

76. Bowen, "Becoming Sons and Daughters," 1.

77. Book of Mormon (1830 ed.), 166.

78. Bowen, "Becoming Sons and Daughters," 6.

79. John W. Welch, "Parallelism and Chiasmus in Benjamin's Speech," in *King Benjamin's Speech Made Simple*, ed. John W. Welch and Stephen D. Ricks (Provo, UT: FARMS, 1999), 283.

80. Book of Mormon (1830 ed.), 167.

81. David E. Bokovoy and John A. Tvedtnes, *Testaments: Links between the Book of Mormon and the Hebrew Bible* (Tooele, UT: Heritage, 2003), 152.

82. Bowen, "Becoming Sons and Daughters," 2.

83. James F. White, *Protestant Worship: Traditions in Transition* (Louisville, KY: Westminster John Knox Press, 1989), 121.

84. White, *Protestant Worship*, 119.

85. Edward Palmer Thompson, *The Making of the English Working Class* (New York: Pantheon Books, 1964), 48.

86. Nardi Reeder Campion, *Mother Ann Lee: Morning Star of the Shakers* (Lebanon, NH: University Press of New England, 1990), 78.

87. Brown, *In Heaven as It Is on Earth*, 211.

88. History, 1838–1856, volume A-1 [23 December 1805–30 August 1834], *The Joseph Smith Papers*, http://josephsmithpapers.org/paperSummary/history-1838-1856-volume-a-1-23-december-1805-30-august-1834?p=93.

89. Samuel Brown, "I Believe! The Origin of 'Strange' Mormon Beliefs," OUPBlog, January 20, 2012, http://blog.oup.com/2012/01/origin-Mormon-beliefs/.

90. John Pack, 1809–1885, Book of Abraham Project, http://www.boap.org/LDS/Early-Saints/JHPack.html.

91. Brown, *In Heaven as It Is on Earth*, 225.

92. Brown, *In Heaven as It Is on Earth*, 249.

93. Rodney Stark, "The Rise of a New World Faith," in *Latter-day Saint Social Life: Social Research on the LDS Church and Its Members* (Provo, UT: Religious Studies Center, Brigham Young University, 1998), 2.

94. See Dean W. Collinwood and James W. McConkie, review of *Temple Theology: An Introduction*, by Margaret Barker, *BYU Studies* 45/2 (2006): 175.

95. Terryl L. Givens, "The Prophecy of Enoch as Restoration Blueprint" (paper presented at the Leonard J. Arrington Mormon History Lecture, Utah State University, Logan, Utah, September 16, 2012), 16.

96. Margaret Barker, *The Older Testament: The Survival of Themes from the Ancient Royal Cult in Sectarian Judaism and Early Christianity* (Sheffield, UK: Sheffield Phoenix Press, 2005), 95.

97. Barker, *Older Testament*, 240.

98. Book of Mormon (1830 ed.), 6.

99. Kevin Christensen, "The Temple, the Monarchy, and Wisdom: Lehi's World and the Scholarship of Margaret Barker," in *Glimpses of Lehi's Jerusalem*, ed. John W. Welch, David Rolph Seely, and Jo Ann H. Seely (Provo, UT: FARMS, 2004), 453.

100. Margaret Barker, "Joseph Smith and the Preexilic Israelite Religion," in *The Worlds of Joseph Smith: A Bicentennial Conference at the Library of Congress*, ed. John W. Welch (Provo, UT: Brigham Young University Press, 2006), 76, emphasis added.

101. Book of Mormon (1830 ed.), 64–65. See also 2 Nephi 2:14–30.

102. Romans 5, Matthew Henry Commentary on the Whole Bible (Complete), http://www.biblestudytools.com/commentaries/matthew-henry-complete/romans/5.html.

103. Book of Mormon (1830 ed.), 544.

104. Book of Mormon (1830 ed.), 546.

105. Mormon scholars John Welch and Thomas Valletta identify this passage as a Nephite temple text. According to Welch: "Based on the appearance of the following elements in Alma 12–13, the Nephite temple ceremony utilized familiar temple motifs, including abundant creation imagery regarding the fall of Adam and Eve (see 12:22–26), the redemption (see 12:25–33), the issuance of commandments (see 12:31–32), one's calling (see 13:3–8), clothing (see 13:11–12), the facing of judgment (see 12:14, 32–35), and symbolic entrance into the presence of God (see 12:36; 13:12)." John W. Welch, "The Temple in the Book of Mormon: The Temples at the Cities of Nephi, Zarahemla, and Bountiful," in *Temples of the Ancient World: Ritual and Symbolism*, ed. Donald W. Parry (Salt Lake City: Deseret Book and FARMS, 1994), 366. See also Thomas R. Valletta, "Conflicting Orders: Alma and Amulek in Ammonihah," in *The Temple in Time and Eternity*, ed. Donald W. Parry and Stephen D. Ricks (Provo, UT: FARMS, 1999), 183–231.

106. Book of Mormon (1830 ed.), 248.

107. Book of Mormon (1830 ed.), 255.

108. Book of Mormon (1830 ed.), 256.

109. Book of Mormon (1830 ed.), 257.

110. Book of Mormon (1830 ed.), 268. See also Alma 12–13 for the broader text containing these elements.

111. Symbols and themes present in Alma's temple discourse and *missing* from Lehi's visions and blessings are references to (1) priests or priesthood, (2) sanctification or purification, (3) sacred garments, and (4) entering into the rest of the Lord at the end of one's spiritual journey.

112. Andrew F. Ehat, "Joseph Smith's Introduction of Temple Ordinances and the 1844 Mormon Succession Question" (master's thesis, Brigham Young University, 1982), 18.

113. Don Bradley, "Piercing the Veil: Temple Worship in the Lost 116 Pages," 2012 FAIR Conference, The Foundation for Apologetic Information and Research, August 2–3, 2012, http://www.fairlds.org/fair-conferences/2012-fair-conference/2012-piercing-the-veil-temple-worship-in-the-lost-116-pages.

114. Bradley, "Piercing the Veil."

115. According to Trent C. Butler, "Badger Skins," in the *Holman Bible Dictionary* (1991): "[The] NRSV reads 'fine leather' with a note that the meaning of the Hebrew is uncertain. Some have proposed the simple translation, 'leather,' noting the similarity of the Hebrew and Egyptian words for leather (TEV)." http://www.studylight.org/dic/hbd/view.cgi?n=641.

116. Bradley, "Piercing the Veil."

117. Old Testament Revision 1, A Revelation given to Joseph the Revelator June 1830, *The Joseph Smith Papers*, http://josephsmithpapers.org/paperSummary/old-testament-revision-1?p=9. See Moses 5:10–11.

118. Revelation Book 1, Revelation, September 1830–A [D&C 29], *The Joseph Smith Papers*, http://josephsmithpapers.org/paperSummary/revelation-book-1?p=23. See also D&C 29:34–42.

119. Old Testament Revision 1, A Revelation given to Joseph the Revelator June 1830, Dec 1rst, <The Plan of Salvation>, *The Joseph Smith Papers*, http://josephsmithpapers.org/paperSummary/old-testament-revision-1?p=17. See also Moses 7:3–4, 22–32.

120. Revelation Book 1, Vision, 16 February 1832 [D&C 76], *The Joseph Smith Papers*, http://josephsmithpapers.org/paperSummary/revelation-book-1?p=124. See D&C 76:56–58.

121. Book of Mormon (1830 ed.), 259–60.

122. Givens, "Prophecy of Enoch," 9.

123. Harold Bloom, *The American Religion: The Emergence of the Post-Christian Nation* (New York: Simon & Schuster, 1992), 101.

3. Sacred Rituals, Symbols, and Narratives of Sacrament, Baptism, and Zion

1. See James F. White, *Protestant Worship: Traditions in Transition* (Louisville, KY: Westminster John Knox Press, 1989), 154.

2. White, *Protestant Worship*, 154. Thanks to Terryl Givens for his suggestions on this essential dichotomy.

3. Milton V. Backman Jr., "Awakenings in the Burned-Over District: New Light on the Historical Setting of the First Vision," *BYU Studies* 9/3 (1969): 301–20; and Milton V. Backman Jr., *Joseph Smith's First Vision: Confirming Evidences and Contemporary Accounts* (Salt Lake City: Deseret Book, 1971). Catholics had no organized congregation but were present in the region, especially since the commencement of the Erie Canal, which began in 1817 with the employ of many Irish Catholic immigrant workers.

4. White, *Protestant Worship*, 173–74.

5. History, 1838–1856, volume A-1 [23 December 1805–30 August 1834], *The Joseph Smith Papers*, http://josephsmithpapers.org/paperSummary/history-1838-1856-volume-a-1-23-december-1805-30-august-1834?p=2.

6. Mormons use the term *sacrament* to refer to commemoration of the Lord's Supper, instituted by Christ the night before his crucifixion in Jerusalem (Luke 22:14–20) and, after his resurrection, at the Bountiful temple in ancient America (3 Nephi 18:1–11). Nineteenth-century theologian Rev. Charles Buck described sacrament as "derived from the Latin word *sacramentum*, which signifies an oath. . . . The word was adopted by the writers of the Latin [Catholic] church, to denote those ordinances of religion by which Christians came under an obligation of obedience to God. . . . Protestant churches admit of but two [sacraments] . . . baptism and the Lord's supper. . . . The Romanists, however, add to this number confirmation, penance, extreme unction, ordination, and marriage, holding in all seven sacraments." Rev. Charles Buck, *A Theological Dictionary Containing All Religious Terms* (Philadelphia: Edwin T. Scott, 1823), 530. By contrast, Mormons describe sacrament and baptism as *ordinances*, along with confirmation, ordination, various forms of priesthood blessings, and temple ordinances. Buck defined *Eucharist* as "the sacrament of the Lord's supper. The word properly signifies giving thanks." Buck, *Theological Dictionary*, 170. Paul in the New Testament linked the term *communion* with the Lord's Supper: "The cup of blessing which we bless, is it not the communion of the blood of Christ? The bread which we break, is it not the communion of the body of Christ? For we being many are one bread, and one body: for we are all partakers of that one bread" (1 Corinthians 10:16–17). Eighteenth-century theologian Matthew Henry said: "Is not this sacred rite an instrument of communion with God? Do we not therein profess to be in friendship, and to have fellowship, with him? Is it not a token whereby we professedly hold communion with Christ, whose body was broken, and blood shed, to procure remission of our sins, and the favour of God?" 1 Corinthians 10, Matthew Henry Commentary on the Whole Bible (Complete), http://www.biblestudytools.com/commentaries/matthew-henry-complete/1-corinthians/10.html.

7. "Liturgy of the Mass: Name and Definition," in *Catholic Encyclopedia*, http://www.newadvent.org/cathen/09790b.htm.

8. See Grant Underwood, "Expulsion from Zion," in *Joseph Smith, the Prophet and Seer*, ed. Richard Neitzel Holzapfel and Kent P. Jackson (Provo, UT: Religious Studies Center, Brigham Young University, 2010), 127–50; also Dennis Lancaster, "Dixie Wine" (master's thesis, Brigham Young University, 1972), 128; and Loren R. Webb, "Southern

Utah Memories: The Dixie Wine Mission," WCSG Television, WCSG.com, published July 20, 2012.

9. History, 1838–1856, volume A-1 [23 December 1805–30 August 1834], *The Joseph Smith Papers*, http://josephsmithpapers.org/paperSummary/history-1838-1856-volume-a-1-23-december-1805-30-august-1834?p=47.

10. Minute Book 2, *The Joseph Smith Papers*, http://josephsmithpapers.org/paperSummary/minute-book-2?p=7.

11. This reference to *sacrament* may have been terminology used by nineteenth-century Baptists and not merely Kimball's use of Mormon terminology of sacrament. Even though modern Baptists refer to the ceremony of the Lord's Supper as *communion*, in fact, earlier Baptists used the term *sacrament* and even saw Christ's acts as sacramental. American Baptist church historian William Joseph McGlothlin, in the fifty-first of his "Propositions and Conclusions concerning True Christian Religion," wrote in 1911: "That Christ Jesus, according to the flesh and history of His doings and suffering, is a great mystery, and divine sacrament of Himself." W. J. McGlothlin, *Baptist Confessions of Faith* (Philadelphia: American Baptist Publication Society, 1911), 75. He further quoted from the General Baptists' "Orthodox Creed" of 1678: "Those two sacraments, viz. Baptism, and the Lord's-supper, are ordinances of positive, sovereign, and holy institution, appointed by the Lord Jesus Christ . . . and to be administred by those only who are rightly qualified, and thereunto called, according to the command of Christ." McGlothlin, *Baptist Confessions of Faith*, 144.

12. "Extracts from the Journal of Heber C. Kimball," Book of Abraham Project, http://www.boap.org/LDS/Early-Saints/HCKimball.html.

13. History, 1838–1856, volume A-1 [23 December 1805–30 August 1834], *The Joseph Smith Papers*, http://josephsmithpapers.org/paperSummary/history-1838-1856-volume-a-1-23-december-1805-30-august-1834?p=57.

14. History, 1838–1856, volume A-1 [23 December 1805–30 August 1834], *The Joseph Smith Papers*, http://josephsmithpapers.org/paperSummary/history-1838-1856-volume-a-1-23-december-1805-30-august-1834?p=57. According to James White, "[In Methodism] the year 1876 brought the first recommendation of the use of 'pure unfermented juice of the grape' for the Lord's supper. This eventually became mandatory until 1988. Such a move resulted from the work of a pious dentist, Dr. Thomas B. Welch (1825–1903), who discovered in 1869 a means of pasteurizing grape juice that prevented fermentation." White, *Protestant Worship*, 159. Wesley also introduced love feasts; White explained: "Occasionally, the love feast would be held when eucharists were not possible. Administered with bread and water, this derived from the ancient church via the Moravians and was an occasion for sharing of prayer, testimony, and hymn singing." White, *Protestant Worship*, 155.

15. History, 1838–1856, volume A-1 [23 December 1805–30 August 1834], *The Joseph Smith Papers*, http://josephsmithpapers.org/paperSummary/history-1838-1856-volume-a-1-23-december-1805-30-august-1834?p=58.

16. The five phases to the Mass consist of Introductory Rites, Liturgy of the Word, Liturgy of the Eucharist, Communion Rite, and Concluding Rite.

17. Source for this description of the Tridentine form of the Catholic Mass: "Mass of the Faithful to the Canon, Liturgical Texts, 1962 Missal, Mass of the 1962 Missal." The Catholic Liturgical Library, http://www.catholicliturgy.com. See also Wikipedia, "Tridentine Mass," http://en.wikipedia.org/wiki/Tridentine_Mass.

18. See "Liturgy of the Mass," in *Catholic Encyclopedia* (New York: Appleton, 1913).

19. Wikipedia, "Words of Institution," http://en.wikipedia.org/wiki/Words_of_Institution.

20. Stanley R. Hall, "Grateful Words: The eucharistic prayer is the table grace of the people of God," Reformed Worship: Resources for Planning and Leading Worship, http://www.reformedworship.org/article/june-1998/grateful-words-eucharistic-prayer-table-grace-people-god.

21. White, *Protestant Worship*, 162.

22. White, *Protestant Worship*, 162.

23. White, *Protestant Worship*, 158.

24. Backman, "Awakenings in the Burned-Over District," 309.

25. Catholics and Anglicans would have used the term *altar*; Methodists, Presbyterians, Baptists, and others used the term *communion table*.

26. Book of Mormon (1830 ed.), 575.

27. Book of Mormon (1830 ed.), 575–76.

28. Robert J. Woodford, "The Articles and Covenants of the Church of Christ and the Book of Mormon," in *Sperry Symposium Classics: The Doctrine and Covenants*, ed. Craig K. Manscill (Provo, UT: Religious Studies Center, Brigham Young University, 2004), 103–16. Also, Scott H. Faulring, "The Book of Mormon: A Blueprint for Organizing the Church," *Journal of Book of Mormon Studies* 7/1 (1998): 60–69.

29. Book of Mormon (1830 ed.), 490.

30. "Purpose of the sacrament of the Lord's Supper, May 2, 1946," in James R. Clark, *Messages of the First Presidency* (Salt Lake City: Deseret Book, 1975), 6:253.

31. Book of Mormon (1830 ed.), 490. See also 3 Nephi 18:1–11.

32. Book of Mormon (1830 ed.), 506.

33. Book of Mormon (1830 ed.), 576.

34. There were three other possible sacramental references that most theologians rejected as sacramental occurrences: First, Jesus "took bread, and blessed it, and brake, and gave to them" on the road to Emmaus (Luke 24:30); second, on the Day of Pentecost when the new converts "continued steadfastly in the apostles' doctrine and fellowship, and in breaking of bread, and in prayers" (Acts 2:42); and third, during Paul's journey to Rome in which "he took bread, and gave thanks to God in presence of them all" (Acts 27:35). Nineteenth-century Methodist theologian Adam Clarke rejected these; of the occurrence on the Rome journey, for example, he said: "Some think that he celebrated the holy eucharist here: but this is by no means likely: he would not celebrate such a mystery among ungodly sailors and soldiers, Jews and heathens; nor was there any necessity for such a measure." *Adam Clarke Commentary*, http://www.studylight.org/com/acc/view.cgi?bk=43&ch=27.

35. "On the first day of the week, when we met to break bread, Paul was holding a discussion with them; since he intended to leave the next day, he continued speaking until midnight" (Acts 20:7 NRSV).

36. White, *Protestant Worship*, 154.

37. White, *Protestant Worship*, 175.

38. Book of Mormon (1830 ed.), 490, emphasis added.

39. "This is my body, which is given for you. Do this in remembrance of me" (Luke 22:19 NRSV).

40. John Welch, "3 Nephi 15–18: Sacrament Prayers and Implications of the Sermon at the Temple," lecture 100 in *Teachings of the Book of Mormon*, part 4, by Hugh Nibley (Provo, UT: FARMS, 2004), 157.

41. Michael G. Reed, *Banishing the Cross: The Emergence of a Mormon Taboo* (Independence, MO: John Whitmer Books, 2012), 27–28.

42. Reed, *Banishing the Cross*, 33.

43. *Journal of Discourses*, 6:194.

44. Martin Luther, *CRUX sola est nostra Theologia*, Weimarer Ausgabe 5.176.32.

45. The King James Version preserves 12,601 words on Christ's crucifixion.

46. John Dominic Crossan, *Jesus: A Revolutionary Biography* (New York: HarperOne, 2009), 145.

47. Book of Mormon (1830 ed.), 477.

48. Book of Mormon (1830 ed.), 477.

49. The 1830 edition of the Book of Mormon preserves 17,133 words on the risen Christ.

50. The King James Version preserves 3,654 words on the risen Christ.

51. Book of Mormon (1830 ed.), 508.

52. Gordon B. Hinckley, "The Symbol of Christ," *Ensign*, May 1975, 92.

53. Backman, "Awakenings in the Burned-Over District," 315.

54. William Smith, *William Smith on Mormonism* (Lamoni, IA: Herald Steam Book and Job Office, 1883), 6–7. Joseph Smith noted: "My mind at different times was greatly excited ~~for~~ the cry and tumult were so great and incessant. The Presbyterians were most decided against the Baptists and Methodists, and used all their powers of either reason or sophistry to prove their errors, or at least to make the people think they were in error. On the other hand the Baptists and Methodists in their turn were equally Zealous in endeavoring to establish their own tenets and disprove all others." History, 1838–1856, volume A-1 [23 December 1805–30 August 1834], *The Joseph Smith Papers*, http://josephsmithpapers.org/paperSummary/history-1838-1856-volume-a-1-23-december-1805-30-august-1834?p=2.

55. Backman, "Awakenings in the Burned-Over District," 317.

56. White, *Protestant Worship*, 174.

57. Lucy Smith, George A. Smith, and Elias Smith, *History of the Prophet Joseph* (Salt Lake City: Improvement Era, 1902), 45–56.

58. Smith, Smith, and Smith, *History of the Prophet Joseph*, 54.

59. John Matzko, "The Encounter of the Young Joseph Smith with Presbyterianism," *Dialogue: A Journal of Mormon Thought* 40/3 (2007): 68–84.

60. "John Calvin - Of Baptism - Institutes Book 4.15.1," http://www.piney.com/RefCalInst4-15-1.html.

61. History, 1838–1856, volume A-1 [23 December 1805–30 August 1834], *The Joseph Smith Papers*, http://josephsmithpapers.org/paperSummary/history-1838-1856-volume-a-1-23-december-1805-30-august-1834?p=2.

62. Smith, *William Smith on Mormonism*, 7.

63. Oliver Cowdery, "Letter III to W. W. Phelps," *Messenger and Advocate* 1 (December 1834): 42.

64. Smith, *William Smith on Mormonism*, 6.

65. Larry C. Porter, "Reverend George Lane—Good 'Gifts,' Much 'Grace,' and Marked 'Usefulness,'" *BYU Studies* 9/3 (1969): 321–40.

66. Mark C. Trotter, "A United Methodist Understanding of Baptism," http://www.umc.org/what-we-believe/baptism.

67. John Wesley and Joseph Benson, *The Works of the Rev. John Wesley* (London: Conference Office, 1812), 13:428, emphasis in the original.

68. Paul Bradshaw, *The New Westminster Dictionary of Liturgy & Worship* (Louisville, KY: SCM, 2002), 42–43.

69. *Evening and the Morning Star* 2/22 (July 1834): 171.

70. *Messenger and Advocate* 1/1 (October 1834): 15.

71. History, 1838–1856, volume A-1 [23 December 1805–30 August 1834], *The Joseph Smith Papers*, http://josephsmithpapers.org/paperSummary/history-1838-1856-volume-a-1-23-december-1805-30-august-1834?p=23.

72. History, 1838–1856, volume A-1 [23 December 1805–30 August 1834], *The Joseph Smith Papers*, http://josephsmithpapers.org/paperSummary/history-1838-1856-volume-a-1-23-december-1805-30-august-1834?p=23.

73. History, 1838–1856, volume A-1 [23 December 1805–30 August 1834], *The Joseph Smith Papers*, http://josephsmithpapers.org/paperSummary/history-1838-1856-volume-a-1-23-december-1805-30-august-1834?p=24.

74. Book of Mormon (1830 ed.), 478.

75. Faulring, "Blueprint for Organizing the Church," 66, emphasis in the original.

76. Luis Ladaria, S.J., "The Question of the Validity of Baptism Conferred in the Church of Jesus Christ of Latter-Day Saints," *L'Osservatore Romano*, Weekly Edition in English, August 1, 2001, page 4. *L'Osservatore Romano* is the newspaper of the Holy See. Cited from Eternal *Word Television Network*, http://www.ewtn.com/library/theology/mormbap1.htm. United Methodists took a similar stand in 2000 but as of 2002 were considering rescinding the original resolution. Peggy Fletcher Stack, "Methodists Debate Rebaptism," *Salt Lake Tribune*, May 30, 2002, cited from Worldwide Religious News, http://wwrn.org/articles/2868/?&section=methodist. See also Linda Green, "United Methodists adopt guidelines for Mormons joining church," umc.org, News Archives, May 10, 2000, http://archives.umc.org/interior.asp?ptid=2&mid=3558.

77. "Text of: 806–NonDis," General Conference 2000, May 2–12, Cleveland, Ohio: The United Methodist Church. See also *Presbyterians and Latter-Day Saints*. Ecumenical and Interfaith Relations, Presbyterian Church (USA), Louisville, KY; and "Should

Lutherans rebaptize former Mormons who are joining the congregation?" Evangelical Lutheran Church in America, http://www.elca.org/Growing-In-Faith/Worship/Learning-Center/FAQs/Rebaptism.aspx.

78. Ladaria, "Question of the Validity of Baptism."

79. Ladaria, "Question of the Validity of Baptism," emphasis added.

80. Book of Mormon (1830 ed.), 78, 81.

81. Book of Mormon (1830 ed.), 192.

82. Joseph Smith Jr., trans., *The Book of Mormon*, 3rd ed. (Nauvoo, IL: Robinson and Smith, 1840), 53. See 1 Nephi 20:1, cf. Isaiah 48:1, emphasis added.

83. Terryl Givens provided this helpful insight.

84. Inexplicably, the Prophet's inserted phrase of the Isaiah 48 passage, "or out of the waters of baptism," was left out of the next edition, the 1841 Liverpool edition; this edition was remotely commissioned "By order of the Translator [Joseph Smith]" to British missionaries Brigham Young, Heber C. Kimball, and Parley P. Pratt, and thus was done without the Prophet's direct involvement. Still, somehow the phrase remained absent from LDS editions until the 1920 Salt Lake City edition, when it was restored again and has remained in subsequent LDS editions: the 1921, 1981, and present 2013 Salt Lake City editions. The phrase "or out of the waters of baptism" was also included in an 1858 New York unauthorized edition of the Book of Mormon, which was used by the Reorganized Church of Jesus Christ of Latter Day Saints (now Community of Christ). Similarly, the 1874 edition used by the RLDS Church included the phrase; it was finally dropped from the RLDS Church's official 1908 Iowa edition, suggesting that its meaning to the RLDS had been lost. See Facsimiles of Historic Book of Mormon Editions, http://bookofMormononline.net/#/fax; also Royal Skousen, ed., *The Book of Mormon: The Earliest Text* (New Haven: Yale University Press, 2009).

85. *Evening and the Morning Star* 1/10 (March 1833): 73, emphasis added.

86. Book of Mormon (1830 ed.), 118, emphasis added.

87. Old Testament Revision 1, *The Joseph Smith Papers*, http://josephsmithpapers.org/paperSummary/old-testament-revision-1?p=16.

88. Andrew F. Ehat and Lyndon W. Cook, comps. and eds., *The Words of Joseph Smith: The Contemporary Accounts of the Nauvoo Discourses of the Prophet Joseph* (Provo, UT: Religious Studies Center, Brigham Young University, 1980), 49.

89. *Evening and the Morning Star* 2/18 (March 1834): 143.

90. History, 1838–1856, volume A-1 [23 December 1805–30 August 1834], *The Joseph Smith Papers*, http://josephsmithpapers.org/paperSummary/history-1838-1856-volume-a-1-23-december-1805-30-august-1834?p=23.

91. Bruce M. Metzger and Bart D. Ehrman, *The Text of the New Testament: Its Transmission, Corruption, and Restoration*, 4th ed. (Oxford: Oxford University Press, 1992).

92. *The New American Standard New Testament Greek Lexicon*, based on *Thayer's and Smith's Bible Dictionary*, plus others, http://www.biblestudytools.com/lexicons/greek/nas/.

93. The NRSV reads: "Have mercy on me, O God, according to your steadfast love; according to your abundant mercy blot out my transgressions. Wash me thoroughly

from my iniquity, and cleanse me from my sin. For I know my transgressions, and my sin is ever before me. . . . Purge me with hyssop, and I shall be clean; wash me, and I shall be whiter than snow" (Psalm 51:1–2). In the law of Moses the hyssop was used in various forms of symbolic purification, that is, applied to the doorposts on the night of Passover (Exodus 12:22), used in cleansing the leper (Leviticus 14:1–6, 51), or used to sprinkle water upon all persons or effects touched by "one slain, or one dead, or a grave" (Numbers 19:18). When Jesus was on the cross "they filled a spunge with vinegar, and put it upon hyssop, and put it to his mouth" (John 19:29).

94. The King James Version reads: "Arise, and be baptized, and wash away thy sins, calling on the name of the Lord" (Acts 22:16).

95. The New Revised Standard Version of this quoted sentence is the same.

96. Jonathan D. Lawrence, *Washing in Water: Trajectories of Ritual Bathing in the Hebrew Bible and Second Temple Literature* (Atlanta, GA: Society of Biblical Literature, 2006), 3–4, emphasis added. According to Lawrence, 286 potential miqva'ot were discovered archaeologically from the Second Temple period of Judaism; 262 are located in Judea, 151 in Jerusalem, and another 31 in Jericho. According to Christian author Ron Moseley: "Historically, we know that there were many ritual immersion baths (mikvaot) on the Temple Mount including one in the Chamber of Lepers situated in the northwest corner of the Court of Women (Mid. 2:5). Josephus tells us that even during the years of war (66–73 A.D.) the laws of ritual immersion were strictly adhered to (Jos. Wars, 4:205). The Temple itself contained immersion baths in various places for the priests to use, even in the vaults beneath the court (Commentary to Tam. 26b; Tam. 1:1). The High Priest had special immersion pools in the Temple, two of which are mentioned in the Mishnah. We are told one of these was in the Water Gate in the south of the court and another was on the roof of the Parva Chamber (Mid. 1:4; Mid. 5:3). There was an additional place for immersion on the Mount of Olives which was connected with the burning of the red heifer (Par. 3:7). A special ramp led to the mikveh on the Mount of Olives from the Temple Mount, which was built as an arched way over another arched way to avoid uncleanness from the graves in the valley below. Recent archaeological excavations have found 48 different mikvaot near the Monumental Staircase leading into the Temple Complex."

97. "Baptism," in *Jewish Encyclopedia*, http://www.jewishencyclopedia.com/articles/2456-baptism.

98. "Baptism," in *Jewish Encyclopedia*.

99. Rivkah Slonim, "The Mikvah," The Jewish Woman, Chabad.org, http://www.chabad.org/theJewishWoman/article_cdo/aid/1541/jewish/The-Mikvah.htm.

100. Ladaria, "Question of the Validity of Baptism."

101. Ladaria, "Question of the Validity of Baptism."

102. History, 1838–1856, volume A-1 [23 December 1805–30 August 1834], *The Joseph Smith Papers*, http://josephsmithpapers.org/paperSummary/history-1838-1856-volume-a-1-23-december-1805-30-august-1834?p=3.

103. Book of Mormon (1830 ed.), 119–20.

104. As part of a much larger, broad-based critique of the Book of Mormon, Alexander Campbell questioned how Nephi could speak of baptism "2300 years ago," or how Alma baptized in the waters of Mormon "100 years before Christ was born"; see Alexander Campbell, "An Analysis of the Book of Mormon," *Millennial Harbinger* 2 (1831): 94. Such criticisms directed at Campbell's competitor, Smith, blended with what Givens called "religious propaganda, political polemics, and prurient sensationalism," speaking of another popular form of nineteenth-century religious denigration: anti-Catholic novels. Terryl L. Givens, *The Viper on the Hearth: Mormons, Myths, and the Construction of Heresy* (New York: Oxford University Press, 1997), 113.

105. "Truth Will Prevail," *Times and Seasons* 3/9 (March 1, 1842): 710.

106. Grant Underwood, *The Millenarian World of Early Mormonism* (Champaign: University of Illinois Press, 1999), 76–79.

107. Bushman, *Rough Stone Rolling*, 122.

108. Revelation Book 1, *The Joseph Smith Papers*, http://josephsmithpapers.org/paperSummary/revelation-book-1?p=25.

109. Bushman, *Rough Stone Rolling*, 122.

110. "Mormonism -- Nos. VIII – IX," *Ohio Star*, December 8, 1831.

111. "And I saw the holy city, the new Jerusalem, coming down out of heaven from God, prepared as a bride adorned for her husband" (Revelation 21:2 NRSV).

112. Donald Burke, "New England New Jerusalem, the Millenarian Dimension of Transatlantic Migration: A Study in the Theology of History" (PhD diss., Wayne State University, 2006).

113. Samuel Sewall, *Phaenomena quaedam Apocalyptica ad aspectum Novi Orbis configurata. Or, some few lines towards a description of the New Heaven (1697)*, University of Nebraska—Lincoln, Electronic Texts in American Studies, DigitalCommons@University of Nebraska—Lincoln, 2, emphasis added.

114. This summary of Protestant American religionist views of New Jerusalem comes from Craig S. Campbell, *Images of the New Jerusalem: Latter-Day Saint Faction Interpretations of Independence, Missouri* (Knoxville: University of Tennessee Press, 2004), 6–8.

115. W. A. Morris, *The Writings of Alexander Campbell: Selections Chiefly from the Millennial Harbinger* (Austin, TX: Eugene Von Boeckmann, 1896), 280.

116. "I saw that while Jesus was in the Most Holy place he would be married to the New Jerusalem, and after his work should be accomplished in the Holiest, he would descend to earth in kingly power and take the precious ones to himself who had patiently waited his return." Ellen G. White, *The Great Controversy between Christ and Satan* (1858; repr., Charleston, SC: BiblioBazaar, 2008), 115.

117. Roy W. Doxey, *The Doctrine and Covenants Speaks* (Salt Lake City: Deseret Book, 1973), 1:80.

118. Book of Commandments, 1833, *The Joseph Smith Papers*, http://josephsmithpapers.org/paperSummary/book-of-commandments-1833?p=18. See also D&C 6:1–3.

119. Actually the concept of Zion appears many times in 1 Nephi and 2 Nephi, and Joseph Smith thus would have encountered these mentions of Zion while working with scribe Martin Harris and, perhaps to a much lesser extent, Joseph's wife, Emma. But

these companions apparently did not motivate Joseph to seek clarification from God. So the first evidence of what I would call "clarifying" latter-day revelations to the Prophet comes while working with Oliver Cowdery. Oliver's formal legal training would have taught him to question and clarify the meaning and interpretation of concepts. Oliver was a spirited project companion: he and Joseph debated whether John, the beloved disciple of Jesus, had died or tarried in the flesh, which led to the clarifying revelation in D&C 7. He tried unsuccessfully to translate the plates as Joseph had done (see D&C 8–9). Then together they "inquire[d] of the Lord respecting baptism for the remission of sins, that we found mentioned in the translation of the plates," which led to ordination to the Aaronic Priesthood (D&C 13). Thus we see a flurry of revelations on Zion at precisely the time when Smith and companion Cowdery sequentially encountered Zion in the Book of Mormon text, initially in Mosiah, then 3 Nephi, and then Ether, and finally in 1 Nephi and 2 Nephi as they returned to the beginning to replace the lost pages of Lehi.

120. Book of Mormon (1830 ed.), 182, emphasis added.

121. Matthew O. Richardson, "Establishing Zion in Missouri," in *Joseph: Exploring the Life and Ministry of the Prophet*, ed. Andrew C. Skinner and Susan Easton Black (Provo, UT: Deseret Book, 2005), 157.

122. Book of Mormon (1830 ed.), 499, 501.

123. Richardson, "Establishing Zion in Missouri," 157.

124. Book of Mormon (1830 ed.), 566.

125. "Joseph is a fruitful bough . . . whose branches run over the wall . . . unto the utmost bound of the everlasting hills . . . that was separate from his brethren" (Genesis 49:22, 26 KJV). "Joseph is a fruitful bough . . . his branches run over the wall . . . the bounties of the everlasting hills . . . who was set apart from his brothers" (NRSV).

126. Revelation, 6 April 1830 [D&C 21], *The Joseph Smith Papers*, http://josephsmithpapers.org/paperSummary/revelation-6-april-1830-dc-21?p=1. See D&C 21:7–8.

127. Campbell, in *Images of the New Jerusalem*, noted that this idea of an agrarian inheritance was influenced by Jeffersonian America in the early nineteenth century. Thomas Jefferson declared: "Those who labor in the earth are the chosen people of God, if ever He had a chosen people, whose breasts He has made His peculiar deposit for substantial and genuine virtue. It is the focus in which he keeps alive that sacred fire, which otherwise might escape from the face of the earth." Quoted in Leo Marx, *The Machine in the Garden: Technology and the Pastoral Ideal in America* (New York: Oxford University Press, 1964), 157.

128. Robin Scott Jensen, Robert J. Woodford, and Steven C. Harper, eds., *Manuscript Revelation Books*, facsimile edition, first volume of the Revelations and Translations series of *The Joseph Smith Papers*, edited by Dean C. Jessee, Ronald K. Esplin, and Richard Lyman Bushman (Salt Lake City: Church Historian's Press, 2009), 39. See D&C 25:1.

129. History, 1838–1856, volume A-1 [23 December 1805–30 August 1834], *The Joseph Smith Papers*, http://josephsmithpapers.org/paperSummary/history-1838-1856-volume-a-1-23-december-1805-30-august-1834?p=55.

130. The King James Version reads: "And Enoch walked with God: and he was not; for God took him" (Genesis 5:24).

131. Old Testament Revision 1, *The Joseph Smith Papers*, http://josephsmithpapers.org/paperSummary/old-testament-revision-1?p=20. See Moses 7:69.

132. Givens, "Prophecy of Enoch as Restoration Blueprint," 3–4.

133. Old Testament Revision 1, *The Joseph Smith Papers*, http://josephsmithpapers.org/paperSummary/old-testament-revision-1?p=20. See Moses 7:62–64.

134. Upon his arrival, Smith recorded: "But our reflections were great: coming as we had from a highly cultivated state of society in the east, and standing now upon the confines, or western limits of the united States, and looking into the vast wilderness of those that sat in darkness, how natural it was to observe the degredation, leanness of intellect, ferocity and jealousy of a people that were nearly a century behind the times; and to feel for those who roamed about without the benefit of civilization, refinement or religion!—yea, and exclaim in the language of the prophets:—when will the wilderness blossom as the rose; when will Zion be built up in her glory, and where will thy Temple stand unto which all nations shall come in the last days?" History, 1838–1856, volume A-1 [23 December 1805–30 August 1834], *The Joseph Smith Papers*, http://josephsmithpapers.org/paperSummary/history-1838-1856-volume-a-1-23-december-1805-30-august-1834?p=133.

135. See Matthew B. Brown and Paul Thomas Smith, *Symbols in Stone: Symbolism on the Early Temples of the Restoration* (American Fork, UT: Covenant Communications, 1997).

136. Book of Mormon (1830 ed.), 497.

137. Book of Mormon (1830 ed.), 566.

138. History, 1838–1856, volume A-1 [23 December 1805–30 August 1834], *The Joseph Smith Papers*, http://josephsmithpapers.org/paperSummary/history-1838-1856-volume-a-1-23-december-1805-30-august-1834?p=93. See Moses 7:62.

139. "If you conquer, I will make you a pillar in the temple of my God; you will never go out of it. I will write on you the name of my God, and the name of the city of my God, the new Jerusalem that comes down from my God out of heaven, and my own new name" (Revelation 3:12 NRSV).

4. Influences on the Temple of the Early Restoration

1. "Facts and Statistics," Newsroom, Church of Jesus Christ of Latter-day Saints, http://www.mormonnewsroom.org/facts-and-stats.

2. "Temples of the Church of Jesus Christ of Latter-day Saints," LDS Church Temples.com, http://www.ldschurchtemples.com/statistics/units/.

3. Adney Y. Komatsu, "The House of the Lord," *Ensign*, November 1983, 27.

4. Truman G. Madsen, "The Temple and the Restoration," in *The Temple in Antiquity: Ancient Records and Modern Perspectives*, ed. Truman G. Madsen (West Valley City, UT: Bookcraft, 1984), 2.

5. History, 1834–1836, 13 December 1835 • Sunday, *The Joseph Smith Papers*, http://josephsmithpapers.org/paperSummary/history-1834-1836?p=150.

6. Glen M. Leonard, *Nauvoo: A Place of Peace, a People of Promise* (Salt Lake City: Shadow Mountain Publishing, 2002), 204.

7. Andrew F. Ehat, "Joseph Smith's Introduction of Temple Ordinances and the 1844 Mormon Succession Question" (master's thesis, Brigham Young University, 1982), 18.

8. "drove out all who were selling and buying in the temple. . . . He said to them, 'It is written, "My house shall be called a house of prayer"'" (Matthew 21:12–13 NRSV).

9. "Now every year his parents went to Jerusalem for the festival of the Passover" (Luke 2:41 NRSV).

10. Regarding the annual pilgrimage requirement, LDS apostle Bruce R. McConkie said: "By the time of Jesus, however, it was no longer possible for all males—scattered among many nations, as they were—to go up three times a year to the City of God. Instead twenty-four courses of lay attendants were appointed to stand in the temple as representatives of all the people; attendance at the feasts became something that could be delegated, as it were." Bruce R. McConkie, *The Mortal Messiah: From Bethlehem to Calvary* (Salt Lake City: Deseret Book, 1979), 1:160.

11. "shall bring the sheaf of the first fruits of your harvest to the priest" (Leviticus 23:10 NRSV).

12. "Jesus went throughout Galilee, teaching in their synagogues and proclaiming the good news of the kingdom and curing every disease and every sickness among the people" (Matthew 4:23 NRSV).

13. "went to Capernaum; and when the sabbath came, he entered the synagogue and taught. They were astounded at his teaching, for he taught them as one having authority, and not as the scribes" (Mark 1:21–22 NRSV).

14. "who belonged to the synagogue of the Freedmen (as it was called), Cyrenians, Alexandrians, and others of those from Cilicia and Asia" (Acts 6:9 NRSV).

15. "The Jews incited the devout women of high standing and the leading men of the city, and stirred up persecution against Paul and Barnabas, and drove them out of their region" (Acts 13:50 NRSV). Research suggests that New Testament Christians indeed practiced a dual form of worship. Researcher Marcus von Wellnitz observed: "Christ and his disciples were deeply involved with the temple *and* the synagogue. . . . It appears obvious that the early Christians not only had their Sunday services, either in a Jewish synagogue or a member's domicile, but also that they still retained the periodic visit to the temple and saw no conflict in the dual nature of their worship." Marcus von Wellnitz, "The Catholic Liturgy and the Mormon Temple," *BYU Studies* 21/1 (1981): 5, emphasis added. Luke, eyewitness to the emerging New Testament Church, confirmed this dual form of worship in the book of Acts: "And they [the disciples], continuing daily with one accord [1] *in the temple*, and [2] *breaking bread [the sacrament] from house to house*, did eat their meat with gladness and singleness of heart, Praising God, and having favour with all the people" (Acts 2:46–47, emphasis added). "Day by day, as they spent much time together in the temple, they broke bread at home and ate their food with glad and generous hearts, praising God and having the goodwill of all the people" (NRSV).

16. The Old Testament reference to *synagogue* is a prayer of lamentation on the destruction of the temple; in this one instance we see the framework of dualistic worship in the Psalmist's life, but not much else: "They have cast fire into thy sanctuary [the temple], they have defiled by casting down the dwelling place of thy name to the ground. They said in their hearts, Let us destroy them together: they have burned up all the synagogues of God in the land" (Psalm 74:7–8 KJV). "They set your sanctuary on fire; they desecrated the dwelling place of your name, bringing it to the ground. They said to themselves, 'We will utterly subdue them;' they burned all the meeting places of God in the land" (Psalm 74:7–8 NRSV).

17. Book of Mormon (1830 ed.), 492.

18. Book of Mormon (1830 ed.), 8.

19. Book of Mormon (1830 ed.), 108.

20. While the temple dates back to nearly the second millennium BC, synagogue worship as an institution is more recent, though still uncertain. In fact, so little information about the synagogue is contained in the Hebrew Bible that rabbinical scholars differ considerably over the emergence of the synagogue: One theory says the synagogue emerged during the period of Solomon's temple in the tenth century BC; another during Josiah's great temple centralization in 622 BC, when the synagogue became a place of local spiritual activity to complement the temple; still another that the synagogue emerged after the destruction of the Jerusalem temple in 586 BC, either in the Diaspora (in Babylonia) or during the period of the Second Temple under Ezra and Nehemiah. See Lee I. Levine, *The Ancient Synagogue: The First Thousand Years* (New Haven, CT: Yale University Press, 2005).

21. Book of Mormon (1830 ed.), 268.

22. Book of Mormon (1830 ed.), 313.

23. Book of Mormon (1830 ed.), 492.

24. David Whitmer, *An Address to All Believers in Christ: By a Witness to the Divine Authenticity of the Book of Mormon* (Richmond, MO, 1887), 32–33.

25. "Mormonism -- Nos. VIII – IX," *Ohio Star*, December 8, 1831.

26. Bushman, *Rough Stone Rolling*, 216.

27. Historical Introduction, History, circa summer 1832, *The Joseph Smith Papers*, http://josephsmithpapers.org/paperSummary/history-circa-summer-1832?p=4.

28. Historical Introduction, History, circa summer 1832, *The Joseph Smith Papers*, http://josephsmithpapers.org/paperSummary/history-circa-summer-1832?p=4.

29. Of the time frame for these historical accounts, Prince wrote: "Several lines of evidence suggest that this account [of Moroni], though cast in a setting of 1823, reflects the understanding of 1838 and is thus anachronistic. . . . Earlier accounts of Moroni's visit failed to mention either Elijah or priesthood. Also, no Restoration reference to Elijah prior to the 1838 account mentions or infers a relationship between Elijah and priesthood. The sequential redactions of Malachi 4:6, which formed the basis of a developing theology of afterlife, demonstrate a continuum." See Gregory A. Prince, *Power from on High: The Development of Mormon Priesthood* (Salt Lake City: Signature Books, 1995), 37.

30. History, 1838–1856, volume A-1 [23 December 1805–30 August 1834], *The Joseph Smith Papers*, http://josephsmithpapers.org/paperSummary/history-1838-1856-volume-a-1-23-december-1805-30-august-1834?p=5.

31. Journal, 1835–1836, *The Joseph Smith Papers*, http://josephsmithpapers.org/paperSummary/journal-1835-1836?p=26.

32. Journal, 1835–1836, *The Joseph Smith Papers*, http://josephsmithpapers.org/paperSummary/journal-1835-1836?p=26.

33. Out of sixty-nine verses quoted by Moroni. Some passages referenced multiple themes, so totals do not sum to 100 percent. My research, based on Oliver Cowdery's "Letter VI, to W.W. Phelps, Esq.," *Messenger and Advocate* 1/7 (April 1835): 109–12, and Smith, History, 1838–1856, volume A-1 [23 December 1805–30 August 1834].

34. "See, I am sending my messenger to prepare the way before me, and the Lord whom you seek will suddenly come to his temple. The messenger of the covenant in whom you delight—indeed, he is coming, says the Lord of hosts" (Malachi 3:1 NRSV). Smith recorded in his history that Moroni "first quoted part of the third chapter of Malachi" (History, 1838–1856), which by inference would be verses 1–4 since they relate directly to the remainder of Moroni's quotation of Malachi: "And he quoted also the fourth or last chapter of the same prophecy," that is, Malachi 4:1, 5. Historian B. H. Roberts wrote: "This [verses 1–4] undoubtedly would be the first part of the third chapter of Malachi [quoted by Moroni], as that part of the chapter has undoubtedly a direct bearing on the coming forth of God's work in the last days." B. H. Roberts, *New Witnesses for God* (1909; repr., Salt Lake City: Deseret Book, 1950), 2:73 note h.

35. See Adam Clarke, "Commentary on Malachi 3," in *The Adam Clarke Commentary*, http://www.studylight.org/com/acc/view.cgi?bk=38&ch=3; also Malachi 3, Matthew Henry Commentary on the Whole Bible (Complete), http://www.biblestudytools.com/commentaries/matthew-henry-complete/malachi/3.html.

36. History, circa June 1839–circa 1841 [Draft 2], *The Joseph Smith Papers*, http://josephsmithpapers.org/paperSummary/history-circa-june-1839-circa-1841-draft-2?p=5. "Lo, I will send you the prophet Elijah before the great and terrible day of the Lord comes. He will turn the hearts of parents to their children and the hearts of children to their parents, so that I will not come and strike the land with a curse" (Malachi 4:5–6 NRSV).

37. Book of Commandments, 1833, CHAPTER XXXVII, Revelation, 7 December 1830 [D&C 35], *The Joseph Smith Papers*, http://josephsmithpapers.org/paperSummary/book-of-commandments-1833?p=80. See D&C 35:4. This revelation was the first recorded chronologically giving reference to Elijah in the early restoration; see also Prince, *Power from on High*.

38. History, 1838–1856, volume B-1 [1 September 1834–2 November 1838], *The Joseph Smith Papers*, http://josephsmithpapers.org/paperSummary/history-1838-1856-volume-b-1-1-september-1834-2-november-1838?p=182. See D&C 110:13–16.

39. Prince, *Power from on High*, 35.

40. Andrew F. Ehat and Lyndon W. Cook, comps. and eds., *The Words of Joseph Smith* (Provo, UT: Religious Studies Center, Brigham Young University, 1980), 329.

41. Boyd K. Packer, *The Holy Temple* (Salt Lake City: Deseret Book, 1980), 137.

42. Ronald E. Romig, "Temple Lot Discoveries and the RLDS Temple," in *Regional Studies in LDS History: Missouri* (Salt Lake City: Deseret Book, 1994).

43. In fact, the Hebrew Bible, or Old Testament, records various accounts of sanctioned altar worship at places away from the temple altar at Jerusalem, usually overlooked by a nonthorough examination, including Jethro (Exodus 18:12), Gideon (Judges 6:23–36), Manoah (Judges 13:19–20), Samuel (1 Samuel 1:1; 7:9, 15–17), Saul (1 Samuel 14:35), and David (2 Samuel 24:24–25).

44. Book of Mormon (1830 ed.), 72.

45. According to Joseph Modrzejewski the Elephantine temple "was not a house of prayer, like the future synagogues in the Land of Israel and the Diaspora, but a genuine temple with its complement of priests to whom the tithe was paid, and where worship took place according to the biblical precepts, with burnt offerings, oblations, and incense, as was the practice in Jerusalem. This, then, was one of the 'high places' condemned by the Deuteronomic reform [of King Josiah], which ordained their elimination." Joseph Modrzejewski, *The Jews of Egypt: From Rameses II to Emperor Hadrian* (Princeton: Princeton University Press, 1997), 36.

46. Josephus, *Antiquities of the Jews* 13.3.3.

47. Book of Mormon (1830 ed.), 72.

48. See Menahem Haran, *Temples and Temple Service in Ancient Israel* (Winona Lake, IN: Eisenbrauns, 1995). See also Joseph Modrzejewski, *The Jews of Egypt: From Rameses II to Emperor Hadrian* (Princeton: Princeton University Press, 1997), 25–26.

49. Solomon Zeitlin, "The Offspring of Intermarriage," *Jewish Quarterly Review*, n.s., 51/2 (1960): 139.

50. Based on their research, John Lundquist and John Welch noted: "Covenant ceremonies at temples were essential to the successful creation of ancient states. For a charismatic figure to merely become king did not assure or perpetuate the state. Without inward commitments and outward symbols of the temple, Nephi's little community looked like a mere splinter group, lacking divine and social sanction. With these observances, however, they laid an enduring foundation for the reign of Nephite kings for over four hundred years to come." "Kingship and Temple in 2 Nephi 5–10," in *Reexploring the Book of Mormon*, ed. John W. Welch (Salt Lake City: Deseret Book and FARMS, 1993), 68.

51. Book of Mormon (1830 ed.), 155–56, emphasis added.

52. "You shall live in booths for seven days; all that are citizens in Israel shall live in booths, so that your generations may know that I made the people of Israel live in booths when I brought them out of the land of Egypt" (Leviticus 23:42–43 NRSV).

53. See John A. Tvedtnes, "King Benjamin and the Feast of Tabernacles," in *By Study and Also by Faith*, ed. Stephen D. Ricks and John M. Lundquist (Salt Lake City: Deseret Book and FARMS, 1990), 2:197–237.

54. Book of Mormon (1830 ed.), 157.

55. Why would Christ not come to the temple of Zarahemla? The city of Zarahemla fell into decline and apostasy in the years leading up to the coming of Christ to America.

Wracked with civil war and secret societies, the people of Zarahemla abandoned the higher forms of Nephite government instituted two hundred years earlier by King Mosiah$_2$ and dissolved into primitive tribes and tribal alliances. Soon thereafter seismic destruction changed the very geography of the Book of Mormon lands in the Americas, and "that great city Zarahemla [was] burned with fire, and the inhabitants thereof." Book of Mormon (1830 ed.), 472.

56. John W. Welch, "The Temple in the Book of Mormon: The Temples at the Cities of Nephi, Zarahemla, and Bountiful," in *Temples of the Ancient World: Ritual and Symbolism*, ed. Donald W. Parry (Salt Lake City: Deseret Book and FARMS, 1994), 367–68.

57. The issue for early Catholicism was how to reconcile the early common Christian desire for the long-held deep meaning of the temple, which was Jewish, and the new Christian sacramental worship established by Christ. The resolution seemed inevitable: the temple would be subsumed into the church. Marcus von Wellnitz describes some of these early Catholic innovations as the church assumed symbolic features of the temple: "[Like the temple, the] earliest basilicas were divided into three parts: first, the atrium or forecourt; then the church proper with the area for the congregation; and, finally, set off by a barrier, the holy place for the altar and the officiating clergy. Thus the church became a temple, because it is a place 'where the Christians perform a sacrifice.' With the introduction of the [temple] altar in the church, the mixture of temple and synagogue became even more complete. Yet the altar was a structure of the outside [temple] court and not of the sacred temple interior, but the affiliation of both places was soon established. The locale of the altar in the church was converted into a sanctuary and the purpose and function of the ark of the covenant in the [temple] Holy of Holies was transferred to the [church] altar. With the real temple in Jerusalem destroyed and the Catholic Church as its self-appointed successor, the site of the church altar now symbolized the most holy place, the sanctum sanctorum. This was dramatically emphasized by Renaissance and Baroque architects who often surrounded the [church] altar with statues of angels representing the cherubim of the Lord's presence on the ark of the covenant [in the temple]." Wellnitz, "Catholic Liturgy and the Mormon Temple," 7, 21, 23.

58. Book of Mormon (1830 ed.), 266.

59. Book of Mormon (1830 ed.), 412.

60. Book of Mormon (1830 ed.), 412.

61. Book of Mormon (1830 ed.), 268, emphasis added.

62. "and the sanctuaries of Israel shall be laid waste" (Amos 7:9 NRSV).

63. Haran, *Temples and Temple Service in Ancient Israel*, 16.

64. *Journal of Discourses*, 3:372, emphasis added.

65. Gordon B. Hinckley, "Some Thoughts on Temples, Retention of Converts, and Missionary Service," *Ensign*, November 1997, 49, emphasis added.

66. Bushman, *Rough Stone Rolling*, 216.

67. History, 1838–1856, volume A-1 [23 December 1805–30 August 1834], *The Joseph Smith Papers*, http://josephsmithpapers.org/paperSummary/history-1838-1856-volume-a-1-23-december-1805-30-august-1834?p=96. See also D&C 38:32, 37–39.

68. "so stay here in the city until you have been clothed with power from on high" (Luke 24:49 NRSV).

69. "All of them were filled with the Holy Spirit and began to speak in other languages, as the Spirit gave them ability" (Acts 2:4 NRSV).

70. "Endowment," in Noah Webster, *American Dictionary of the English Language* (1828 Facsimile Edition), Foundation for American Christian Education, Facsimile of 1st edition (June 1, 1967), http://1828.mshaffer.com.

71. History, 1838–1856, volume A-1 [23 December 1805–30 August 1834], *The Joseph Smith Papers*, http://josephsmithpapers.org/paperSummary/history-1838-1856-volume-a-1-23-december-1805-30-august-1834?p=262. See D&C 88:127, received January 3, 1833; the version using the phrase "school of the prophets" was added in 1835.

72. History, 1838–1856, volume A-1 [23 December 1805–30 August 1834], *The Joseph Smith Papers*, http://josephsmithpapers.org/paperSummary/history-1838-1856-volume-a-1-23-december-1805-30-august-1834?p=254. See D&C 88:38–40, received December 27, 1832.

73. *Lectures on Faith* (1835), lecture 2, paragraph 18.

74. Harold Bloom, *The American Religion: The Emergence of the Post-Christian Nation* (New York: Simon & Schuster, 1992), 99.

75. Revelation Book 1, Revelation, 6 May 1833 [D&C 93], *The Joseph Smith Papers*, http://josephsmithpapers.org/paperSummary/revelation-book-1?p=167. See D&C 93:1, 20, 36.

76. Revelation Book 1, Revelation, 1 June 1833 [D&C 95], *The Joseph Smith Papers*, http://josephsmithpapers.org/paperSummary/revelation-book-1. See also D&C 95:8–9.

77. Book of Mormon (1830 ed.), 435.

78. Minute Book 1, 166, *The Joseph Smith Papers*, http://josephsmithpapers.org/paperSummary/minute-book-1?p=166.

79. According to tradition, the day of the first Christian Pentecost described in Acts 2 took place in the Upper Room, where Jesus held the last supper. Alternative interpretations suggest that the location was instead the House of God, or Herod's temple, probably Solomon's Porch or the Court of the Gentiles, both public meeting spaces that were not connected to formal temple ritual. See "Herod's Temple," *Easton's Bible Dictionary*, http://www.biblestudytools.com/dictionaries/eastons-bible-dictionary/temple-herods.html. Also "Solomon's Porch," *Scripture Backdrops*, http://www.bible-history.com/backd2/solomons_porch.html.

80. Andrew Ehat provides an excellent summary of the New Testament and Nephite endowment in "'Who Shall Ascend into the Hill of the Lord?' Sesquicentennial Reflections of a Sacred Day: 4 May 1842," in *Temples of the Ancient World: Ritual and Symbolism*, ed. Donald W. Parry (Salt Lake City: Deseret Book and FARMS, 1994).

81. Book of Mormon (1830 ed.), 494–95.

82. History, 1838–1856, volume B-1 [1 September 1834–2 November 1838], *The Joseph Smith Papers*, http://josephsmithpapers.org/paperSummary/history-1838-1856-volume-b-1-1-september-1834-2-november-1838?p=177.

83. History, 1838–1856, volume B-1 [1 September 1834–2 November 1838], *The Joseph Smith Papers*, http://josephsmithpapers.org/paperSummary/history-1838-1856-volume-b-1-1-september-1834-2-november-1838?p=307.

84. History, 1838–1856, volume B-1 [1 September 1834–2 November 1838], *The Joseph Smith Papers*, http://josephsmithpapers.org/paperSummary/history-1838-1856-volume-b-1-1-september-1834-2-november-1838?p=180.

85. Another ritual ordinance introduced at the Kirtland Temple was a washing of feet by the First Presidency and Quorum of the Twelve Apostles, similar in form to the New Testament account of Jesus washing the feet of his disciples at the last supper (see John 13:5–17). At Kirtland this was a special ordinance for a select few of the congregation.

86. History, 1838–1856, volume B-1 [1 September 1834–2 November 1838], *The Joseph Smith Papers*, http://josephsmithpapers.org/paperSummary/history-1838-1856-volume-b-1-1-september-1834-2-november-1838?p=149.

87. Book of Mormon (1830 ed.), 477.

88. Book of Mormon (1830 ed.).

89. Reed Durham summarizes these occasions: "1. At the close of the famous Sidney Rigdon Salt Sermon at Missouri in 1838; 2. By the twelve before leaving for their missions to England, 1838; 3. Upon arrival on English soil, Brigham Young and the rest of the Twelve with him, April 6, 1840; 4. At a secret council of fifty meeting in Nauvoo, March 11, 1844, and April 11, 1844; 5. At the laying of the capstone of the Nauvoo Temple, May 24, 1845; 6. Upon entering the Salt Lake Valley for the first time; 7. At several general conferences—April 11, 1852; October 6, 1862; April 9, 1882; 8. At a 24th of July celebration in Brigham City—July 24, 1875; 9. Occasionally, at a ward or stake conference. When the proper occasion arises for this spiritious [*sic*] congregational shout of praise and rejoicing (and it is now used only on rather special occasions), when the spirit guides the proper ecclesiastical authority, and when the congregation has been properly tutored and instructed in the sacredness and pattern of it, the Hosanna Shout is one of the most dramatic and impressive ceremonies in the Church." Reed Durham, "What Is the Hosanna Shout?," Q&A: Questions and Answers, *New Era*, September 1973, 14–15.

90. Dean C. Jessee, "The Kirtland Diary of Wilford Woodruff," *BYU Studies* 12/4 (1972): 390.

91. N. B. Lundwall, *Temples of the Most High* (Salt Lake City: Deseret Book, 1941), 23–24.

92. Book of Mormon (1830 ed.), 494.

93. Book of Mormon (1830 ed.), 494, 495. In 3 Nephi 19:22, Jesus added, "They pray unto me because I am with them."

94. Book of Mormon (1830 ed.), 495.

95. Truman O. Angell records the following: "Frederick G. Williams, one of President Smith's counselors, came into the temple, when the following dialogue took place in my presence. Carpenter Rolph said: 'Doctor, what do you think of the house? He answered: 'It looks to me like the pattern precisely.' Then he related the following: 'Joseph received the word of the Lord for him to take his two counselors, Williams and Rigdon, and come before the Lord, and He would show them the plan or model of the house to

be built. We were upon our knees, called on the Lord, and the building appeared within viewing distance. I being the first to discover it. Then all of us viewed it together. After we had taken a good look at the exterior, the building seemed to come right over us; and the make-up of this hall seemed to coincide with what I there saw to a minutia.' Joseph was accordingly enabled to dictate to the mechanics, and his counselors stood as witnesses." Truman O. Angell, *Autobiography*, 4–5, cited in Matthew B. Brown and Paul Thomas Smith, *Symbols in Stone: Symbolism on the Early Temples of the Restoration* (American Fork, UT: Covenant Communications, Inc., 2003), 76.

96. Edward W. Tullidge, "Eliza R. Snow's Graphic Description of the Temple and Its Dedication—Hosannas to God—His Glory Fills the House," *The Women of Mormondom* (New York, 1877), 81–82, emphasis added. See also Kip Sperry, *Kirtland, Ohio: A Guide to Family History and Historical Sources* (Provo, UT: Religious Studies Center, Brigham Young University, 2005), 225–26.

97. History, 1838–1856, volume B-1 [1 September 1834–2 November 1838], *The Joseph Smith Papers*, http://josephsmithpapers.org/paperSummary/history-1838-1856-volume-b-1-1-september-1834-2-november-1838?p=181. See D&C 110:2, 3, 5, 7.

98. Jessee, "Kirtland Diary of Wilford Woodruff," 385–86.

99. Jessee, "Kirtland Diary of Wilford Woodruff," 386.

100. Marilyn Chiat, *North American Churches* (Lincolnwood, IL: Publications International, 2004), 72.

101. "Virtual Tour of the Temple," Community of Christ, http://www.cofchrist.org/visit/virtual/default.asp.

102. Ehat and Cook, *Words of Joseph Smith*, 49.

103. History, 1838–1856, volume C-1 [2 November 1838–31 July 1842], *The Joseph Smith Papers*, http://josephsmithpapers.org/paperSummary/history-1838-1856-volume-c-1-2-november-1838-31-july-1842?p=323. See D&C 124:31, 33–34.

104. History, 1838–1856, volume C-1 [2 November 1838–31 July 1842], *The Joseph Smith Papers*, http://josephsmithpapers.org/paperSummary/history-1838-1856-volume-c-1-2-november-1838-31-july-1842?p=324. See D&C 124:39–40.

5. Priesthood Restorations, Origins, and Influences

1. "You shall anoint Aaron and his sons, and consecrate them, in order that they may serve me as priests" (Exodus 30:30 NRSV).

2. "And he appointed twelve, whom he also named apostles, to be with him, and to be sent out to proclaim the message, and to have authority to cast out demons" (Mark 3:14–15 NRSV). Luke 6:13 called these twelve *apostles*: "He called unto him his disciples: and of them he chose twelve, whom also he named apostles" (KJV), and "he called his disciples and chose twelve of them, whom he also named apostles" (NRSV).

3. Walter Augustus Shirley, *The Supremacy of Holy Scripture: Four Lectures Composed for Delivery before the University of Oxford in Lent and Easter Terms 1847* (London: Oxford, 1847).

4. Martin Luther, *The Babylonian Captivity of the Church: A Prelude 1520, Jesus*, 7.9 (Project Wittenberg, Concordia Theological Seminary), http://www.lutherdansk.dk/Web-Babylonian%20Captivitate/Martin%20Luther.htm.

5. Revelation Book 1, *The Joseph Smith Papers*, http://josephsmithpapers.org/paperSummary/revelation-book-1?p=16. See D&C 22:2.

6. In 1834 Cowdery described this experience: "What Joy filled our hearts, and with what surprise we must have bowed, (for who would not have bowed the knee for such a blessing?) when we received under his hand the holy priesthood, as he said, ["] upon <you> my fellow servants, in the name of Messiah I confer this priesthood, and this authority, which shall remain upon earth, that the sons of Levi may yet offer an offering into the Lord in righteousness!" History, 1834–1836, *The Joseph Smith Papers*, http://josephsmithpapers.org/paperSummary/history-1834-1836?p=51. Cowdery then recorded in 1835: "He [Joseph] was ordained by the angel John, unto the lesser or Aaronic priesthood, in company with myself, in the town of Harmony, Susquehannah County, Pennsylvania, on Fryday, the 15th day of May, 1829, after which we repaired to the water, even to the Susquehannah River, and were baptized, he first ministering unto me and after—I to him." Blessing for Joseph Smith Sr., circa September 1835, *The Joseph Smith Papers*, Blessing given by Joseph Smith Jr. to Oliver Cowdery, 18 Dec. 1833, Kirtland, Ohio, transcribed 2 Oct. 1835, Patriarchal Blessing Book 1, pp. 8–9, Historical Dept., Archives Division, The Church of Jesus Christ of Latter-day Saints, Salt Lake City. Joseph Smith recorded this vision later in 1838: "While we were thus employed praying and calling upon the Lord, a Messenger from heaven, descended in a cloud of light, and having laid his hands upon us, he ordained us, saying unto us; "Upon you my fellow servants in the name of Messiah I confer the priesthood of Aaron." History, 1838–1856, volume A-1 [23 December 1805–30 August 1834], *The Joseph Smith Papers*, http://josephsmithpapers.org/paperSummary/history-1838-1856-volume-a-1-23-december-1805-30-august-1834?p=23. See also D&C 13.

7. History, 1838–1856, volume A-1 [23 December 1805–30 August 1834], *The Joseph Smith Papers*, http://josephsmithpapers.org/paperSummary/history-1838-1856-volume-a-1-23-december-1805-30-august-1834?p=86. See D&C 36:5–7.

8. Many New York religions had a dearth of educated and trained ministers willing to leave their clerical positions on the East Coast and move west to settle new lands and service rough, less civilized, and less religiously inclined colonizers. Consequently, some faiths instituted clergy innovations out of necessity. The Baptists "solved the problem of a shortage of ministers by not requiring their elders to be college graduates, but ordained many men who claimed an inward call to preach," explained Mormon historian Milton Backman. "For most Baptist elders of the early Republic, preaching was an avocation rather than a profession. They did not rely on parish contributions for their support, earning much of their livelihood from farming and other economic pursuits. . . . [In Methodism] resident ministers were generally assigned to communities where there

was a Methodist meetinghouse, [and] most groups were served by traveling ministers. After preaching locations were determined within the circuits, itinerants were appointed to preach regularly in the designated places of worship. The circuits were called two-week, three-week, or four-week circuits, depending on the period required to contact the members at each station. . . . Since members of the Society of Friends [Quakers] did not believe in a paid ministry, lay members were appointed to supervise the ecclesiastical activities of these Christians." Milton V. Backman, *Joseph Smith's First Vision: Confirming Evidences and Contemporary Accounts* (Salt Lake City: Deseret Book, 1971), 56–57, 61.

9. David Holland, "Priest, Pastor, and Power: Joseph Smith and the Question of Priesthood," in *Archive of Restoration Culture: Summer Fellows' Papers 1997–1999* (Provo, UT: Joseph Fielding Smith Institute for Latter-day Saint History, 2000), 9–16.

10. An 1835 addition to an 1830 revelation [D&C 27] confirmed this apostolic ordination: "And also with Peter, and James, and John, whom I have sent unto you, by whom I have ordained you and confirmed you to be apostles and especial witnesses of my name, and bear the keys of your ministry." History, 1838–1856, volume A-1 [23 December 1805–30 August 1834], *The Joseph Smith Papers*, http://josephsmithpapers.org/paperSummary/history-1838-1856-volume-a-1-23-december-1805-30-august-1834?p=58. See also D&C 27:12.

11. Catholic historian Rev. Thomas Donohue wrote: "The state laws, condemning Catholic priests to imprisonment and even death, were not repealed until 1784; and up to this time there did not exist a single Catholic congregation within the limits of the State of New York. . . . When the great project of building the Erie canal, to connect Lake Erie with the Atlantic Ocean was begun it attracted thousands of the laboring class from Europe, but more especially from Ireland; and in three years, from 1816 to 1819, more than ten thousand Irish emigrants landed at the port of New York. The Erie canal was begun in October, 1817, at Rome, New York, and the greater number of these Irish emigrants were undoubtedly employed on this great work. Nearly all of these were Catholics, yet no priests came to attend them. . . . There was no priest to preach the word of God to the hundreds of Catholics laboring along the canal, or to light up the last hours of many faithful sons of the Church who contracted mortal maladies in the swamps and forests along the line of this great work. There were not priests enough to attend the established congregations [in New York City], much less to travel through the State to administer the sacraments to the scattered Catholic population. . . . Even as late as 1822, there were only eight priests in the entire diocese, and but one. Rev. Patrick Kelly, in all Western New York." Rev. Thomas Donohue, *History of the Catholic Church in Western New York, Diocese of Buffalo* (Buffalo: Catholic Historical Publishing, 1904), 110–12.

12. Richard L. Bushman, *Joseph Smith: Rough Stone Rolling* (New York: Knopf, 2005),157.

13. For instance, according to Mormon scholar William Hartley, "The Book of Mormon was [Joseph's] first primer on priesthood and how it functioned in ancient times." See William G. Hartley, "'Upon You My Fellow Servants': Restoration of the Priesthood," in *Prophet Joseph: Essays on the Life and Mission of Joseph Smith*, ed. Larry C.

Porter and Susan Easton Black (Salt Lake City: Deseret Book, 1988), 1. Prince affirmed, "In addition to authorizing and initiating Smith's ministry, the Book of Mormon served as a blueprint for the early church. The form of the early church beginning in the summer of 1829 paralleled that described in the Book of Mormon." Gregory A. Prince, *Power from on High* (Salt Lake City: Signature Books, 1995), 10.

14. According to the *Catholic Encyclopedia*, "In 1688 [due to] the Stuart Revolution in England, . . . the Province of New York immediately followed the example of the mother-country in all its bitter intolerance and persecution by the law of the Catholic Church and its adherents. . . . [This included] the enactment by the provincial legislature from time to time of proscriptive laws against the Catholic Faith and its adherents—laws which are savage in their malignity. Catholic priests and teachers were ordered to keep away from the province or, if they by any chance came there, to depart at once. Severe penalties were provided for disobedience to these laws extending to long imprisonment or even death. These laws were directed in many cases principally against the Catholic missionaries among the Iroquois, who were almost exclusively Frenchmen. . . . [I]n the case of the unfortunate schoolmaster John Ury . . . [in] the so-called Negro Plot of 1741 he was actually tried in New York and executed under these statutes for the crime of being a 'Popish priest' and teaching his religion. . . . The [American] Revolution of 1776 overthrew entirely the system of government churches and all religious proscription by law, and the [New York] State Constitution of 1777 provided . . . for general religious liberty. The [New York] legislature in 1784 carried out the declaration. It provided 'that an universal equality between every religious denomination, according to the true spirit of the Constitution, toward each other shall forever prevail.'" "State of New York," in *Catholic Encyclopedia*, http://www.newadvent.org/cathen/11029a.htm. As late as 1838, according to Doris Kearns Goodwin, Governor-elect William Seward's proposal to support Catholic parochial schools to help get Irish and German Catholic immigrant children off the street "provoked a violent reaction among nativist Protestants. They accused him of plotting 'to overthrow republican institutions' . . . that Seward was 'in league with the Pope' and schemed to throw Protestant children into the hands of priests." Doris Kearns Goodwin, *Team of Rivals: The Political Genius of Abraham Lincoln* (New York: Simon & Schuster, 2005), 83.

15. See "Anglican Community of St Mary the Virgin" and "Society of St. John the Evangelist," at "Anglican Religious Communities," http://communities.anglicancommunion.org/communities/index.cfm; "Methodist Diaconal Order," http://methodistdiaconalorder.org.uk/index.php?page=history-of-the-mdo; "Frequently Asked Questions," Order of Lutheran Franciscans, http://www.lutheranfranciscans.org/FAQ.html.

16. History, 1838–1856, volume C-1 [2 November 1838–31 July 1842], *The Joseph Smith Papers*, http://josephsmithpapers.org/paperSummary/history-1838-1856-volume-c-1-2-november-1838-31-july-1842?p=481.

17. Revelation Book 1, Revelation, 22–23 September 1832 [D&C 84], *The Joseph Smith Papers*, http://josephsmithpapers.org/paperSummary/revelation-book-1?p=137. See D&C section 84. This section was the earliest revelation mentioning a "priesthood [confirmed] upon Aaron and his seed" (84:18), in September 1832. Section 27, dated

August or September 1830, also affirms that a priesthood of Aaron had been given to the Prophet: "to ordain you unto this first priesthood which you have received, that you might be called and ordained even as Aaron" (27:8). However, this verse was part of a later revelation included in section 27 as verses 6 through 13, originally appearing in the 1835 edition of the Doctrine and Covenants. Similarly, section 68, dated November 1, 1831, in the Book of Commandments and Revelations speaks of the bishop's right to preside over "this priesthood," alluding to the priesthood of Aaron. But this revelation also was inserted later as section 22 of the 1835 edition of the Doctrine of Covenants.

18. Book of Mormon (1830 ed.), 259–60.

19. John Whitmer, History, 1831–circa 1847, *The Joseph Smith Papers*, http://josephsmithpapers.org/paperSummary/john-whitmer-history-1831-circa-1847?p=31.

20. Minute Book 2, 3 June 1831 • Friday, *The Joseph Smith Papers*, http://josephsmithpapers.org/paperSummary/minute-book-2?p=5.

21. Ezra Booth, "Mormonism—No. II," *Ohio Star*, October 20, 1831.

22. See Revelation Book 1, Revelation, 11 November 1831–B [D&C 107 (partial)], *The Joseph Smith Papers*, http://josephsmithpapers.org/paperSummary/revelation-book-1?p=108.

23. William V. Smith, "Early Mormon Priesthood Revelations: Text, Impact, and Evolution," *Dialogue: A Journal of Mormon Thought* 46/4 (2013): 63n15.

24. Matthew C. Godfrey, "A Culmination of Learning: D&C 84 and the Doctrine of the Priesthood," in *You Shall Have My Word: Exploring the Text of the Doctrine and Covenants* (Provo, UT: Religious Studies Center, Brigham Young University, 2012), 170.

25. Smith, "Early Mormon Priesthood Revelations," 66n32.

26. Godfrey, "Culmination of Learning," 176.

27. Revelation Book 1, *The Joseph Smith Papers*, http://josephsmithpapers.org/paperSummary/revelation-book-1?p=138.

28. Godfrey, "Culmination of Learning," 176.

29. Doctrine and Covenants, 1844, Instruction on Priesthood, circa April 1835 [D&C 107], *The Joseph Smith Papers*, http://josephsmithpapers.org/paperSummary/doctrine-and-covenants-1844?p=103.

30. History, 1838–1856, volume A-1 [23 December 1805–30 August 1834], *The Joseph Smith Papers*, http://josephsmithpapers.org/paperSummary/history-1838-1856-volume-a-1-23-december-1805-30-august-1834?p=24.

31. History, 1838–1856, volume A-1 [23 December 1805–30 August 1834], *The Joseph Smith Papers*, http://josephsmithpapers.org/paperSummary/history-1838-1856-volume-a-1-23-december-1805-30-august-1834?p=24.

32. Hartley, "'Upon You My Fellow Servants,'" 4. See note 6 in this chapter.

33. "By August 1829 as Mormons began proselyting adult male converts were ordained to one of the three offices described in the Book of Mormon: teacher, priest, and elder/disciple." Prince, *Power from on High*, 48.

34. One explanation for the early priesthood confusion is that it is possible that in Smith's later accounts he retrospectively interpreted what happened in 1829 in light of later knowledge he acquired through the 1830s from different priesthood revelations

(D&C sections 68, 84, 107). In other words, Peter, James, and John did in fact restore the Melchizedek Priesthood in 1829, and John the Baptist the Aaronic Priesthood, but the Prophet didn't realize that until later. Thanks to Terryl Givens for this insight.

35. "Excerpts from the Autobiography of William Farrington Cahoon," Book of Abraham Project, http://www.boap.org/LDS/Early-Saints/WFCahoon.html.

36. "William E. McLellin, 1806–1883," History and Writings of William E. McLellin, Book of Abraham Project, http://www.boap.org/LDS/Early-Saints/Mcllelin.html.

37. "Autobiography of Charles Henry Hales," Selections from *Windows: A Mormon Family*, Book of Abraham Project, http://www.boap.org/LDS/Early-Saints/HalesF.html.

38. "Diary of Lorenzo Brown," Journal Vol. 1 (1823–1846), Book of Abraham Project, http://www.boap.org/LDS/Early-Saints/LBrown.html.

39. Revelation Book 1, Revelation, 22–23 September 1832 [D&C 84], *The Joseph Smith Papers*, http://josephsmithpapers.org/paperSummary/revelation-book-1?p=138. See D&C 84:19–20.

40. Revelation Book 1, Revelation, 22–23 September 1832 [D&C 84], *The Joseph Smith Papers*, http://josephsmithpapers.org/paperSummary/revelation-book-1?p=138. See D&C 84:26–27.

41. History, circa June 1839–circa 1841 [Draft 2], *The Joseph Smith Papers*, http://josephsmithpapers.org/paperSummary/history-circa-june-1839-circa-1841-draft-2?p=24. To be sure, this 1838 rendering reflects the Prophet's evolved understanding of priesthood, after 1835. According to William Smith, "When Smith quoted John the Baptist saying, "Upon you my fellow servants, in the name of Messiah I confer the Priesthood of Aaron," this meant that Smith and Cowdery were thereby made 'priests.'" Three years later Smith's 1835 priesthood revelation (D&C 107) "establishes two authority 'pools' from which all Mormon priesthood offices are drawn. These pools are the Melchizedek Priesthood and the Aaronic Priesthood. . . . Here we have a *new* definition of '[Aaronic] priesthood.' It no longer refers just to the office of priest, as it does in D&C 84 for example." Smith, "Early Mormon Priesthood Revelations," 13, 20, 22.

42. Smith, "Early Mormon Priesthood Revelations," 45–46, quoting from *General Handbook of Instructions, Book 2* (The Church of Jesus Christ of Latter-day Saints, 2010), 20.7.1. A current version is available online at http://www.lds.org.

43. Smith, "Early Mormon Priesthood Revelations," 66n32.

44. Dan Vogel, *Religious Seekers and the Advent of Mormonism* (Salt Lake City: Signature Books, 1988), 126n65.

45. "A Meeting of Ministers Opposed to Freemasonry," *New-York Baptist Register*, November 25, 1828, 4, cited in Rick Grunder, *Mormon Parallels: A Bibliographic Source* (LaFayette, NY: Rick Grunder—Books, 2008), 1364.

46. "Now if perfection had been attainable through the levitical priesthood—for the people received the law under this priesthood—what further need would there have been to speak of another priest arising according to the order of Melchizedek, rather than one according to the order of Aaron?" (Hebrews 7:11 NRSV).

47. Citing a text from the Dead Sea Scrolls, biblical historian Margaret Barker elaborated: "The Qumran Melchizedek text (11 QMelch) [describes a] heavenly deliverer,

Melchizedek, the great high priest and leader of the sons of heaven, [who] comes to deliver the [priesthood] sons of light from the hand of Satan." Margaret Barker, "Atonement: The Rite of Healing," *Scottish Journal of Theology* 49/1 (1996): 17. Theologian Adam Clarke wrote of Melchizedek: "He was a *priest of the most high God.* The word *cohen*, which signifies both *prince* and *priest*, because the patriarchs sustained this double office, has both its root and proper signification in the Arabic; [Arabic] *kahana* signifies *to approach, draw near, have intimate access to*; and from hence *to officiate as priest before* God, and thus have intimate access to the Divine presence: and by means of the sacrifices which he offered he received *counsel* and *information* relative to what was *yet to take place*, and hence another acceptation of the word, to *foretell, predict future events, unfold hidden things or mysteries;* so the lips of the priests preserved knowledge, and they were often the interpreters of the will of God to the people." Adam Clarke, "Commentary on Genesis 14," in *The Adam Clarke Commentary*, http://www.studylight.org/com/acc/view.cgi?book=ge&chapter=014, emphasis in the original.

48. Adam Clarke, "Commentary on Hebrews 7:11–12," in *The Adam Clarke Commentary*, http://www.studylight.org/com/acc/view.cgi?book=heb&chapter=007, emphasis in the original.

49. Mark Lyman Staker, *Hearken, O My People: The Historical Setting of Joseph Smith's Ohio Revelations* (Salt Lake City: Greg Kofford Books, 2009), 149.

50. Staker, *Hearken, O My People*, 150.

51. Of Alma's words to the Ammonihah community, one-third (33 percent) relate to the high priesthood, and another 30 percent relate to Nephite temple teachings (see chapter 4). Alma 12–13 documents Alma's words to the people of Ammonihah, for a total of 2,601 words spoken by Alma. Further, 514 words in Alma 12 and 440 words in Alma 13 address the plan of salvation, 785 words in Alma 12 address temple teachings and 862 words in Alma 13 address the high priesthood and Melchizedek.

52. Book of Mormon (1830 ed.), 259–60.

53. "The Lord has sworn and will not change his mind, 'You are a priest forever according to the order of Melchizedek'" (Psalm 110:4 NRSV).

54. "So also Christ did not glorify himself in becoming a high priest, but was appointed by the one who said to him, 'You are my Son, today I have begotten you;' as he says also in another place, 'You are a priest forever, according to the order of Melchizedek'" (Hebrews 5:5–6 NRSV).

55. Old Testament Revision 1, *The Joseph Smith Papers*, http://josephsmithpapers.org/paperSummary/old-testament-revision-1?p=35.

56. Hebrews 7:3 JST, "Joseph Smith Translation: Excerpts Too Lengthy for Inclusion in Footnotes," Appendix, *The Holy Bible* (Salt Lake City: The Church of Jesus Christ of Latter-day Saints, 1979), 811.

57. History, 1838–1856, volume B-1 [1 September 1834–2 November 1838], Priesthood, *The Joseph Smith Papers*, http://josephsmithpapers.org/paperSummary/history-1838-1856-volume-b-1-1-september-1834-2-november-1838?p=36.

58. Barker, "Atonement: The Rite of Healing,"17.

59. Margaret Barker, *Adam the High Priest in the Paradise Temple*, The Fourth Temple Studies Group Symposium, Saturday, 6 November 2010, Temple Church, London, 2.

60. "according to the order of Melchizedek" (Hebrews 5:6 NRSV).

61. As we saw earlier in the chapter, Freemasonry also included select high priests as part of its hierarchical structure. Samuel Brown remarked: "To not be at least dimly aware of Masonry in western New York in the middle to late 1820s was impossible. This need not and likely does not imply any rigorous esoteric training derived from these encounters, but the young Joseph Smith was almost certainly aware of [Masonry's] basic social structures." Samuel Morris Brown, *In Heaven as It Is on Earth: Joseph Smith and the Early Conquest of Death* (New York: Oxford University Press, 2012), 174. However, there is no evidence that Freemasonry had any significant connection with Mormonism during the early restoration—there is no mention of it among contemporary sources even amid the anti-Masonic hostility of the late 1820s. Brown concluded: "That [Joseph Smith's] contemporaries reasonably versed in Masonry and harshly antipathetic to Mormonism and Masonry did not make these comparisons suggests a lack of traction for this interpretation [of a connection between the two]. Smith's engagement of formal Masonry during this period seems to have been relatively minor." Brown, *In Heaven as It Is on Earth*, 176.

62. Minute Book 2, *The Joseph Smith Papers*, http://josephsmithpapers.org/paperSummary/minute-book-2?p=13.

63. Quoted in Eber D. Howe, *Mormonism Unvailed* (Painesville, OH: Howe, 1834), 180.

64. Bushman, *Rough Stone Rolling*, 159–60.

65. Book of Mormon (1830 ed.), 259, emphasis added.

66. Book of Mormon (1830 ed.), 259.

67. Book of Mormon (1830 ed.), 260.

68. Instruction on Priesthood, between circa 1 March and circa 4 May 1835 [D&C 107], *The Joseph Smith Papers*, http://josephsmithpapers.org/paperSummary/instruction-on-priesthood-between-circa-1-march-and-circa-4-may-1835-dc-107?p=3.

69. According to the revelation, a literal descendant of Aaron could serve alone as bishop without counselors. Instruction on Priesthood, between circa 1 March and circa 4 May 1835 [D&C 107], *The Joseph Smith Papers*, http://josephsmithpapers.org/paperSummary/instruction-on-priesthood-between-circa-1-march-and-circa-4-may-1835-dc-107?p=6.

70. Doctrine and Covenants, 1844, *The Joseph Smith Papers*, http://josephsmithpapers.org/paperSummary/doctrine-and-covenants-1844?p=103.

71. History, 1838–1856, volume C-1 [2 November 1838–31 July 1842], *The Joseph Smith Papers*, http://josephsmithpapers.org/paperSummary/history-1838-1856-volume-c-1-2-november-1838-31-july-1842?p=481.

72. Charles A. Young, *Biographical Sketch of the Life of Walter Scott*, http://www.therestorationmovement.com/_states/kentucky/scott,walter.htm.

73. Journal, December 1841–December 1842, *The Joseph Smith Papers*, http://josephsmithpapers.org/paperSummary/journal-december-1841-december-1842?p=76. See D&C 128:18.

74. Prince, *Power from on High*, 63.

75. Compared to the Book of Mormon, the New Testament mentions a more diverse set of priesthood offices: apostle, prophet, teacher, evangelist, pastor, elder, bishop, and deacon. The offices of priest, Levite, and high priest—central offices of the Old Testament religion—are clearly absent from this list. Furthermore, unlike the Book of Mormon, there appears to be no evident consistency between these New Testament offices and the more ancient Old Testament offices. New Testament *prophets* seem to have had precedent in the Old Testament religion, and *elders* may have had as well, appearing with Moses and the Seventy Elders of Israel; the *Jewish Encyclopedia* says: "The Mishnah speaks of the elders as the recipients of the oral law from Joshua (Abot i. 1), and as the forerunners of the Sanhedrin (Sanh. 2a). The institution of elders flourished during the period of the Babylonian Exile (Ezek. viii. 1, xiv. 1, xx. 1), and continued in Palestine during the Persian and Greek periods" ("ELDER, or ZAḲEN," *Jewish Encyclopedia* [2002–2011], http://www.jewishencyclopedia.com/articles/5517-elder), suggesting precedent before Christ and possible continuity after Christ's coming similar to the Book of Mormon's continuity over time with the office of elder.

76. "but when the complete comes, the partial will come to an end" (1 Corinthians 13:10 NRSV).

77. Hugh Nibley, "Christian Envy of the Temple," in *Mormonism and Early Christianity* (Salt Lake City: Deseret Book and FARMS, 1987), 403.

78. Dean W. Collinwood and James W. McConkie, review of *Temple Theology: An Introduction*, by Margaret Barker, *BYU Studies* 45/2 (2006): 173.

79. Margaret Barker, *Temple Theology: An Introduction* (London: Society for Promoting Christian Knowledge, 2004), 11.

80. Taylor G. Petrey, "Purity and Parallels: Constructing the Apostasy Narrative of Early Christianity," in *Standing Apart: Mormon Historical Consciousness and the Concept of Apostasy*, ed. Miranda Wilcox and John D. Young (New York: Oxford University Press, 2014), 180.

81. See also Matthew 10:1; 11:1; 20:17; Luke 9:1.

82. "While the Book of Mormon uses both *disciples* and *apostles*, distinguishing between the twelve 'disciples' in America and the twelve 'apostles' in Jerusalem, the terms seem to refer to comparable offices. This revelation uses the term *disciple* to describe the calling of the twelve, but it is unclear whether in 1829 JS and Cowdery thought of the terms *disciple* and *apostle* as interchangeable, as they did later. When JS and Cowdery convened a meeting to select twelve apostles in February 1835, they referred to the proceedings as being a fulfillment of this [June 1829, D&C 18] revelation. Similarly, although the text featured here (from the 1833 Book of Commandments) refers to the calling of 'disciples,' the 1835 edition of the Doctrine and Covenants describes the purpose of the same revelation as the 'calling of twelve apostles,' as does JS's history begun in 1838." Historical Introduction, Revelation, June 1829–B

[D&C 18], *The Joseph Smith Papers*, http://josephsmithpapers.org/paperSummary/revelation-june-1829-b-dc-18?p=1.

83. Prince identified eight that he believes may have been called to the earliest office of apostle in the restoration by November 1830: Joseph Smith, Oliver Cowdery, David Whitmer, John Whitmer, Peter Whitmer, Ziba Peterson, Samuel H. Smith, and Orson Pratt. See Prince, *Power from on High*, 13–14n40.

84. Prince, *Power from on High*, 13.

85. Prince, *Power from on High*, 13.

86. Brigham Young said of David Whitmer: "Joseph Smith, Oliver Cowdery, and David Whitmer were the first Apostles of this dispensation, though in the early days of the Church David Whitmer lost his standing, and another took his place." *Journal of Discourses*, 6:320. In an 1877 interview Whitmer was recorded as saying: "Soon after his [Whitmer's] return [1 June 1829] from his little mission to bring Joseph the Prophet and Company from Pa. Joseph Babtized him and Ordained him as the 3d Elder in the Church." Letter of Edward Stevenson to President Wilford Woodruff, October 6, 1891, LDS Church Archives.

87. David Whitmer, *An Address to All Believers in Christ: By A Witness to the Divine Authenticity of the Book of Mormon* (Richmond, MO, 1887), 29, 32.

88. My analysis of 3 Nephi 11–28, by verse.

89. Book of Mormon (1830 ed.), 478.

90. Book of Mormon (1830 ed.), 478–79.

91. Book of Mormon (1830 ed.), 487.

92. Book of Mormon (1830 ed.), 479. This paralleled the apostolic requirement established by the eleven apostles in Jerusalem following Jesus's ascension that the next (twelfth) apostle, called to fill the vacancy left by Judas, must "be ordained to be a witness with us of his resurrection" (see Acts 1:21–26).

93. Book of Mormon (1830 ed.), 507. See also 3 Nephi 27:3–21. Later, Mormon clarified the parallel ministries of the *twelve* of ancient America and the original *twelve* of Jerusalem, saying: "I write unto all the ends of the earth; yea, unto you, twelve tribes of Israel, which shall be judged according to your works, by the twelve whom Jesus chose to be his disciples in the land of Jerusalem. And I write also unto the remnant of this people, which shall also be judged by the other twelve whom Jesus chose in the land of Jerusalem." Book of Mormon (1830 ed.), 524. See Mormon 3:18–19. Amid these intricate designs of priesthood governance, Mormon's explanation seemed consistent with Christ's promise to the twelve in Jerusalem that "when the Son of Man is seated on the throne of his glory, you who have followed me will also sit on twelve thrones, judging the twelve tribes of Israel" (Matthew 19:28 NRSV).

94. Revelation, June 1829–B [D&C 18], *The Joseph Smith Papers*, http://josephsmithpapers.org/paperSummary/revelation-june-1829-b-dc-18?p=2. See D&C 18:9.

95. "Articles of the Church of Christ," June 1829, *The Joseph Smith Papers*, http://josephsmithpapers.org/paperSummary/articles-of-the-church-of-christ-june-1829?p=3.

96. Mariella Marks, ed., *Memoirs of the Life of David Marks, Minister of the Gospel* (Dove[r], NH: Free-Will Baptist Printing Establishment, 1846), 236–37. The first edition was published in 1831; see Prince, *Power from on High*, 56.

97. Articles and Covenants, circa April 1830 [D&C 20], *The Joseph Smith Papers*, http://josephsmithpapers.org/paperSummary/articles-and-covenants-circa-april-1830-dc-20. See D&C 20:2–3.

98. History, 1838–1856, volume B-1 [1 September 1834–2 November 1838], *The Joseph Smith Papers*, http://josephsmithpapers.org/paperSummary/history-1838-1856-volume-b-1-1-september-1834-2-november-1838?p=37. See D&C 107:23.

99. Book of Mormon (1830 ed.), 575.

100. Book of Mormon (1830 ed.), 73.

101. Book of Mormon (1830 ed.), 72.

102. Book of Mormon (1830 ed.), 124.

103. Joseph Fielding Smith, then an LDS apostle, offered an alternative explanation of Book of Mormon priesthood: "It is true that Nephi 'consecrated Jacob and Joseph' that they should be priests and teachers over the land of the Nephites, but the fact that plural terms *priests* and *teachers* were used indicates that this was not a reference to the definite office in the priesthood in either case, but it was a general assignment to teach, direct, and admonish the people. Otherwise the terms *priest* and *teacher* would have been given, in the singular." Joseph Fielding Smith, "The Priesthood of the Nephites," *Answers to Gospel Questions* (Salt Lake City: Deseret Book, 1957), 1:124. In their Book of Mormon commentary, Robert Millet and Joseph Fielding McConkie offered a similar view, commenting on Alma 15:13 in which Alma "consecrated priests and teachers in the land" of Sidom: "We note that both the priests and the teachers were given the authority to baptize [they infer this from Alma 15:13]. As we have discussed earlier in this work, so far as we know there was no Aaronic Priesthood among the Nephites (because there were no Levites), at least until the coming of the resurrected Lord to them in the meridian of time. Thus priests and teachers among the Nephites held the Melchizedek Priesthood, and the words *priests* and *teachers* describe their ministerial duties, not the offices to which they were ordained." Robert L. Millet and Joseph Fielding McConkie, "Alma Establishes the Church in Sidom: Alma 15:13–19," in *Doctrinal Commentary on the Book of Mormon* (Salt Lake City: Deseret Book, 1991), 3:116–17.

104. Prince, *Power from on High*, 50.

105. Joseph Smith's contemporary critic Alexander Campbell concluded after reading the Book of Mormon: "Before Nephi died, which was about 55 years from the flight of Lehi from Jerusalem, he had preached to his people every thing which is now preached in the state of New York, and anointed or ordained his brother Jacob priest over his people, called the Nephites. Jacob brought up his son Enos 'in the nurture and admonition of the Lord,' gave him the plates, and left him successor in office over the people of Nephi." Alexander Campbell, *Millennial Harbinger* 2/1 (1831): 87.

106. John Welch noted: "The prophecies and rules issued by Nephi in 2 Nephi 5:19–25 and the 'covenant speech' given by Jacob under the direction of Nephi (see 2 Nephi 6–10) were, in my opinion, most likely all delivered at the temple. They were probably

proclaimed at or around Nephi's coronation and the temple's dedication. Indeed, the text in 2 Nephi 5–10 makes good sense as a temple text and features several themes of constitutional force among the Nephites." John W. Welch, "The Temple in the Book of Mormon: The Temples at the Cities of Nephi, Zarahemla, and Bountiful," in *Temples of the Ancient World: Ritual and Symbolism*, ed. Donald W. Parry (Salt Lake City: Deseret Book and FARMS, 1994), 328.

107. Book of Mormon (1830 ed.), 74.

108. Welch, "Temple in the Book of Mormon," 330.

109. Book of Mormon (1830 ed.), 123.

110. "They teach Jacob your ordinances, and Israel your law; they place incense before you, and whole burnt offerings on your altar" (Deuteronomy 33:10 NRSV; see also verses 8–11).

111. Roland de Vaux, *Ancient Israel: Its Life and Institutions* (Grand Rapids, MI: Eerdmans, 1997), 356. There is, however, considerable dispute among Hebrew scholars, some arguing that the entire tribe of Levi, the Levites, could also officiate at the altar. According to de Vaux: "The entire tribe of Levi was set apart to carry the Ark, to serve God and to bless the people (Dt 10:8), and members of this tribe are called 'the priests, the Levites' (Dt 17:9, 18; 18:1; 21:5; 24:8; 31:9). The text of Dt 18:1 should be translated: 'the Levite priests, all the tribe of Levi', with the two phrases in apposition. . . . Dt 18:6–7 makes provision for a Levite, when he comes to the central sanctuary, to perform the functions of a priest together with all his brother Levites" (pp. 362–63).

112. Moses Buttenwieser, "Priest," in *Jewish Encyclopedia*, http://www.jewishencyclopedia.com/articles/12358-priest.

113. Book of Mormon (1830 ed.), 167.

114. Book of Mormon (1830 ed.), 193.

115. Book of Mormon (1830 ed.), 211.

116. Book of Mormon (1830 ed.), 313.

117. Book of Mormon (1830 ed.), 209. Alma 4:6–7 provides a similar example of the guardianship role of teachers, where "the people of the church began to wax proud, because of their exceeding riches. . . . [T]his was the cause of much affliction to Alma, yea, and to many of the people whom Alma had consecrated to be teachers, and priests, and elders over the church; yea, many of them were sorely grieved for the wickedness which they saw had begun to be among their people." Here teachers are mentioned first in this guardianship hierarchy, as a primary role; but they act under the direction of priests and elders.

118. Book of Mormon (1830 ed.), 208.

119. Book of Mormon (1830 ed.), 155–56.

120. Numbers 3:9 says: "And thou shalt give the Levites unto Aaron and to his sons [the priests]"; see Numbers 3:1–10. De Vaux elaborated: "One branch within this tribe [of Levi] received the promise of a perpetual priesthood [as priests], as a result of which the other Levites were relegated to a subordinate position and restricted to the less important functions of the cult: this branch was the family of Aaron, Moses' brother (Ex 29:9, 44; 40:15)." De Vaux, *Ancient Israel*, 360.

121. "For according to the last words of David these were the number of the Levites . . . but their duty shall be to assist the descendants of Aaron for the service of the house of the Lord, having the care of the courts and the chambers, the cleansing of all that is holy, and any work for the service of the house of God; to assist also with the rows of bread, the choice flour for the grain offering, the wafers of unleavened bread, the baked offering, the offering mixed with oil, and all measures of quantity or size. And they shall stand every morning, thanking and praising the Lord, and likewise at evening, and whenever burnt offerings are offered to the Lord on sabbaths, new moons, and appointed festivals, according to the number required of them, regularly before the Lord. Thus they shall keep charge of the tent of meeting and the sanctuary, and shall attend the descendants of Aaron, their kindred, for the service of the house of the Lord" (1 Chronicles 23:27–32 NRSV).

122. According to the Chronicler, the Levites "offer[ed] all burnt sacrifices," suggesting they may have officiated at the altar—probably under the direction of the priests. In a parallel way, priests and teachers in the Book of Mormon both apparently baptized in the land of Sidom (see Alma 15).

123. G. Ernest Wright, "The Levites in Deuteronomy," *Vetus Testamentum* 4 (1954): 329.

124. Wright, "Levites in Deuteronomy," 329.

125. Revelation, June 1829–B [D&C 18], *The Joseph Smith Papers*, http://josephsmithpapers.org/paperSummary/revelation-june-1829-b-dc-18?p=4. See D&C 18:32.

126. Revelation Book 1, *The Joseph Smith Papers*, http://josephsmithpapers.org/paperSummary/revelation-book-1?p=138. See D&C 84:30.

127. This rendition of Cowdery's 1829 "Articles of the Church of Christ" was amended in John Whitmer's 1830 version of the same document to include specific reference to elders. Robin Scott Jensen, Robert J. Woodford, and Steven C. Harper, eds., *Manuscript Revelation Books*, facsimile edition, first volume of the Revelations and Translations series of *The Joseph Smith Papers*, edited by Dean C. Jessee, Ronald K. Esplin, and Richard Lyman Bushman (Salt Lake City: Church Historian's Press, 2009), 23. Cowdery's original Articles document said: "And now I speak unto the Church Repent all ye ends of the Earth & come unto me & be baptized in my name which is Jesus Christ & endure to the end & ye shall be saved." "Articles of the Church of Christ," June 1829, *The Joseph Smith Papers*, http://josephsmithpapers.org/paperSummary/articles-of-the-church-of-christ-june-1829?p=3.

128. *Evening and the Morning Star* 1/1 (June 1832): 1. See also D&C 20:46–57.

129. Whitmer, *An Address to All Believers in Christ*, 32–33.

130. Book of Mormon (1830 ed.), 289.

131. David Whitmer, writing at the end of his life, said that Hyrum was one of the first six *elders* of the restoration, ordained in the summer of 1829. Whitmer, *An Address to all Believers in Christ*, 32. If correct, then Hyrum would have been an elder in 1829, prior to the official organization of the Church, and then ordained a priest later in June 1830, following the church's formal organization April 6, 1830. Apparently ordinations were performed again routinely after the organization of the church in April. Bushman

notes that at this organizational meeting, after "receiving unanimous approval, Joseph ordained Cowdery an elder, and Cowdery ordained Joseph" despite the fact that both had been previously ordained elders in 1829; see Bushman, *Rough Stone Rolling*, 109.

132. Larry C. Porter, "The Colesville Branch and the Coming Forth of the Book of Mormon," *BYU Studies* 10/3 (1970): 365–85, based on the names of those baptized in Colesville. Hyrum went to Colesville in early October 1830. Lucy Smith, *Biographical Sketches of Joseph Smith, the Prophet, and His Progenitors for Many Generations* (Liverpool: Richards, 1853), 158–59.

133. Hyrum and Newel worked side by side as priests, coleading the Colesville Branch from about October 1830 until March 3, 1831, when Hyrum was called to go to Kirtland. Newel organized the members of the Colesville Branch and led them to Kirtland in April and May 1831. Both Hyrum and Newel were ordained elders sometime prior to June 3, 1831, for they were both listed among the elders present at the fourth General Conference of the church held on that date. Minutes, circa 3–4 June 1831, *The Joseph Smith Papers*, http://josephsmithpapers.org/paperSummary/minutes-circa-3-4-june-1831?p=1.

134. Minutes, circa 3–4 June 1831, *The Joseph Smith Papers*, http://josephsmithpapers.org/paperSummary/minutes-circa-3-4-june-1831?p=2. Also see Hezekiah Peck Biography, *The Joseph Smith Papers*, http://josephsmithpapers.org/person?name=Hezekiah+Peck.

135. According to the *Evening and the Morning Star*, "Soon after the Book of Mormon came forth, containing the fulness of the gospel of Jesus Christ, the church was organized on the sixth of April, in Manchester; soon after, a branch was established in Fayette, and the June following, another in Colesville, New York. We shall not give, at this time, the particulars attending the organization of these branches of the church. . . . Twenty more were added to the church in Manchester and Fayette, in the month of April; and on the 28th of June, thirteen were baptized in Colesville. . . . In October, (1830) the number of disciples had increased to between seventy and eighty, when four of the elders started for the west, and founded a branch of the church at Kirtland, Ohio." *Evening and the Morning Star* 1/11 (April 1833): 84.

136. License for Joseph Smith Sr., 9 June 1830, *The Joseph Smith Papers*, http://josephsmithpapers.org/paperSummary/license-for-joseph-smith-sr-9-june-1830?p=1.

137. Ordained a teacher by October 5, 1830. License, John Whitmer and JS to William Smith, Hiram, OH, October 5, 1831; handwriting of John Whitmer with signatures of John Whitmer and JS; one page; CCLA. "William Smith's certificate is unusual in that the church did not hold a conference or special meeting on or about 5 October 1831. Moreover, he had been identified as holding the priesthood office of teacher during the June 1831 conference. Since he had apparently been ordained a teacher earlier, this 5 October 1831 certificate may have been a replacement for a previous document." License for William Smith, 5 October 1831, *The Joseph Smith Papers*, http://josephsmithpapers.org/paperSummary/license-for-william-smith-5-october-1831.

138. *Messenger and Advocate* 3/4 (January 1837): 441.

139. Heber C. Kimball, 1801–1868, Book of Abraham Project (citing *Times and Seasons* 2 (1841); 6 (1845)), http://www.boap.org/LDS/Early-Saints/HCKimball.html. Also see *Millennial Star* 26 (1864): 632.

140. Brigham Young (1801–1877), Book of Abraham Project, citing *Manuscript History of Brigham Young*, 1801–1844, comp. Elden Jay Watson (Salt Lake City: Smith Secretarial Service, 1968), http://www.boap.org/LDS/Early-Saints/MSHBY.html.

141. Parley P. Pratt, *The Autobiography of Parley Parker Pratt, One of the Twelve Apostles of the Church of Jesus Christ of Latter-Day Saints* (New York: Russell Brothers, 1874), 348.

142. Dean C. Jessee, ed., *Personal Writings of Joseph Smith* (Salt Lake City: Deseret Book, 1984), 182–83.

143. Jessee, *Personal Writings of Joseph Smith*, 185–86.

144. *Manuscript History of Brigham Young*, 1801–1844.

145. *Manuscript History of Brigham Young*, 1801–1844.

146. *Evening and the Morning Star* 1/1 (June 1832): 1. See D&C 20:46–57.

147. "The Confessional," *Millennial Star* 49/10 (March 7, 1887): 157.

148. Quoted in William G. Hartley, "From Men to Boys: LDS Aaronic Priesthood Offices, 1829–1996," *Journal of Mormon History* 22/1 (1996): 85–86.

149. William G. Hartley, "Ordained and Acting Teachers in the Lesser Priesthood, 1851–1883," *BYU Studies* 16/3 (1976): 382.

150. Hartley, "From Men to Boys," 87–88.

151. Hartley, "Ordained and Acting Teachers," 390.

152. Hartley, "Ordained and Acting Teachers," 379.

153. William G. Hartley, "Bishop, History of the Office," in *Encyclopedia of Mormonism*, 1:119–20.

154. Hartley, "Ordained and Acting Teachers," 379.

155. Hartley, "Ordained and Acting Teachers," 388.

156. Hartley, "Ordained and Acting Teachers," 388.

157. Hartley, "Ordained and Acting Teachers," 389.

158. Hartley, "From Men to Boys," 114–15.

159. "Practical Duties for Members of the Lesser Priesthood," *Improvement Era*, July 1916, 847.

160. "Practical Duties for Members of the Lesser Priesthood," 847.

6. The Meaning of the Book of Mormon in the Early Restoration

1. Grant Hardy, introduction to *The Book of Mormon: The Earliest Text*, ed. Royal Skousen (New Haven: Yale University Press, 2009), xxvii.

2. Grant Hardy, *Understanding the Book of Mormon: A Reader's Guide* (New York: Oxford University Press, 2010), xiv.

3. Andrew F. Ehat and Lyndon W. Cook, comps. and eds., *The Words of Joseph Smith: The Contemporary Accounts of the Nauvoo Discourses of the Prophet Joseph* (Provo, UT: Religious Studies Center, Brigham Young University, 1980), 34–35.

4. Hardy, *Understanding the Book of Mormon*, 11.

5. Book of Mormon (1830 ed.), 490. See 3 Nephi 18:7.

6. "This is my body, which is given for you. Do this in remembrance of me" (Luke 22:19 NRSV).

7. Evangelical leaders published a statement to defend against liberal conceptions of scripture. International Council on Biblical Inerrancy, *The Chicago Statement on Biblical Inerrancy* (Dallas: Dallas Theological Seminary Archives, 1978).

8. Revelation Book 1, Revelation, 1 November 1831–A [D&C 68], *The Joseph Smith Papers*, http://josephsmithpapers.org/paperSummary/revelation-book-1?p=99.

9. Hardy, introduction to *Book of Mormon: The Earliest Text*, xx.

10. Book of Mormon (1840 ed.), title page.

11. Revelation, circa August 1830 [D&C 27], *The Joseph Smith Papers*, http://josephsmithpapers.org/paperSummary/revelation-book-1.

12. Robin Scott Jensen, Robert J. Woodford, and Steven C. Harper, eds., *Manuscript Revelation Books*, facsimile edition, first volume of the Revelations and Translations series of *The Joseph Smith Papers*, edited by Dean C. Jessee, Ronald K. Esplin, and Richard Lyman Bushman (Salt Lake City: Church Historian's Press, 2009), xxix.

13. Rodney Stark, "The Rise of a New World Faith," in *Latter-day Saint Social Life: Social Research on the LDS Church and Its Members* (Provo, UT: Religious Studies Center, Brigham Young University, 1998), 2.

14. Harold Bloom, *The American Religion: The Emergence of the Post-Christian Nation* (New York: Simon & Schuster, 1992), 85.

15. History, 1838–1856, volume A-1 [23 December 1805–30 August 1834], *The Joseph Smith Papers*, http://josephsmithpapers.org/paperSummary/history-1838-1856-volume-a-1-23-december-1805-30-august-1834?p=469.

16. John W. Welch, "The Book of Mormon as the Keystone of Church Administration," in *A Firm Foundation: Church Organization and Administration*, ed. David J. Whittaker and Arnold K. Garr (Provo, UT: Religious Studies Center, Brigham Young University, 2011), 30.

17. Dan Jones, "The Martyrdom of Joseph Smith and His Brother Hyrum," trans. Ronald D. Dennis, *BYU Studies* 24/1 (1984): 101.

Illustration Credits

Figs. 1, 5, 6, 10, 18. Courtesy Church History Library.

Fig. 2. Colton, Zahm & Roberts, lithographer, © 1872. Prints and Photographs Division, Library of Congress.

Fig. 3. Courtesy Community of Christ Archives.

Fig. 4. *Pioneers in the Great Religious Reformation of the Nineteenth Century*. Steel engraving by J. C. Buttre, after a drawing by J. D. C. McFarland, c. 1885. Prints and Photographs Division, Library of Congress.

Fig. 7. Rare Books Division, The New York Public Library, Astor, Lennox and Tilden Foundations.

Fig. 8. Clay County Museum, Liberty, Missouri. Jacob Hicks Photo Collection.

Fig. 9. Courtesy Joseph Smith Jr. and Emma Hale Smith Historical Society (www.josephsmithsr.com).

Fig. 11. Benjamin G. Ferris, *Utah and the Mormons* (New York: Harper & Brothers, 1854), 138. L. Tom Perry Special Collections, Harold B. Lee Library, Brigham Young University, Provo, Utah (hereafter Perry Special Collections).

Fig. 12. M. Dubourg, engraver; Jacques Gérard Milbert, artist. Prints and Photographs Division, Library of Congress.

Fig. 13. Photo by Val Brinkerhoff, courtesy Community of Christ Archives.

Fig. 14. Lithograph by P. S. Duval, ca. 1801, from Joseph Smith, Old Redstone. Copyprint. Philadelphia: 1854. General Collections, Library of Congress.

Fig. 15. Baptism in the Schuylkill River, woodcut illustration, in Morgan Edwards, *Materials towards a History of the American Baptists*. Historical Society of Pennsylvania in The Library Company of Philadelphia. Historical Society of Pennsylvania.

Fig. 16. Prints and Photographs Division, Library of Congress.

Fig. 17. Photograph courtesy of Kent P. Jackson.

Fig. 19. Mitchell's National Map of the American Republic, 1843. Perry Special Collections.

Fig. 20. 1903 (c 1893?) Rand McNally map of Utah, http://wchsutah.org/maps/maps.php.

Fig. 21. Photo by C. Ed Miller, courtesy Community of Christ Archives.

Fig. 22. Photo by Jack Martin. Community of Christ Archives. Digital Photo Collection.

Fig. 23. James Linforth, ed., *Route from Liverpool to Great Salt Lake Valley*, with steel engravings from sketches made by Frederick Piercy (Liverpool: Richards, 1855), following p. 70.

Scripture Index

Index